HOMELESSNESS IN NEW

Homelessness in New York City

Policymaking from Koch to de Blasio

Thomas J. Main

NEW YORK UNIVERSITY PRESS
New York

NEW YORK UNIVERSITY PRESS
New York
www.nyupress.org

First published in paperback in 2017.

References to Internet websites (URLs) were accurate at the time of writing. Neither the author nor New York University Press is responsible for URLs that may have expired or changed since the manuscript was prepared.

Library of Congress Cataloging-in-Publication Data
Names: Main, Thomas James, 1955- author.
Title: Homelessness in New York City : policymaking from Koch to De Blasio / Thomas J. Main.
Description: New York : New York University, [2016] |
Includes bibliographical references and index.
Identifiers: LCCN 2016010259| ISBN 9781479896479 (cl : alk. paper) |
ISBN 9781479846870 (pb : alk. paper)
Subjects: LCSH: Homelessness—Government policy—New York (State)—New York. |
Homelessness—New York (State)—New York—History. | Public welfare—
New York (State)—New York—History.
Classification: LCC HV4506.N6 M35 2016 | DDC 362.5/92561097471—dc23
LC record available at https://lccn.loc.gov/2016010259

New York University Press books are printed on acid-free paper, and their binding materials are chosen for strength and durability. We strive to use environmentally responsible suppliers and materials to the greatest extent possible in publishing our books.

Manufactured in the United States of America

10 9 8 7 6 5 4 3 2 1

Also available as an ebook

To my wife, Carla Main

CONTENTS

ACKNOWLEDGMENTS

I wish to thank the following people for assistance that made this book possible. Lawrence M. Mead of New York University has been my friend and colleague for many years and provided me with invaluable criticism and inspiration. The School of Public Affairs at Baruch College, City University of New York, my professional home for more than twenty years, has been a supportive community throughout; colleagues at the school who have been especially supportive include Sanders D. Korenman, Dahlia Remler, Jerry Mitchell, James A. Krauskopf, and David S. Birdsell. Lawrence M. Mead, Nicole P. Marwell, Neil J. Sullivan, and Daniel W. Williams read early drafts of the book and provided valuable advice. Two anonymous reviewers for NYU Press also made useful suggestions. Any remaining errors or omissions are my own. Kardi Teknomo of the School of Science and Engineering, Ateneo de Manila University, Philippines, did the queuing theory analysis that appears in chapter 3, table 3.1, concerning the debate over the *Callahan* consent decree plumbing ratios. Clara Platter and Constance Grady were wonderful editors. Benjamin Gillespie did a great job putting the book's tables and charts into order, and Diana Lazov helped me prepare the final manuscript file. My wife, Carla Main, endured my long process of writing this book and provided wise counsel and indispensable inspiration. My sons, Henry Main and Joshua Main, my brother, William Main, and my cousin, Margaret Gallacher, kept my spirits up. To my parents, George Main and Catherine Main, and my grandmother, Catherine Gallacher, who raised me, I owe greater thanks than I can express here. Finally, I would like to acknowledge the importance of the people who have been homeless in New York City over the past thirty-five years and express my admiration for all the actors who have worked to improve their lot.

This book contains excerpts from the following articles that I have previously written: "Quantum Change in the Fragmented Metropolis: Political Environment and Homeless Policy in New York City," *Review of Policy Research* 23, no. 4 (2006); "Shelters for the Homeless Men in New York City: Toward Paternalism through Privatization," in Lawrence M. Mead, ed., *The New Paternalism* (Washington, DC: Brookings Institution Press, 1997); "Hard Lessons about Homelessness: The Education of David Dinkins," *City Journal*, Summer 1993; "The Homeless of New York," *Public Interest* no. 72 (Spring 1983).

PREFACE TO THE PAPERBACK EDITION

Homeless Policy under de Blasio

THOMAS J. MAIN AND PETER NASAW

During the course of his overwhelmingly successful campaign for mayor, Bill de Blasio made poverty and income inequality his main issues. As the liberal journalist and fervent de Blasio supporter Eric Alterman put the matter, "De Blasio made economic inequality the central issue in his campaign and attempted to tie nearly every issue he addressed to that problem."[1] Homelessness was obviously such an issue, and so when de Blasio took office in January 2014, expectations were high that he would address that problem effectively.

Unfortunately, as of April 2017, under the new mayor, the homelessness problem had, by several important measures, gotten worse. The month de Blasio assumed office there were 53,615 people in the Department of Homeless Services (DHS) shelter system. That number has hovered around sixty thousand people since December 2014. The annual enumeration of street dwellers—the HOPE count—is down from 3,537 people in 2014 to about 2,794 in 2016, which is a positive trend but not a dramatic improvement. And the DHS budget remains high: $1.29 billion for fiscal year 2017.

Voters and other observers are not impressed. Quite surprisingly, given the emphasis de Blasio put on poverty and homelessness in his campaign, a March 2017 Quinnipiac University poll found that voters rated this the weakest aspect of the mayor's performance, with 55 percent disapproving. And the *New York Times*, which supported de Blasio's mayoral run, recently concluded, "The rise in homelessness is arguably the mayor's biggest failure in that goal to close the gap between the haves and the have-nots."[2] How did the mayor end up in this position, and what is he doing about it?

To put de Blasio's situation in context, we have to back up to 2004, when Mayor Bloomberg developed a five-year plan to "make the condition of chronic homelessness effectively extinct in New York."[3] Preventing homelessness would be emphasized through a "Home Base" program that would intervene with at-risk families to keep them housed. Analysis would show that Home Base did lower homelessness and even paid for itself. More supportive housing—that is, apartments with services for the mentally ill and other disabled street dwellers—was to be developed. This goal was accomplished in 2005, when the city and state signed the "New York/New York III Agreement," which produced nine thousand such units. Under the "Housing First" philosophy, street dwellers would be moved into supportive housing as quickly as possible, an approach that both reduced street homelessness and encouraged enrollment in rehabilitative services. Shelter use was to be cut by rehousing long-term shelter stayers. And, very importantly, shelter clients were to be moved out through rent subsidies, which, a key document noted, "must continue to be available in shelter to re-house chronically homeless individuals and families."[4] Bloomberg pledged to reduce the shelter census—36,399 people in June of 2004—by two-thirds in five years, to about 12,000 persons by 2009.

On October 19, 2004, DHS abandoned its long-term policy of giving shelter residents priority for entering public housing and for federal Section 8 rent vouchers. Commissioner of DHS Linda Gibbs believed that moving one shelter family to public housing would draw at least one new family into the system. But economists found that to draw one family into the system requires placing seven families into subsidized housing. Perverse incentives are real but too weak to drive up the shelter census. Nonetheless, shelter families lost preferential access to public housing and Section 8 vouchers; instead, they were eligible for a temporary five-year rent subsidy, Housing Stability Plus, replaced in 2007 by the Advantage two-year-maximum rent-subsidy program, which was funded jointly by the state and the city.

By Bloomberg's deadline of June 2009, the shelter census had not dropped appreciably. Then, as a result of a falling out between the city and the state over funding, Advantage ended. At that point no subsidies of any kind were offered to move families out of the shelter system. The number of people in the DHS shelter system began going up, and in January 2014 de Blasio inherited a record high shelter census. De Blasio's challenge was to create a new rent subsidy, implement it effectively, and hang on until it took hold. How well did he meet that challenge?

First off, the new administration made striking changes in personnel as well as policy. Steven Banks, the Legal Aid lawyer who since 1983 had litigated against the city for the right to shelter for homeless families, became commissioner of HRA. Lilliam Barrios-Paoli, a former Catholic nun who served in the city's social service bureaucracy under Koch, Giuliani, and Bloomberg, became deputy mayor for Health and Human Services. And Gilbert Taylor, formerly executive deputy commissioner for the Administration for Children's Services, was appointed commissioner of the Department of Homeless Services.

The new administration's biggest initiative in homeless policy is the Living in Communities (LINC) programs, which are a batch of rental-subsidy programs designed to help various sorts of shelter clients move out of the system. But the new programs had implementation problems. Getting LINC started required cooperation from New York State and thus between de Blasio and Governor Cuomo. The necessary small adjustments were not accomplished in a timely manner. LINC did not get fully up to speed until December 2014, and the nonpartisan Independent Budget Office concluded that "the homeless shelter population has remained stubbornly high this year. This is largely due to a slower than anticipated start to the LINC rental assistance programs."[5]

The ongoing Cuomo/de Blasio turbulence also delayed the development of more supportive housing. Supportive housing provided through the New York/New York Agreements is one of the great policy successes in homeless policy and has been demonstrated to keep the disabled off the streets and reduce the cost of their care. The last of these agreements was signed in November 2005, and by 2014 most of its units were occupied. Thus the homeless remained on the streets, where they attracted the attention of unsympathetic media and the general public and fostered the perception of a homeless crisis. In fact, despite the declining street homeless population documented by the HOPE count, the March 2017 Quinnipiac poll reported that 54 percent of city voters believe that they now see more homeless people on the streets and in parks and subways than they did a few years ago.

The de Blasio team made a big misstep when in 2015 it decided to halt development of new shelters for eight months due to community opposition. When the delayed LINC program did not reduce the shelter census, the city was forced to rely on various unsatisfactory stopgaps to put up homeless clients.

One such stopgap is the cluster site program, which was initiated by the Bloomberg administration and harshly criticized by de Blasio before he became mayor. Under this program, DHS rents out a "cluster" of private apartments to shelter homeless families. Private landlords own the apartments while nonprofit providers under contract with DHS provide the families with services, and the buildings have a mix of homeless families and private rent-paying tenants.

The cluster site program is a policy disaster. It is premised on putting shelter families in apartments that would otherwise have gone to still-independent families, thus making an already tight low-income housing market even worse. And cluster site apartments are of poor quality. In March 2015, the Department of Investigation (DOI), which is a nonmayoral agency, released a scathing, 180-page report[6] on family shelters that focused mostly on cluster site apartments. The DOI report found DHS's cluster sites to be "poorly monitored" and said that they "provide the least adequate social services to families." Among the issues were rodent infestations, fire safety code violations, defective window guards, a lack of furniture, and units in need of major repair. Landlords can charge three times the market rent for such low-quality apartments. Moreover, as the buildings are privately owned, DHS is unable to monitor who is using the apartment, security guards cannot screen guests, and there are many unauthorized visitors. Assaults, prostitution, gang activity, and other crimes are frequent. DHS is even renting from landlords who are on the Public Advocate's list of the city's one hundred worst landlords. Well before he became mayor, de Blasio was aware of these problems and pledged to end the use of cluster sites. But his moratorium on building new shelters and continuing high demand left him unable to do so. Given the vastness of the cluster site program—three thousand families—improvement will take years.

De Blasio inherited the cluster site program from Bloomberg, but is himself responsible for reviving the old and unfortunate practice of placing shelter system clients in commercial hotels. In the late 1980s, the common practice was to place homeless families in private, for-profit "welfare hotels" where conditions were infamously poor. Eventually the federal government refused to fund these hotels, and the practice was curbed.

But because of increased demand, de Blasio has had to return to using commercial hotels. Unlike with traditional, Tier II shelters, use of commercial hotels does not require community board notification, for the city is able to claim that it is not actually opening up a "facility," but merely renting out hotel rooms. DHS has to make sure its clients maintain a low profile in these hotels to avoid protests from other guests. Further, providing social services in a private facility is difficult. DHS clients in commercial hotels, although they may like the relative independence hotels offer compared to Tier IIs, are thus less likely to receive the necessary assistance to obtain permanent housing. Also, security at the hotel is poor. Visitors are not monitored and only recently have security guards been stationed at hotels. In February of 2016, there was a triple homicide at the Staten Island Ramada Inn. Michael "Da Kid" Sykes murdered his girlfriend, and her two children, one of whom was his own. Had this hotel had the same security and monitoring that is provided in Tier II shelters, it is unlikely that this tragedy would have occurred.

The new administration was set back when Barrios-Paoli, a seasoned administrator and voice of moderation, left the administration just twenty months after she had joined it with much fanfare. Moreover, Gilbert Taylor did not work out as DHS commissioner and stepped down on December 15,

2015. Thus, for about the first two years of his administration, while he was being battered in the press and in public opinion over the issue of homelessness, de Blasio tolerated the presence of an ineffective point person on this crucial issue. With Taylor's departure, HRA commissioner Banks took temporary charge of DHS.

Thus by mid-December 2015, city homeless policy was perhaps not in crisis but certainly less than optimal. Responsibility was widespread. Bloomberg failed to follow up on promising beginnings, eliminated housing subsidies, and drove up the shelter census. Candidate de Blasio underestimated how difficult a reversal would be. The conflict between de Blasio and Cuomo delayed the renewal of rent subsidies and kept the shelter census higher than it would have been. The feud also put off a fourth New York/New York agreement, leaving the city with few supportive housing units for the unsheltered mentally ill, who remained on the streets to be seen by all. The mayor responded slowly to the resulting media flap. Putting off building new shelters forced the city to rely on cluster sites and commercial hotels. Letting Lilliam Barrios-Paoli leave and Gilbert Taylor stay was a mistake. If de Blasio was to prove that a progressive could govern New York City, he would have to pick up his game, and he tried to do so.

To deal with the perception that street homelessness was out of control, the administration introduced the Home-Stat program. Sixty workers from the Mayor's Office of Operations now patrol the streets and call in sightings of homeless people to the city's nonemergency phone number, 311. Funding to private outreach nonprofits will be increased so that they can expand their street outreach teams from 175 to 312 workers and thus be able to respond to 311 calls within one hour. The Police Department will redeploy forty officers to its Homeless Outreach Unit. Two extra mini-counts of street homeless will be done each year for a total of four yearly counts. The idea is to identify street homeless individuals quickly and bring them to shelter rapidly. It may also be that the administration finally realized that more frequent and more accurate enumerations of street homelessness will be likely to rebut the belief that this population has exploded.

Further, it seems that a way around the Cuomo/de Blasio impasse, as it concerns supportive housing, may have developed. There is still no New York/New York IV Agreement, but there is what might be called a New York/New York IV Disagreement. In his State of the State Speech of January 13, 2013, Governor Cuomo announced plans for the state to develop twenty thousand supportive housing units over fifteen years. Earlier, de Blasio pledged that the city would develop fifteen thousand such units over the same period. In other words, since the mayor and governor cannot get along well enough to sign a formal agreement, each will undertake part of the job on his own. Supporters of a New York/New York IV Agreement had been calling for thirty thousand more units and are pleased that together the city and state plan to create thirty-five thousand units. The New York/New York Agreements were strikingly successful ventures in intergovernmental cooperation, so it is a pity that that process has apparently been abandoned for largely personal reasons. No one knows yet whether the lack of a formal agreement will prove to be a problem.

* * *

A key part of this effort to get on top of the homeless issue was the partial remerger of DHS with HRA. Homeless services were spun off from HRA in 1994. In April of 2016, a ninety-day review authored by City Hall with the help of outside management consultants PriceWaterhouseCoopers argued that having two different agencies provide services to these largely overlapping populations was inefficient. The mayor's solution was to have both HRA and DHS report to Banks, who was now dubbed commissioner of social services. The review projected $38 million in savings from the combined management structure.

But this partial merger may not be a good idea. As an independent agency, DHS was able to communicate and bargain with other city entities. Most homeless services are provided, not directly by DHS, but by contracted providers, who are generally not enthusiastic about the new arrangement. Most providers prefer to deal with a small agency focused on their specific issue rather than a very large but possibly more powerful superagency. Bureaucratic coordination via consolidation is rarely achieved in America's fragmented administrative system. Agency effectiveness is more likely to be achieved by smaller, mission-driven organizations. But if the new, better-integrated structure is to work, the mayor needs to get serious about it: so far, no new head of DHS has been appointed.

Another problem for the de Blasio administration is that the LINC subsidies are not having as much of an effect as was hoped. According to a report from the Independent Budget Office, as of December 2015, the program had assisted only half as many families as had originally been planned. LINC has faced obstacles in recruiting landlords who are still angry over the Advantage debacle. Analysts believe that since the end of Advantage, housing prices have risen, and so LINC vouchers are too paltry (between about $1,200 and $1,550, depending on household size). Also, finding suitable units for LINC clients is difficult, partly because many of the very apartments that would be assigned to LINC voucher holders are still being used as cluster site units.

The de Blasio administration initiated another housing voucher program, CITYFEPS. FEPS stands for Family Eviction Prevention Services, and is designed for families that have experienced eviction. Landlords are reluctant to rent to tenants who have a history of eviction, so the CITYFEPS program has guarantees attached to it such that if the family is no longer able to pay its portion of the rent, the city will pay. The CITYFEPS vouchers provide the same support as LINC vouchers.

But the CITYFEPS program has serious problems. All apartments that participate in low-income voucher programs—Section 8, NYCHA, LINC, and TBRA—are inspected by the city department of Housing, Preservation, and Development (HPD) in order to meet federal standards for habitation. However, CITYFEPS units are not inspected by HPD. According to an HRA spokesperson, "For CITYFEPS, not-for-profit service providers generally do an assessment of the units, including a walk-through of the units."[7] But providers are judged by DHS partly by the number of families they place in independent apartments. Underperforming providers are at risk of losing their contract. So providers have an interest in approving apartments that can undermine their objectivity.

* * *

The HPD inspection process is time tested; their inspectors are trained and regulated, and there are rules in place to prevent conflicts of interest. CITYFEPS apartments need to be inspected by HPD in order to protect vulnerable families from being exploited by unscrupulous landlords. Allowing potentially self-interested shelter providers to inspect CITYFEPS units is incautious and likely to provoke criticism when it comes to light.

A major factor that has driven demand, but has rarely been spoken about in public, is the eligibility process for families that apply to the shelters. The city must direct scarce housing resources to those who are most in need, and the eligibility process is designed to keep out families that are not actually homeless.

The city shelter system is regulated by the state welfare department, these days known as the Office of Temporary and Disability Assistance (OTDA). In December of 2015, OTDA issued a new regulation that drastically loosened eligibility rules. Very often, families applying for shelter had previously been living in an apartment leased to a family member or friend. Essentially, the new administrative directive made it much easier for the primary tenant of an apartment to refuse to let a family applying for shelter return to the apartment where it had been staying.

Often, prior housing history, public assistance records, and close family ties would show that despite the primary tenant's refusal, the applicant was in fact lawfully permitted to reside at the address of origin. With the new rules, any applicant who told eligibility specialists that they were not allowed to return to their former apartment would be found eligible for shelter. In effect, the primary tenant now had a greater power to evict family members than did the city marshal. According to the Coalition for the Homeless, "the 2015 change in policy resulted in a decrease of the percentage of families denied shelter."[8] No doubt many needy families now received shelter, but the census was also driven up. Whether this was on balance a good deal may be doubted. In any case, almost one year later, in December 2016, a new OTDA regulation allowed the city to retighten eligibility standards. In effect, eligibility standards were loosened, more families were found eligible, the shelter census went up, and then the standards were tightened again. Fiddling with the eligibility standards at the very time when the new rent-subsidy programs were supposed to drive the shelter census down was probably not a good idea.

* * *

In response to the growing shelter census, the de Blasio administration has released a new plan, "Turning the Tide on Homelessness," which features an ambitious proposal to build ninety new shelters within a five-year period. The multipronged approach also touts the mayor's success in enhancing shelter security and addressing code violations, which is particularly warranted given the state of disrepair found in many cluster site apartments.

Perhaps the most striking thing about the new plan is its tone, which is markedly more realistic than de Blasio's campaign rhetoric was. When he was a candidate, de Blasio's determination that the city could indeed successfully take on the daunting problem of inequality raised expectations about what could be done to deal with homelessness. Now, his new plan tells us that "[w]e must be clear-eyed: it will take many years to reset the unacceptable status quo we see today. . . . There are no silver bullets here. We will not solve this crisis overnight. It will be a long hard fight."[9] The more realistic tone is certainly welcome. But wouldn't it have been better to *start out* by lowering expectations, which de Blasio could have afforded to do given the big lead he enjoyed in the general election campaign?

If the city indeed succeeds in building ninety new shelters, it will be able to end the use of commercial hotels and cluster site housing. But the greatest challenge to the construction of new shelters is community opposition. De Blasio's new plan therefore calls for improved community relations and better outreach to community boards in order to curb resistance to new shelters. Unfortunately, the mayor's promises to consult communities thoroughly sound all too much like those of his mentor, David Dinkins, who in 1991 proposed to overcome local opposition to his plan of opening a mere twenty shelters through "Early and Meaningful Community Involvement," "Fair Distribution of New Facilities around the City," and "Undertaking a Comprehensive Approach to Siting." Dinkins's plan was to win over hostile neighborhoods by being too impeccably fair to dispute. Communities would have none of it. The highly visible plan merely called attention to itself and gave communities an obvious target. The fact is, the less noticeable such siting efforts are, the easier they are for the city to accomplish.

Another problem for de Blasio's plan is that where and how to place new shelters is governed by the city's "Fair Share" law, which was incorporated into the City Charter in 1989. The law is outdated and confusing, and over the past twenty-five years, poor neighborhoods have in fact received more shelters than is equitable. In response to this unfairness, the City Council is now considering a proposal to reform the Fair Share law and push better-off communities to accept more shelters. Fair enough, it would seem, but a disproportionate number of shelter residents come from those same poor communities. Locating more shelters in better-off neighborhoods would mean that more homeless people would be sheltered far away from their places of origin, a practice that advocacy groups such as Coalition for the Homeless already dislike. How the de Blasio administration will square this circle is not at all clear.

Two courses of action for the city seem clear. One is to reform the CITYFEPS voucher program. As it stands, CITYFEPS is unlikely to meet its goals of rehousing families with histories of eviction, since families are returning to the shelters because they are being placed in apartments that do not meet minimal standards for habitation. The practice of having CITYFEPS units inspected by potentially self-interested service providers should end. The responsibility of inspecting apartments should be taken over by HPD, who already have a set of standards that is enforceable. They also are trained and equipped to perform this function. If the reintegration of DHS and HRA is successful, perhaps better coordination with HPD and other agencies will improve the administration of CITYFEPS.

The cluster site program should end, and the apartments it made use of should be converted into permanent housing for LINC voucher holders. But as the Independent Budget Office notes, the greatest challenge to this initiative is that the landlords will be paid half as much from LINC as they are already being paid to run a cluster site. Landlords are also reluctant to resume business relationships with the city after the fallout from the abrupt termination of the Advantage program in 2011. However, the city should be able to use the threat of withdrawing funding for cluster site housing as leverage in convincing landlords to participate in the LINC program.

* * *

The experience of the de Blasio administration also sheds light on two conceptual issues. First of all, it seems that the issue of perverse incentives needs to be reexamined. The studies that undermined the perverse incentive theory and cleared the way for the reintroduction of rent subsidies are now eighteen years old and need to be updated. The introduction of LINC was supposed to drive the census down, but it has in fact gone up, which does not imply causality but does suggest that the issue of how policy affects shelter demand needs to be revisited. DHS needs to improve its forecasting ability to more accurately predict the likely results of changes in rent subsidies, eligibility, and other policies.

Also important is what recent experience with homelessness policy says about the prospects for the progressive coalition in New York City. A striking feature of city homelessness policy is that it was developed mostly under conservative mayors: Koch, Giuliani, and Bloomberg. From the beginning of modern homeless policy in the late 1970s to the end of Bloomberg's term in 2014, the one-term mayoralty of David Dinkins was the only interregnum of progressive rule. As readers of this book will learn, coming to grips with homelessness proved difficult for Dinkins, who found that he had to rethink some of the progressive conceptions he had brought to the issue. Dinkins's indecisiveness and his failure to make a dent in a problem he had decried as a candidate seemed to justify Giuliani's criticism that progressives lacked the managerial skills necessary to govern New York City. De Blasio's reelection prospects seem pretty good right now, but his lackluster record with an issue that was central to his political vision will not be helpful. To be fair, de Blasio was dealt a bad hand regarding the homeless problem, but he has not always played his cards well. The problem has not been fundamentally wrongheaded policy but lack of managerial and political deftness. Can progressives govern New York City? Not if they don't get their act together.

Introduction

In America, homelessness, defined as living in public spaces or in facilities that accommodate people who otherwise would be living in public spaces, continues to be a large and intractable problem. The scholarly literature includes a study that estimates the number of people nationwide who, over a five-year period, have experienced a spell of homelessness at nearly six million.[1] A recent survey conducted by the federal Department of Housing and Urban Development (HUD) found that nationally, on a single night in January 2013, there were 591,768 homeless persons and that about 1.42 million people spent at least one night during that year in an emergency shelter or a transitional housing program.[2] The federal government spent $4.042 billion on projects targeted to the homeless in fiscal year 2012.[3] This is, of course, not very much in an over $3 trillion federal budget. However, there is a lot of federal spending that is not directly targeted to homeless people but nevertheless serves them. For example, many homeless people are served by the Medicaid program, but we do not have data about how many such people there are. How much in total is spent by all state and local governments on homelessness is also not known. The National Alliance to End Homelessness estimates that, at a minimum, each federal dollar spent on the homeless is matched at the state or local level.[4]

Even so, it cannot be said that America spends a great deal, relatively speaking, on the homeless. However, homelessness has a greater salience than budget figures imply. To be without shelter is to be without a basic necessity of life. The conditions under which many homeless people live can be very bad. The quality of life for even the sheltered homeless can also be poor. Further, homeless people often suffer from other debilitating conditions. Thus, according to a 2010 HUD report, 34.7 percent of sheltered homeless people were substance abusers, 26.2 percent were severely mentally ill, 12.3 percent were victims of domestic violence, and 3.9 percent were persons with HIV/AIDS.[5] It is not surprising, then, that a March 2013 Gallup Poll found that 75 percent of the American public said they worry either a "great deal" or a "fair amount" about homelessness and hunger.[6] In short, homelessness is widely recognized as an important social problem.

The ability of the American political system to deal effectively with pressing social problems has often been questioned. Much political science and public administration literature has claimed that change, when it happens in policymaking and implementation, occurs slowly and incrementally.[7] Claims that national policymaking has ground to a halt are frequent today as a Republican Congress faces off against a Democratic president.[8] But concern over gridlock and drift goes back to at least the early 1960s and has continued through the following decades and into the twenty-first century.[9] As one introduction to the American policymaking process notes, "One of the most enduring criticisms of American government has been its seeming inability to respond quickly and responsibly to important policy issues of the day."[10]

How effective, then, has our political system been at dealing with the pressing problem of homelessness? For various reasons it is best to address this question by looking not at the federal level but at lower levels of government. To begin with, probably the majority of the money spent on homelessness is spent at the state and local levels.[11] Almost all shelters and other services delivered to the homeless are operated by nongovernmental organizations under contract to local governments, or by local governments themselves. And the key experience that results in much of the public concern over homelessness is that of seeing and confronting a homeless person, which is, in its nature, an event that takes place at the local level.

The jurisdiction that has developed the most ambitious policy to address the problem of homelessness is New York City. In April 2015, New York City sheltered 59,285 homeless people (including both single individuals and members of families), and an estimate based on a street survey done in February of that year indicates that there were an additional 3,182 persons living in public spaces.[12] In fiscal year 2011 the city's Department of Homeless Services spent $1.47 billion. No other American city spends nearly as much on the homeless as New York or has close to as large a shelter system. The poor quality of life for at least some of the city's homeless has received wide attention. New York City's infamous welfare hotels were icons of the suffering of the urban poor.[13] Just as disturbing are reports of a small population of homeless people who live in the city's tunnels and other underground spaces.[14]

New York City is also the jurisdiction with the longest history of coping with homelessness. The plight of the so-called disaffiliated alcoholics of the Bowery was documented in the early 1960s and had been dealt with by the city in various ways for decades before then. The 1960s also saw the development of "hotel families," that is, families that had been burned out of or otherwise lost their housing and were put up in hotels at the city's expense.[15] These episodes belong to what might be called the prehistory of homelessness policy in New York.

A whole new policy framework was created by the signing of a consent decree in the case of *Callahan v. Carey* on August 26, 1981. As a result of this and other litigation by advocates for the homeless, the city is one of the few local governments with a court-recognized and enforceable policy of providing shelter to anyone who requests it. New York City is therefore the main stage on which the pressing national problem of homelessness has been addressed.

But just as there is a literature on the shortcomings of the national policy process, there is a similar literature on the limits of urban politics, especially New York City politics. Urban policymaking especially is held to be slow and incremental. A standard textbook on urban politics sums up the consensus of the literature on the nature of urban politics as follows: "Urban political structures change slowly in an incremental, evolutionary fashion."[16] Classic statements of pluralist and corporatist theories of urban politics predict that urban politics, in particular New York City politics, will tend towards "stasis" as proposed changes are fought by the many interest groups with stakes in the status quo to defend.[17] Later, structuralist accounts of urban politics have argued that various sorts of economic, constitutional, and social structures drastically limit the possibilities for change.[18]

Urban politics generally, New York City politics particularly, and New York City public bureaucracies especially are held to be resistant to change. In her analysis of the city's agencies, Blanche Blank begins with the observation that "[i]t may be the very essence of any bureaucracy to move cautiously, even ponderously," and concludes that "[c]hange is always incremental as it is too in New York City government."[19] And in their updating of Wallace Sayre and Herbert Kaufman's work, the authors of *Power Failure: New York City Politics and Policy since 1960* hold that "[t]here is much inertia within the system, which makes change difficult. . . . The major difficulty is in putting forward changes, regardless of the direction of the change."[20] And finally, of all bureaucracies, street-level bureaucracies—that is, public service agencies that employ a significant number of front-line workers who interact with the public with substantial discretion—are held to be very resistant to change. Thus in his classic account of street-level bureaucracies, Michael Lipsky writes, "I have argued that the determinants of street-level practice are deeply rooted in the structure of the work. . . . These observations contribute to our understanding of the stability of the institutions and their unlikely response to significant reform activities."[21]

Some recent literature has challenged this picture of slow change and has argued that more dramatic change is possible. The most comprehensive statement of this challenge is *The New Politics of Public Policy*, edited by Marc Landy and Martin Levin (1995). The contributors to this volume argue that the combination of the professionalization of reform, a fragmented institutional framework, divided government, a highly competitive political environment, and the rights revolution have encouraged various types of policy entrepreneurs to compete with each other to have the best claim to popular political ideas. The result has been that "[a] shift has taken place from a 'politics of interests' (which tend to be fixed and thus to change slowly) to a 'politics of values and ideas' (which tend to be more open, fluid, and responsive to change and reason)."[22] However, the contributors to *New Politics* are concerned with national political developments and have little to say about urban politics. The question is, Can this new paradigm of change, which we can call the ideational paradigm, be usefully applied to the supposedly very static forum of city politics?

This book is part of an ongoing effort to test the validity of the received wisdom on urban political change, and the usefulness of the ideational paradigm, by examining in detail various efforts that have been made by successive mayoral administrations to introduce major changes in New York City's public welfare policy and bureaucracy. I have elsewhere argued that throughout the last thirty years, homelessness and welfare policy in New York City have developed in a series of quantum or nonincremental jumps with dramatic, short-term changes in funding, administration, and policy "philosophy."[23] Put another way, nonincremental change is the product of the "politics of values and ideas," with its key features of expertise, policy entrepreneurs, institutional fragmentation, competitive political environments, and, especially, public ideas. My purpose here is to develop this account in more detail and at greater length in the context of the city's efforts to deal with the challenging social problem of homelessness.

Another theme broached by this case history is that of what might be called the perversity thesis, which is the idea that addressing a social problem can actually make it worse. An obvious problem with the jerry-built system as it developed in the 1980s was the poor quality of the shelter it provided. Many clients, both single individuals and families, were quartered in large barracks-style shelters. Welfare hotels for families were also of low quality. One solution to these problems was to move families to *in rem* apartments that the city had come to own as a result of tax delinquency and abandonment by their former owners and that had been refurbished. This solution was pursued vigorously in the early days of the Dinkins administration.

Rapid rehousing to renovated apartments seemed to have created a perverse incentive to become homeless in order to qualify for housing. Many people in the Dinkins administration came to believe this as the number of families entering the system rose for a time. A blue ribbon advisory commission established by Dinkins and headed by Andrew Cuomo later endorsed this claim, as did the present author.

Later scholarship, at the least, cast serious doubt on the reality of perverse incentives in the city's shelter system.[24] Michael Cragg and Brendan O'Flaherty have convincingly argued that the immediate impact of rapidly rehousing a family is to reduce the shelter population by one family and that whatever perverse incentive was created was not strong enough to pull more than one new family into the shelter system. Nonetheless, city administrators and some observers continued to be concerned. Near the end of his administration, Mayor Bloomberg himself suggested that his administration took the possibility of perverse incentives very seriously.[25] New York City's homelessness shows us how ideas, in this case what A. O. Hirschman calls the "perversity thesis," can influence policy.[26]

Let me anticipate some of my findings here by noting that in New York City, the process of establishing shelter as a right has gone through three distinct stages or moments. These are described in the following sections.

Phase One: Entitlement

Simply establishing that there indeed is a right to shelter and then delivering on that entitlement is one of the central challenges to policy. The courts and various advocacy groups such as Coalition for the Homeless are primarily concerned with this aspect of homelessness policy. These interests push policy in the direction of developing a shelter system that is large, court supervised, and primarily concerned with service delivery. Establishing and implementing a right to shelter is one major theme in New York City's policy, a theme that was especially prominent in the early days—that is, through the eighties to the early nineties—of modern homelessness policy.

The right to shelter completely transformed the city's homelessness system. The system grew tremendously in the early eighties. While 7,584 individuals were sheltered in 1982, 21,154 were sheltered in 1985. Spending grew from $6.8 million in 1978, just before the litigation to establish a right to shelter began, to $100 million in 1985.[27] To cope with the rapidly expanding demand, the city rushed to open large, barracks-style shelters where hundreds of clients would sleep in cots laid out in open spaces. During these years the city also relied on commercial welfare hotels to shelter homeless families at the cost of $72 million in 1986. The shelter system during these years was satisfactory neither from a conservative nor from a liberal point of view. The right to shelter was absolute, and unbalanced by any requirements to work, participate in rehabilitation, or seek permanent housing. Moreover, shelter quality was often very poor, and few services were offered to clients. The city had created a system that guaranteed the right to free, low-quality shelter.

Phase Two: Paternalism

Entitlement is one axis around which New York City homelessness policy has spun. As time went by, however, the limits of this purely entitlement-based, emergency-oriented system showed themselves.

The unconditional right to shelter proved to be problematic in various ways. Behavioral problems—such as substance abuse, nonwork, and criminal activity—of some of the homeless required that the entitlement to shelter be conditioned on proper behavior, including participation in work and treatment programs. Strong conceptions of the rights of the mentally ill sometimes had to be limited in order to provide necessary protection and therapy. This set of challenges is of particular concern to mayors and administrators who, unlike the courts or advocates, are responsible for the actual operation of the shelter system. These bureaucracy-based actors therefore push policy in a paternalistic direction, one in which rights are conditioned on good behavior and on participation in programs such as drug treatment, work, and activities designed to move clients out of the shelters as soon as possible.

During the Giuliani administration, the shelter system was much changed from what it had been in the eighties and early nineties, mostly in a paternalistic direction. While in the 1980s most shelters were government run, the system was privatized or, more accurately, not-for-profitized. That change improved shelter quality. Not-for-profitization has also made it possible for the system to impose work or rehabilitation requirements on clients. The city still provided shelter to everyone who asked for it. But not-for-profit shelters can require their clients to work, or participate in rehabilitation, in order to stay in that particular shelter. (Clients who decline to participate are sent back to a city-run, general-intake shelter.) In other words, privatization made paternalism possible.[28]

Family homelessness policy has also over the years shifted away from entitlement and towards paternalism. Throughout the nineties and the early twenty-first century, one of the worst aspects of the shelter system was the intake point for homeless families known as the Emergency Assistance Unit (EAU).[29] During that period, the EAU was typically crowded with families seeking shelter. Processing their requests took many hours and families often slept overnight on the office floor waiting for a determination. One of the main problems was what to do with families that had been found ineligible and who frequently reapplied almost immediately, thus blocking up the process. One knowledgeable observer of city homelessness policy said of the EAU at that time that "[i]t is probably one of the most disturbing places on Earth."[30]

However, since 2003 things are much changed. A court decision that held that DHS may deny shelter to anyone who reapplies within ninety days after his or her application is rejected, unless there has been a change in his or her circumstances, helped end the bottleneck and improve conditions. This was a significant relaxation of the right to shelter, one that allowed DHS to redefine the task performed at the intake point from one of sheltering and determination of eligibility to one of diversion and prevention. Chapter 4, which covers homelessness policy during the Bloomberg administration, describes in detail this process of restructuring intake procedures to the city's family shelter system.

Beginning in the late Dinkins administration and continuing through the Giuliani administration and much of the Bloomberg administration, city homelessness policy developed in a paternalistic direction, one that emphasized the importance of getting homeless people who are able to do so to take responsibility for their housing situation. The drive to develop such a paternalistic policy has required the city to get itself out from under the constraints of the many lawsuits that drive the city's homelessness policy. The city has had to "reinvent" its Department of Homeless Services as a more decentralized and flexible system. In short, New York's homelessness system has evolved from its beginning as a centralized, highly constrained, and entitlement-based system to one that is much more decentralized and privatized and that emphasizes clients' responsibilities as well as their rights.

But paternalism turned out to have its limits, just as entitlement did. Paternalism greatly improved management of homeless services and responded to political demands for more responsibility on the part of recipients. What paternalism did not do was offer much hope of eventually "solving" the problem of homelessness. Despite efforts to diagnose and then treat the "underlying causes" of homelessness, the number of people on the street and of families entering shelters remained frustratingly high. The overall shelter census continued to go up, as did the budget for services for the homeless. The paternalistic reforms, promoted under the Dinkins administration by a special commission led by Andrew Cuomo, and implemented with much fanfare during the Giuliani years, seemed not to be making a dent in these two fundamental measures of success. Paternalism had done a better job at managing homelessness but had failed as a strategy for solving homelessness.

Phase Three: Post-paternalism

The next moment in New York City homelessness policy had its origins in efforts to come up with a strategy that would "solve" homelessness. A crucial part of that effort was what amounted to a redefinition of the homelessness problem by the well-known researcher Dennis Culhane. In the late nineties, only 10 percent of the single homeless persons in New York—who were the most disabled and whom Culhane identified as the "chronic" homeless—accounted for almost half of the shelter days provided by the city. This discovery allowed the homelessness problem to be redefined in such a way that a "solution" seemed within reach: Focus on the relatively small chronic population, house them, thus making a disproportionate impact on reducing shelter use, and declare victory.

The question then became where to house the chronically homeless. The answer was provided by an approach that began to be developed by housing activists in the mid-1980s and that would be expanded between 1990 and 2005 in a series of agreements between New York City and New York State: supportive housing. Supportive housing is subsidized housing for people with various sorts of disabilities who are provided medical and social services on-site so that they can live independently off the streets. Supportive housing was an appropriate place to send the worst-off street dwellers and would receive its largest commitment of resources under the New York/New York III agreement signed during Bloomberg's first term.

In its first iterations, supportive housing projects generally embraced the paternalistic approach and demanded that homeless people sober up, take their medications, and demonstrate that they were "housing ready" before they would be moved into an apartment. The problem was that many street dwellers declined to accept this deal, which made achieving dramatic reductions in street homelessness difficult. Sam Tsemberis, a psychologist experienced in outreach work to the street homeless and founder of the innovative service organization Pathways to Housing, came up with a response. His "Housing First" approach to outreach involved breaking with the paternalist quid pro quo and providing street dwellers with housing before asking them, or perhaps without asking them, for compliance with rehabilitation. Many single homeless people, it turned out, who had previously declined shelter on paternalistic terms were willing to take this deal.

Housing First was developed as an outreach strategy directed to street dwellers but also had an impact on policy toward homeless families. From the eighties to the mid-1990s, it was thought by some observers—including the present author—that homeless families were much more troubled than similar, nonhomeless poor families with problems such as drug use, mental illness, criminal activity, and "underclass" pathologies. Here again, the thought was that there was an underlying cause of the homelessness of many families. By the mid-1990s, research indicated that homeless families, though they suffered higher rate of such problems than similar poor families, were not as dramatically worse as had been thought. In any case, research also showed that whatever their problems, homeless families could generally stay stably placed in permanent housing even if they did not receive any rehabilitative services. The key to rapidly rehousing them was not services, but subsidies. Homeless families, whatever their troubles, could usually live outside the shelter system if they received access to public housing or Section 8 vouchers and other forms of rental subsidy. Thus, under the influence of the Housing First strategy for singles, policy for families began to move away from diagnosing underlying causes and providing appropriate services to planning for rapid rehousing of shelter families, with some form of subsidies being a prominent part of that plan.

The post-paternalistic features of the city's homelessness policy were broached during the early Bloomberg years. It was under Bloomberg that, with much publicity and acclaim, a five-year plan was introduced, the expressed purpose of which was to "overcome" or end homelessness. Ending homelessness really meant having a disproportionate impact on the use of shelters and services by focusing on the chronically homeless, as Culhane had suggested, sending them to supportive housing, and doing so without demanding "good behavior" first, in keeping with the Housing First policy. Implementation of Housing First strategies proceeded apace under Bloomberg, as did the analogous family policy of rapid rehousing, which, in Bloomberg's first term, involved a reliance on various sorts of housing subsidies.

The results of post-paternalism have been mixed, perhaps because this policy philosophy has been incompletely implemented. The Housing First strategy for single homeless people has been effective in considerably reducing the city's population of street dwellers, by about 24 percent between 2005 and 2014.[31] The situation with the shelter population was much different. The census in the shelter system rose throughout the Bloomberg years and was at an all-time high at the end of his final term.

This may be the case because the Housing First strategy was never fully implemented for families. Rapid rehousing consisted mostly in planning to move families out of the shelter almost as soon as they entered, rather than waiting for various sorts of rehabilitative programs to take effect. But a signature Bloomberg policy for dealing with homeless families was "delinking," that is, ending priority access of homeless families to Section 8 vouchers and vacant public housing units. Such delinking was supposed to put an end to the "perverse incentive" of receiving subsidies upon becoming homeless, and was therefore expected to abate the flow of families into the shelter system. Also under Bloomberg, an important rent subsidy for homeless families, the Advantage program, came to an end under complicated circumstances. The delinking strategy and the end of rent subsidies were out of keeping with post-paternalism, which, when applied to families, implied reliance on rent subsidies to achieve rapid access to permanent housing.

We have, then, three stages in the development of homeless policy in New York City: entitlement, paternalism, and post-paternalism. Actually, these stages are more like facets or aspects. Paternalism did not end entitlement; paternalism assumed the homeless had a right to shelter but located the cause of homelessness in the homeless person and demanded that he or she "give something back" in return for shelter and services. Post-paternalism would have undermined paternalism, but has been incompletely implemented. The result is that paternalism has been imposed on top of entitlement, and post-paternalism on top of paternalism. The city's homeless policy is therefore quite complex, and is driven by three distinct "philosophies."

Finally, it is important to note what this book does not do. It does not offer policy prescriptions for how to end homelessness. Such work has been done very ably by Dennis Culhane in his analysis of the problem of chronic homelessness and by Sam Tsemberis and other researchers examining the Housing First approach to sheltering street dwellers. Both these approaches are discussed in the course of the case history told here. This book also does not offer a theory of homelessness. As I have noted elsewhere, the dominant theory of homelessness among academics is a structural theory, that is, one in which longstanding economic and social trends that individuals can have little immediate influence over are held to be the main causes of homelessness while personal characteristics of homeless individuals are held to be of secondary importance.[32] One specific form this structural approach has often taken is to argue that since the late seventies, a decrease in inexpensive housing and an increase in the number of poor people has turned the affordable housing market into a game of "musical chairs," in which some people must end up on the street due to a sheer lack of appropriate units. In this situation it is the weakest—the mentally ill, the addicted, or those who are otherwise incapable of coping—who end up displaced. So, structural features of the housing market and the economy determine the essential fact *that* there will be a certain amount of homelessness, while individual characteristics explain precisely *who* will make up the homeless. This book perhaps could, therefore, begin by elaborating that structural theory in detail as a backdrop against which policy history must be understood.

There are several reasons why I have not begun by laying out this theory. First, developing a theory of homelessness in New York City is beyond the scope of this book, which has the already ambitious objective of chronicling the policy and politics of homelessness. Also, despite excellent work that had been done in applying the structural theory to social reality by authors such as Martha Burt and Brendhan O'Flaherty, I remain somewhat skeptical of the structuralist account and feel that for all its explanatory strength there remains something mysterious about the phenomenon of mass homelessness in New York City. For New York City's population of about sixty thousand (sheltered and unsheltered) homeless people is "small" compared to the total housing stock of the city, which totals 3,084,861 units, including 1,533,107 rentals.[33] It is certainly true that most of these units are too expensive or otherwise not available to the homeless. But more than three million housing units makes for a great deal of physical space with very many unused rooms, attics, basements, garages, and other potential accommodations. Many homeless people have at least some income, if only from welfare and disability payments, and it is reported that a fair number work.[34] Why don't the owners of all that unused space rent it out at a pittance and make at least some money from an otherwise unprofitable asset? In a classic article, Milton Friedman and George Stigler demonstrated that due to such renting out of previously unused space, there was no housing shortage after the San Francisco earthquake of 1906 even though the city's housing stock was reduced by more than half.[35] In New York City today, unused space is often converted—frequently illegally—in this fashion, creating a "housing underground" that has been estimated to include many more than 114,000 apartments.[36] An unknown number of low-income immigrants live in this housing underground, and a recent exploration of this practice among Chinese immigrants found that "[t]he existence of unauthorized apartments provides immigrants, low-wage workers and students a roof over their heads and prevents some of them from becoming homeless."[37] Why doesn't this housing underground expand, perhaps considerably, and take up at least more of the city's "small" homeless population? Working out and testing my skepticism of the dominant structural model of homelessness is a project for another book.

But let's assume this skepticism is unwarranted—that in fact there is no mystery over why people are homeless and that an overview of the structural causes of homelessness could perhaps serve as an introduction to this book. There is another, more important reason for not taking this approach. This project is to a considerable extent historical: it covers a period of more than thirty-five years. The early chapters, at least, are concerned with understanding the actions, decisions, and political judgments of various actors in the past. To understand what people did in *the past*, what is known *now* may or may not be relevant. But what was known *at the time the actors made their decisions* is crucial. Whether or not homelessness should be a mystery to us now, many policy actors of the seventies, eighties, and nineties at least *thought* homelessness was a mystery. As the interviews conducted for this book will bear out, those actors were confused about the roles deinstitutionalization, personal disability, cultural factors, family demographics, policy history, as well as income and housing trends played in creating the homelessness crisis. And they were *legitimately* confused, however certain we may be of things now. Kicking off a history with the very latest account of what happened and then judging past actors according to how closely they approximated that understanding is anachronistic. This is not to say that some mysteries didn't clear up over time. In particular, we have learned much more over time about the phenomenon of perverse incentives as it applies in homeless policy, and about how to improve outcomes in housing mentally ill street dwellers. In these matters, I feel it is fair to say that later actors should have known more than was known at the beginning, and to judge their decisions accordingly. But earlier actors, including the present author, who played a minor role in some of the developments chronicled here, had a right to be unsure.

The following chapters tell the story of New York City's homelessness policy from 1979, when the first work that would lead to the *Callahan v. Carey* consent decree was begun, to the early days of the de Blasio administration up to 2015. The administrations of Koch, Dinkins, Giuliani, Bloomberg, and de Blasio's early years each receives its own chapter. A final chapter draws conclusions about the themes broached in this introduction and about the nature of urban politics.

1

The Beginnings of Homelessness Policy under Koch

In the mid-1970s the problem of homelessness achieved a new visibility on the New York City scene. Literally. Prior to the early 1970s the phenomenon of homelessness—that is, of people who, lacking other accommodations, lived and slept predominantly in public spaces such as the streets, transportation facilities, parks, and other situations not intended for human habitation—was confined mostly to the Bowery, the city's skid row neighborhood. Some classic studies of this milieu began in the early 1960s and reported that the homeless—then often referred to as "derelicts" and "vagrants"—rarely ventured outside of the Bowery on the Lower East Side of Manhattan.[1] Increasingly throughout the seventies, however, the homeless came to be encountered across Manhattan and the city as a whole. Over the years, the *New York Times* and other media documented this spreading crisis.

A *Times* article from 1971, "Alone and Homeless, 'Shutouts' of Society Sleep in Doorways," noted that

> [t]he doorway of the Chase Manhattan Bank is one of half a dozen recessed entry ways on Lexington Avenue between 42nd and 44th Streets that serve as places to sleep for homeless and penniless vagrants drawn to the anonymity of the Grand Central Terminal area. . . .
>
> There are numerous places for doorway sleepers around the city: Pennsylvania Station, the Port Authority bus terminal, Herald Square. Some sites, in Chinatown and along the Upper East Side, are new. All have seen an influx in recent years of derelicts, many of whom formerly slept along the Bowery but who have dispersed largely because of police "clean-up" drives.[2]

The article was illustrated with a photograph captioned "On Lexington Avenue: A person sleeping outside a shoe store north of 42nd Street."

Whether police action was primarily the cause of the dispersion of the homeless is doubtful, but in any case the *Times* continued to document the phenomenon. The title of a 1973 article reported, probably inaccurately, that "The Derelict Population Is Declining" and more cogently added, "But the Whole City Is Its 'Flophouse.'" The article continued:

> For whatever reason, substantial numbers of derelicts are now visible far from the Bowery—in and around Grand Central Terminal and Pennsylvania Station, near Gramercy Park, on Lexington Avenue in the 30's, on Broadway from the 70's through the 90's and in construction sites anywhere, particularly those that have aluminum corridors for pedestrians.
>
> There are also derelicts who regularly sleep in the darkened archways and alleys of city buildings in lower Manhattan. The police report an increase in the number of derelicts living under the Boardwalk at Coney Island, under the Brooklyn Bridge, near the old Police Headquarters at 100 Center Street, and on 125th Street in Harlem.[3]

The article also documented the presence of homeless people in the Bronx and Staten Island and included a photograph of "[a] woman in search of food poring over the contents of a trash receptacle at Third Avenue and 70th Street."

Still on the story in 1976, the *Times* published an article entitled "Vagrants and Panhandlers Appearing in New Haunts," which confirmed that

> [t]he Bowery scene has spread. In the late hours vagrants can now be found singly and in twos and threes in the triangles on Broadway from Herald Square to 72nd Street, along the southern edge of Central Park, in the side streets of Times Square, around the fountained plazas of the Avenue of the Americas, along Lexington Avenue above 42nd Street, in the small parks of the Lower East Side and in Trinity Place. . . .
>
> In a three-mile walk on the West Side one recent summer night, a reporter saw about 50 vagrants. Half a dozen were shopping-bag ladies, who bridled fiercely when approached. The rest were apathetic or asleep, several were dead drunk and many had bottles bulging from pockets.
>
> On a stairway leading to the garage beneath the Coliseum, on Columbus Circle, a barelegged woman in her 30's slept. On the floor of the men's room below a young man sprawled unconscious among his ragged belongings.[4]

This article, too, was accompanied by photographs, one captioned, "In various places in Manhattan, particularly near bright lights, the vagrants may be found sleeping where they can."

By the early 1980s social science research backed up the *Times*' reportage: homeless people were visible all over the city, especially Manhattan. Anthropologist Kim Hopper's ground-breaking ethnographic account of this reality deserves to be quoted at length:

> In the summer of 1980. . . . [o]n the outside plaza of the Garden alone, it was not unusual to find 75 men and women sleeping there at dawn.
>
> Another quick count, made between 5:30 and 6:00 on a summer morning in 1982, revealed 62 men and women sleeping along the southern perimeter of Central Park. The outreach team serving homeless people in the park reported that there were at least a hundred living there on a relatively permanent basis. The director of security for Amtrak at Penn Station estimated that at the time about 150 homeless people "consider[ed] the station home." In a single month, mid-January to mid-February 1984, the outreach team serving the Port Authority Bus Terminal made 2,400 contacts (including, no doubt, many duplications) with homeless people in the station.
>
> In many areas of Manhattan (the region I explored most intensively), men could be found sleeping wherever haven, however tentative, presented itself: in the steam tunnels that ran under Park Avenue, alongside railroad tracks and service yards; in vest-pocket parks, recessed doorways, and storefronts along major thoroughfares; in abandoned buildings and deserted subway stations; in the loading bays of manufacturing firms; in storage bunkers below the entrance ramps to highways; in the lower stairwells and basements of unlocked tenements; under bridges and in parking lots; and in makeshift camps along unused rail lines, closed highways, and derelict freight yards. In the early morning hours, some public places resembled nomadic encampments, with linked cardboard boxes serving as individual sleeping quarters. . . .
>
> Things had changed on the street since the days of skid row, and the changes were apparent to anyone who had spent time there.[5]

Eventually, various groups began to respond to this situation. One of the groups that was most active in the cause of the homeless in the early eighties was Coalition for the Homeless (CFTH). CFTH was born when two streams of social activism that had started independently of each other came together. One stream was that of legal activism, headed by Robert Hayes, a New York lawyer. Another stream was one of advocacy research sponsored by an independent research center, the Community Service Society of New York (CSS) and conducted by Kim Hopper and Ellen Baxter, Columbia University graduate students in medical anthropology and public health, respectively.

Robert Hayes began investigating the condition of the New York City homeless in 1978. Even then the city ran a shelter system, which at the time was a system of lodging houses and auxiliary services for those who had nowhere else to go. Hayes investigated the various kinds of lodging to which the city directed homeless people: the Men's Shelter at 8 East Third Street, which was the principal intake point for the rest of the men's shelter system; the Bowery hotels—or flophouses—to which the Men's Shelter issued vouchers; and later the Keener building (an abandoned mental institution on Wards Island opened in 1979 to accommodate the growing demand for shelter). At the time Hayes began his work, the city sent men applying for shelter to the Bowery hotels, or to Camp LaGuardia, a shelter sixty miles from the city designed to accommodate older clients. If both these places were filled, men slept in the "big room," the largest room of the Men's Shelter. Once the big room was filled, other applicants were simply denied shelter.

Back in the late seventies and early eighties, the Men's Shelter at 8 East Third Street, located in the heart of Manhattan's Bowery, was a frightening place for anyone not inured to life on the streets. On my visits around 1983, there were always many ragged, unclean men loitering on the sidewalk for half a block on either side of the entrance. Even before one entered, a strong unpleasant odor was very noticeable. Inside, scores of men waited in no apparent order to be seen by the "5 x 8 staff," so called because their perfunctory interview produced an index card with some basic information about the applicant. Security was not evident, and on one occasion I was unpleasantly approached by one of the men. Such security as there was focused on protecting the front office from break-ins. The *New York Times* remembered, "Chaos reigned as men checked in for meals and vouchers that purchased beds in nearby flophouses. Between meals, homeless men milled constantly on the street, dealing drugs and panhandling."[6] A staff member once told me that the Men's Shelter sometimes offered internships to students from a nearby university who were getting their degree in social work. Many of those students would take one look, or perhaps sniff, at the Men's Shelter, and that was the end of their aspirations to do social work.

Bonnie Stone, the first assistant deputy administrator at the Human Resources Administration (HRA), which was in charge of services for single homeless men in the late seventies and early eighties, also remembered the old Men's Shelter:

> But the place was frightening. . . . [I]t was a huge building, with huge cavernous spaces and there were echoes everywhere. And you would see hundreds of people going around in very, very bad . . . physical shape. . . . You would drive past them on the Bowery and you'd see them bloody and incoherent on the street, well they would be the same way in the shelter. And there were hundreds of them. And the place was dark and loud and had bad smells and it was a little bit like entering Dante's Inferno. . . . And it had been there for decades.[7]

This remained a fair description of the big room up until the Men's Shelter was renovated in the early nineties.[8]

Hayes continued his interviews with many homeless men and learned, according to CFTH literature, that they "found the streets and subways less dangerous and degrading" than the shelter system. "Streets were [the] preferred option . . . because conditions at the city shelter were so abominable." He therefore felt that "the demand for shelter beds was far lower than the true need since conditions at the municipal shelter effectively deterred many of the homeless from even seeking shelter."[9]

At this point Hayes decided to do something—and what he did seems to have been determined by his belief that what was needed was "recognition with the force of law of a right to shelter." The reasoning, apparently, was that if shelter were recognized as a right, rather than as a matter of social service, then no one could legitimately be deterred from claiming it. The conceptualization of the problem—as one of rights—also determined the avenue through which it would be settled: the courts. CFTH was aware of this implication, and of the problems it might raise. A CFTH report, "Litigation in Advocacy for the Homeless," stated that "[i]t is rare that a 'right to shelter' will be forthrightly espoused in any jurisdiction. Instead, the more probable course would be one which would require creative interpretation of a more general statutory and constitutional language to arrive at an enforceable entitlement."

Such creative work is what Hayes then began. He found entitlements to shelter implied in the New York State Constitution, the New York State Social Service Law, the New York Municipal Law, and even the equal protection provision of the U.S. Constitution. Thus, according to Hayes, the following lines of article 17 from the New York State Constitution imply an enforceable right to shelter: "The aid, care and support of the needy are public concerns and shall be provided by the state and by such of its subdivisions, and in such manner and by such means, as the legislature may from time to time determine."

But whether the New York State Constitution implies a right to shelter is unclear. Unlike the U.S. Constitution, some state constitutions create so-called positive rights to social services such as education and assistance for mentally or physically challenged persons, as well as environmental rights. It has been noted that "[t]he social welfare provision of New York's Constitution is among the strongest in the nation."[10] But the court interpretation of that provision has typically been, as one source says, "Recognition of a Duty, but with Extraordinary or Complete Deference to the Legislature."[11] That is, the court of appeals (New York State's highest court) has found that article 17 makes provision for the needy mandatory but leaves the questions of who is needy and how they are to be provided for largely up to the legislature. Thus, in the 1977 case of *Tucker v. Toya* the court found that

> [i]n New York State, the provision for assistance to the needy is not a matter of legislative grace; rather, it is specifically mandated by our constitution. . . . [T]he Constitution imposes upon the state an affirmative duty to aid the needy and though it provides the legislature with discretion in determining the amount of aid and in classifying recipients and defining the term "needy," it unequivocally prevents the legislature from simply refusing to aid those whom it has classified as needy.[12]

But in another 1977 case, *Bernstein v. Toya*, a case addressing the sufficiency of state grants for housing, the court said of the social welfare provision that "[w]e do not read this declaration as . . . commanding that, in carrying out the constitutional duty to provide aid, care and support of the needy, the State must always meet in full measure all the legitimate needs of each recipient."[13] The court wrote further that "[w]e explicitly recognized in *Tucker* that the legislature is vested with discretion to determine the amount of aid; what we there held prohibited was the legislature's 'simply refusing to aid those whom it has classified as needy.'"[14]

Obviously homeless people are needy, but whether they had been classified by the state as such was not clear in the early eighties. A law review article from that period makes the case that the New York State Constitution should be interpreted to imply a right to shelter but nonetheless acknowledges that "the judiciary, while manifesting a deep concern for the plight of the homeless, has failed to decide the fundamental question of whether a right to shelter exists."[15]

But Hayes believed the right to shelter was more definite than that. He was convinced that advocacy through the courts was crucial to solving the problems of the homeless, and with such arguments in mind, he gathered together several homeless men, including one Robert Callahan, to serve as co-litigants against the city and state.

On October 2, 1979, the *Callahan* suit went before the New York State Supreme Court. The plaintiffs alleged that on cold winter nights homeless men were turned away from the Men's Shelter at 8 East Third Street if it was full to capacity and that men denied shelter suffered hypothermia, frostbite, and death. They sought a temporary mandatory injunction directing state and city officials to provide lodging and shelter to applicants at the Men's Shelter. The plaintiffs presented affidavits from persons who worked with homeless men in the Bowery that some men would freeze to death in the streets that winter if more shelter were not available.[16] George Gutwirth, assistant city corporation counsel, represented the city and argued that "we didn't need a lawsuit to tell us we will have a problem this winter," but state supreme court judge Justice Andrew R. Tyler refused to dismiss the case.[17]

Perhaps in response to the *Callahan* suit, on December 3, 1979, the city opened the Keener building on Wards Island in the East River as a shelter for men. The Keener building was located on the grounds of a former state psychiatric hospital, Manhattan State. To reach it, potential clients could take a city-run van service from the Men's Shelter. Otherwise, they had to take a long trip on public transportation, or cross over a bridge connecting the island to Manhattan at 103rd Street. The Keener building represented a marginal improvement over conditions in the big room. One observer described the building at this time as follows:

> Keener was a paragon of institutional thrift. It was run by a limited and overworked staff. Bedding was rudimentary: light mattresses on metal frames. Walls were bereft of any ornament but graffiti. One concession to relief of tedium was a new mess hall, open only during mealtimes. Few of the televisions in the common rooms worked reliably; newspapers were days, even weeks old; magazines were nowhere to be seen. . . . Men lounged around in various states of undress, in contact with an assortment of realities. Some of the ex-patients among these men had come full circle back to the institution that had originally discharged them—this time as shelter clients, not hospital patients. . . . A limited number of subway and bus tokens were made available to men wishing to go back to Manhattan. . . . But many men left the island only infrequently. In the main they languished in near unbroken torpor, confined to the building through the day but for an occasional supervised walk, inmates in all but name.[18]

Indeed, even Mayor Koch was moved to say no more of the Keener building than "[i]t's not exactly a palace, but it's nice."[19] However unappealing the Keener building then was, it did provide an extra 180 beds. This allowed the city to discontinue use of the big room at the Men's Shelter for purposes of sleeping for the first time in twenty years.[20]

On December 5, 1979, Justice Tyler granted Hayes the temporary injunction he sought and ordered the city and state to open 750 new beds for the "helpless and hopeless men of the Bowery," saying that "Bowery derelicts are entitled to board and lodging."[21] However, it is not correct to say that "Tyler held that the New York State constitution gave homeless men a right to 'adequate shelter.'"[22] City attorneys Doron Gopstein and George Gutwirth later pointed out that except for a footnote in which the plaintiffs' legal authorities were merely cited, the decision did not discuss the legal claims of either party. They also noted that the state constitution claim was eventually rejected by three federal justices, two of whom noted that the decision was instead based on concern that many homeless men were likely to die of hypothermia if the extra beds were not provided. These judges further noted that the granting of a preliminary injunction is not a determination of merits under New York law.[23]

Plaintiffs then asked the court to take the next step and issue a preliminary injunction requiring the defendants to provide an adequate supply of shelter. On December 24, 1979, the court granted the preliminary injunction and "[o]rdered that the State Defendants and the City Defendants provide shelter (including clean bedding, wholesome board, and adequate security and supervision) to any person who applies for shelter at the Municipal Shelter Care Center for Men."[24] The court also ordered that the city provide the plaintiffs every day with a census of the men who had applied for and been given lodging, and that the city grant monitors chosen by the plaintiffs access to the shelter system. Hayes's initial steps had thus been a success.

With this early victory came a challenge. Hayes needed recruits to serve as monitors, and more generally he needed partners to pursue other, nonjudicial courses of action. Thus a cadre of interested parties began to develop. According to Hayes, "During that first part of 1980, you know in pubs and in my studio apartment on Sixteenth Street . . . we brought in a crew of 15 and 20 people . . . the nuns, the saints, the really good people who knew what they were doing. It was not the charitable professional complex people."[25] A rallying point for organizing and publicity suggested itself. That year the Democratic National Convention was held in New York at Madison Square Garden near Penn Station. There were debates about how to take advantage of the situation. According to Hayes,

> So we organized around that and it actually reflected, I thought, the goodness and naiveté and therefore the inadequacy of our little group. There were some people who wanted to do very visible things. Like in 1980 if you had a long bread line in broad daylight on national TV that would have been shocking . . . and there were people who supported that and then people closer to real folks who are homeless said it's not fair to put people on political display because they are hungry. . . . And there was the suggestion to put lice on the floor of the convention. That didn't last long but it was playful. So eventually we worked with one of the groups, the Franciscans, who had the early morning bread line since the Depression around a corner from here at Penn Station. And they

> had developed a Saint Francis residence which was probably the prototype of supported housing. . . . And . . . at Saint Francis of Assisi Church we just set up as a refuge for folks who would be moved away by the police from where they were sleeping then which was in Penn Station and around the [Madison Square] Garden.

The *New York Times* reported on the protest that was set up:

> [A] wrought-iron gate . . . is always open to the courtyard of St. Francis of Assisi Roman Catholic Church. There, kneeling, is an iron St. Francis, and above him hangs a sheet lettered in red with the names of the homeless people who died on New York City's streets in the past year.
>
> Hunched in the darkened recesses of the tiny courtyard are some of the people who ordinarily sleep around Madison Square Garden and in Pennsylvania Station but who have been shooed away this convention week, unsightly men in tattered shirts, women clutching bags of junk.
>
> Standing with them, in round-the-clock vigil each night of the Democratic National Convention, are members of the Community Services Society, the Catholic Worker, Covenant House and other groups that provide shelter for a few thousand of New York's homeless people. The service groups hope their demonstration will attract the attention of political leaders here for the convention and they are calling upon the city to house the 30,000 others they say remain on the streets. One thousand of the wayfarers are believed to have died on sidewalks and in gutters in the last year.[26]

Participants at the vigil report that eventually a camera crew from NBC came around to document the event. One participant, Kim Hopper, was asked just what these various activists represented. On the spot Hopper responded that they were the Coalition for the Homeless. And thus an organization was born.[27] Kim Hopper recalled those early days of CFTH:

> It would have been great if somebody had ever filmed those early Coalition for the Homeless meetings. They were something out of Fellini. All kinds of folks would show up . . . wandering in off the street. . . . It was like running a three ring circus at times. We had lawyers, we had policy makers from Albany, we had city officials, we had people living on the streets, we had folks with active psychiatric problems. Everybody would show up and we would somehow have to hammer out an agenda and actually conduct a semi-orderly meeting. God knows somehow it happened with a kind of, I don't know, folk magic of some sort.[28]

Hopper was then a graduate student in anthropology at Columbia University. Together with Ellen Baxter, a public health graduate student also at Columbia, he had been hired by the Community Service Society (CSS) in December 1979 to conduct a study of the mentally ill homeless on the streets of New York. CSS produced two extensive studies of homelessness, *Private Lives/Public Spaces: Homeless Adults on the Streets of New York City*, by Hopper and Baxter[29] and *One Year Later: The Homeless Poor in New York City, 1982*, in which Lawrence Klein and Stuart Cox joined Hopper and Baxter as coauthors.[30] These works were the products of a research project that had been conceived by Frank G. Caro, director of the Institute for Social Research of CSS, and supported by a fifty thousand dollar grant from the Ittleson Foundation.[31] The CSS reports dealt with the life of the homeless on the streets, and also with the quality of the shelter system. CSS advanced two claims that became especially influential.

First, CSS made an estimate of the number of homeless people in New York City. CSS held that there were thirty-six thousand, this figure being based on estimates made by the New York State Office of Mental Health (OMH).[32] In an internal memo dated October 12, 1979, OMH in turn based its figure of thirty thousand on estimates made by the Men's Shelter that the approximately nine thousand different men they serviced represented 30 percent of the homeless men in the city. CSS then added to this the Manhattan Bowery Corporation's estimate of six thousand to sixty-five hundred "periodically homeless" women to arrive at the thirty-six thousand figure.

CSS made this estimate public in February 1981. According to the New York City Human Resources Administration (HRA), for fiscal year 1980–1981 the overall daily average attendance in the shelters was 2,428.[33] Again, since December 1979 the city had been required to provide shelter to any man who requested it. (In the case of *Eldredge v. Koch*, filed in February 1982, the advocates sought successfully to extend the coverage of the *Callahan* decree to homeless women.) How did CSS explain the fact that, while their estimate of the number of homeless people was thirty-six thousand, not even a tenth of that number had requested shelter from the city?

The answer lies in a second main contention of CSS, which concerned the nature of the shelter system. CSS held that conditions at these facilities were so bad that the homeless refused to use them and preferred to stay on the streets. According to CSS,

> What public resources do exist, moreover, have their own deterrent power. The deplorable conditions of the flophouses and Keener Building, high incidence of violence, routine contempt meted out to applicants for shelter, and the histori-

> cal association of the Bowery as the abode of "bums," all make the Men's Shelter the place of last resort for many homeless men. For different reasons—namely exclusionary policies, limited beds, and the militaristic regime—the Women's Shelter can effectively service only a small proportion of homeless women. . . . Given the state of the public shelters—or perhaps more accurately, given the nature of the personal costs extracted when one submits to their regimes and conditions—the decision made by many homeless people to fend for themselves on the streets gains at least a measure of intelligibility.[34]

In short, CSS came to very much the same conclusions about the plight of New York's homeless and about the condition of the shelter system that Hayes did: The problem was enormous and the shelter system was inadequate to help.

Private Lives/Public Spaces caught the attention of a wide audience right away. The monograph was published in February of 1981. On Sunday, March 8, the *Times*, which had been given exclusive access to the report by CSS,[35] ran a front-page story about Baxter and Hopper's research. The headline trumpeted what the journalist apparently thought was the most salient finding of the study: "Help Is Urged for 36,000 in City's Streets."[36] Thus was born a figure that would be widely repeated in all sorts of media when the issue of homelessness in New York City was broached.

The authors of *Private Lives/Public Spaces* had not expected their work to achieve such wide notice. Baxter would say of the notoriety of the report that "we were totally unprepared . . . and were just . . . stunned."[37] What should not have been so surprising was how much that attention focused on the estimate of thirty-six thousand homeless New Yorkers. In a follow-up to *Private Lives/Public Spaces*, the authors said of the estimate that "its place in that report was less than central."[38] But the very first sentence of the preface to the report featured the thirty-six thousand figure and presented it as based on "official estimates."[39] Cynthia J. Bogard in her book, *Seasons Such as These: How Homelessness Took Shape in America*, offers a detailed, social constructionist account of this estimate that emphasizes the political nature of the process whereby homelessness came to be legitimated as a serious social problem.[40] But her analysis underestimates the importance of one key feature of the estimate: its "official" nature.

In the early eighties there were no scientifically sophisticated estimates of the city homeless population available. Advocates for the homeless who were eager to increase the salience of the homelessness problem were thus faced with a dilemma: how to produce an estimate of the homeless that would be taken seriously by policy actors and the media when no figures derived from objectively collected data and sophisticated statistical methodology were available. If Baxter and Hopper had presented the thirty-six thousand number as simply their own guess, it could have been dismissed as a self-promoting maneuver undertaken by advocates with an interest in exaggerating the problem. But emphasizing the fact that the number was based on estimates made by the Men's Shelter staff and the Manhattan Bowery Corporation imbued it with objectivity. The city had to, at least at first, take seriously an estimate that was generated by the city itself (and a credible nonprofit organization). Baxter and Hopper had pulled off, perhaps unintentionally, a neat piece of rhetorical judo: the city's own credibility was used to validate a claim that placed the city in a very unflattering light. In any case, the estimate drew lots of attention but also lots of criticism. For example, I pointed out that during the winter of 1983 the city shelter system, which at that point was offering shelter to any homeless person who requested it, sheltered only around forty-nine hundred men.[41]

Prodded by the *Callahan* litigation, the city had quickly opened the Keener building as a shelter. Demand for shelter promptly shot up; Keener was filled to overflowing with more than 625 men by early 1980. Partly in response to this situation, the city eventually had a new building constructed on Wards Island—the Schwartz building—which has housed four hundred men almost since it opened in May 1982.

By the summer of 1981 the case of *Callahan v. Carey*, which had thus far resulted in a preliminary injunction, had come to trial. The issue was, What would the final decision of the court be? At this point a compromise was reached: Hayes and the plaintiffs had been demanding not merely recognition of a right to shelter but also that this shelter be "community based," i.e., that shelters be scattered throughout the city and empowered to admit clients directly, to avoid the "deterrent effect" of having clients processed primarily in the Bowery. When the city pointed out that community opposition would make this plan nearly impossible, the requirement was dropped, with the city agreeing to supply all applicants with shelter of a quality to be mandated by the courts. This compromise was the basis for a consent decree, which was signed August 26, 1981, and which amounted to "recognition with the force of law of a right to shelter."

The key provision of the decree, on which the right to shelter would depend, was as follows: "The city defendants shall provide shelter and board to each homeless man who applies for it provided that (a) the man meets the need standard to qualify for the home relief program established in New York State; or (b) the man by reason of physical, mental or social dysfunction is in need of temporary shelter."[42]

As the above text shows, the *Callahan* consent decree did not create a right to shelter on demand for absolutely all homeless men. An applicant had to either meet the standard for home relief or be "by reason of physical, mental or social dysfunction" in need of shelter. But many very poor men qualified for Home Relief, which was the state's welfare program for single men. And the criterion of suffering from physical, mental, or social dysfunction was left undefined and therefore could be interpreted very widely.

But there was more to the decree than the provision of a bare right to shelter. The quality of the shelter was also specified. Beds in city-operated shelters had to be at least "30 inches in width, substantially constructed, in good repair and equipped with clean springs." Each bed had to have a "clean, comfortable, well-constructed mattress" and a "clean, comfortable pillow of average size." Another provision held that "[e]ach resident shall receive two clean sheets, a clean blanket, a clean pillowcase, a clean towel, soap and toilet tissue. A complete change of bed linens and towels will be made for each new resident at least once a week and more often as needed on an individual basis." Clients were to receive a "lockable storage unit" and "laundry services not less than twice a week." Other provisions were as follows:

- "A staff attendant to resident ratio of at least 2 percent shall be maintained in each shelter facility at all times."
- "A staff attendant trained in first aid shall be on duty in each shelter at all times."
- "A minimum of ten hours per week of group recreation shall be available for each resident at each shelter facility."
- "Residents shall be permitted to leave and return to shelter facilities at reasonable hours."
- "Residents of shelter facilities shall be provided with transportation (public or private) to the site where they applied for shelter."
- "Residents shall be permitted to leave the facility by 7:00 a.m. if they so desire."
- "Residents shall be permitted to receive and send mail and other correspondence without interception or interference."
- "The City defendants shall make a good faith effort to provide pay telephones for use by the residents at each shelter facility. The City defendants shall bear any reasonable cost for the installation and maintenance of such telephones."

Client capacities for the Keener building and Camp LaGuardia were also specified. An appendix A provided further crucial requirements:

- "Every facility shall have space for dining and leisure activities." (The size and use of these spaces were specified in detail.)
- "There shall be a minimum one toilet and one lavatory for each six residents and a minimum of one tub or shower for each ten residents."
- "[I]n single occupancy sleeping rooms, a minimum of 80 square feet per resident shall be provided. . . . [I]n sleeping rooms for two or more residents a minimum of 60 square feet shall be provided."
- "[A] minimum of 3 feet, which is included in the per-resident minima, shall be maintained between and for aisles."

Similar provisions applied to the Bowery lodging houses to which some applicants were referred by the city. Appendix B provided for emergency situations, such as snow emergencies, during which time the capacity of the shelters could be temporarily enlarged.

As can be seen, the *Callahan* consent decree, while its provisions were reasonable, represented a challenging set of mandates for the city to execute. Why, then, did the city agree to sign the decree? According to Koch, one important reason why the city decided to sign was that such was the advice of the then corporation counsel, Allen Schwartz. By his own account Koch was reluctant to sign the decree. However, "in the early days [of the Koch administration] the corporation counsel . . . Allen Schwartz . . . said that, it's better that we sign these decrees, because otherwise they'll impose even heavier sanctions."[43] Others, such as George Gutwirth, former assistant city corporation counsel, deny this and claim that no one in the corporation counsel's office ever thought the city would lose. In any case, eventually Koch would come to regret having signed the *Callahan* decree. As he would later say, "We made a mistake, and I am the first one to say it. The city made a mistake when it agreed to the consent decree and now everybody thinks they can tell the city what to do."[44]

Further, at the time of the negotiations, the city was not unsympathetic to Hayes's suit. One of the city officials who was involved in the *Callahan* negotiations was Robert Trobe, deputy commissioner of the Human Resources Administration (HRA) for Family and Adult Services (FAS), which then oversaw services to the single homeless. Trobe was deeply involved in the city's defense from the beginning and was well known at the corporation counsel's office for constantly calling to ask questions and offer advice. According to Trobe,

> we really felt that . . . not signing the consent decree would put us in the position of denying homeless people the right to shelter. We felt we couldn't take the position that if someone came to our doors who was genuinely homeless we

> could turn them away and they would freeze to death. We didn't think that was right. We didn't think it was acceptable from a political point of view.[45]

Of course the city had for years been turning away applicants once the big room in the Men's Shelter was full. But apparently officially stipulating such a policy in court was more than the city could stomach.

Finally, the city was willing to sign the *Callahan* decree because it underestimated how much demand there would be for shelter. Trobe's colleague at HRA FAS, Bonnie Stone, who was also involved in advising the city's lawyers, remembers that

> [w]e . . . certainly underestimated the size of the problem because we thought we could actually—I kind of smile at it—we thought, well, we'll find a thousand beds. We estimated that if we could find a thousand beds for these men on the Bowery and some for the women we could probably take care of it. Well we couldn't have been more wrong because the moment we agreed to do it the floodgates opened because the problem was much, much, much bigger than we had estimated.[46]

Even the advocates underestimated the size of the proposed task. Before signing the *Callahan* decree, the city opened, as has been mentioned, a former psychiatric hospital as the Keener building on Ward's Island in the Hudson River, access to which was gained through a special bus service. Ellen Baxter, one of the founders of Coalition for the Homeless and coauthor of *Private Lives/Public Spaces*, doubted the facility would be much used. She remembered that

> [w]e never thought that people would get on the bus, go over to the grounds of a psychiatric hospital where some of them have had negative histories . . . in a distant place and actually seek shelter. We were sure that selection of that site by the city was a move to sort of contain the issue. And when you looked at the trajectory of how quickly it became overcrowded and beyond capacity, it happened in a matter of about two weeks. So then we thought well I guess we were wrong, that the need is even greater than we had figured.[47]

Hayes has a different perspective on why the city signed the consent decree. He is skeptical of former city actors who now say they never had any problem with the concept of a right to shelter. According to him, the case "was a contested, adversarial proceeding from the get-go." About his own reasons for signing, Hayes said that

> [t]here was no doubt we were the underdogs. A betting person would have been very nervous about us getting thrown out of court. A quirk . . . about New York state litigation against government entities is if you win in a lower court, all the city has to do is file a one-page document called a notice of appeal and the judgment would be stayed . . . through the next level of appeal, which would be a year, and through the next level of appeal, likely, which would be another year. That was a part of it because I did feel some urgency, obviously. . . . I wasn't caring about anything besides having no shelter.[48]

CFTH forced the city to live up to its obligation, and to increase steadily the capacity of the system in order to eliminate the deterrent factor of limited beds. Usually after such an increase, demand for shelter shot up until the new capacity was filled and the city was obliged to find more beds. Thus, six weeks after the consent decree was signed, the city ran out of beds.[49] CFTH then brought the city back into court, where the city was ordered to open another four hundred beds within twenty-four hours. The city complied by housing men at an abandoned Brooklyn school building. Within a month, the school's capacity was reached. Again the city was brought back into court, and again a new shelter was opened, this one in an abandoned armory. But this action did not entirely satisfy the court, and in response to the court's demand that the city meet the growing demand for shelter, the city opened yet another armory to homeless men. After the December injunction, the city made a steady effort to provide for the homeless, and so no longer turned any applicants away.

One must be careful in asserting that the outcome of *Callahan v. Carey* was recognition of a right to shelter. The suit ended with the signing of a consent decree, and left all points of law—including the determination of a right to shelter—legally unsettled. However, it is true that since the December 1979 injunction, the city has been obliged to follow a de facto policy that assumes such a right.

Callahan v. Carey and the publicity brought on by the advocates' work had a large impact on the shelter system, especially in regard to increasing the supply of beds, improving conditions, and generally removing deterrent factors. By the early eighties, the system was already quite different from what it was when Hayes first began his investigations back in 1978. (The emphasis here will be on the facilities for men, since they were the focus of the *Callahan v. Carey* suit, and since the overwhelming majority of the shelter clients were male.)

The intake point to the shelter system for men was the Men's Shelter at Third Street. Very few men actually slept at the Men's Shelter; it contained only a few beds in its infirmary. Rather, clients were generally sent to one of several principal types of lodging. The majority were given housing vouchers, which entitled them to spend the night in one of the Bowery hotels: These were the Union, the Kenton, the Palace, the Sunshine, the Delevan, and the Stevenson. These were among the least comfortable lodgings in the shelter system. Some of the men slept in small cubby-like rooms covered on the top with chicken wire; other accommodations were dormitory style. About 1,150 men slept in the hotels.

After processing at the Men's Shelter, some men were sent to a city-run shelter for lodging. The exact assignment depended on the vacancy rate at the various shelters. The principal city-run shelters were the Charles H. Gay Shelter Center on Wards Island, the East New York Shelter in Brooklyn, and the Harlem Shelter. Men who were assigned to these shelters received free transportation there and back to the Men's Shelter in the morning.

Of these shelters, the Gay Center was by far the largest, lodging 816 men in its two buildings. (East New York housed 350 and the Harlem Shelter held 200.)[50] The Gay Center consisted of the Keener building and the Schwartz building, which was then newly built and which opened in May of 1982. The entire center was run by the private charitable organization, the Volunteers of America, under contract to the city.

Men in the Keener building were assigned to fair-sized "semi-private" rooms, which slept two or three people. Accommodations in the Schwartz building were dormitory style, but still fairly spacious. The Schwartz building, since it was brand new, had a clean and modern look to it. The Schwartz building was dedicated on the same day that CSS released *One Year Later*,[51] which acknowledged that the facility was "clean, spacious, and well appointed." The *Times* described the Schwartz building as a "low, brick dormitory . . . with . . . pine-beamed ceilings and skylights" and quoted the facility's operator as saying, "I didn't think it would be this beautiful. . . . It's like you're going into a student union of some college or university. You wouldn't think these homeless would have such a place."[52] Both buildings had a TV room. The Schwartz building also had kitchen and dining facilities. The center had a medical clinic and mental health services on site.

When the shelters and Bowery hotels were filled, the city sent people to one of the armories it had opened for the homeless with the cooperation of the state. The Flushing Armory and the Lexington Avenue Armory were for women; the Kingsbridge Armory in the Bronx, the Fort Washington Armory in Manhattan, and the Park Avenue Armory were for men. The Fort Washington Armory, which held six hundred people, was the largest of these sites. All the armories were open on a twenty-four-hour basis, which meant that clients could be admitted there directly, without having to go first through the East Third Street site.

The city would continue to rely on low-quality armory shelters up through the late 1990s. But the beginnings of better solutions were made in the early eighties. In 1983 the State Division of Housing and Community Renewal would fund several projects meant to develop SRO (single room occupancy) housing with various supportive services for the mentally ill homeless. One of these grantees, the Committee for the Heights Inwood Homeless, was headed by Ellen Baxter and would by 1986 open a residence that would become a model for future efforts to develop a permanent housing alternative to shelters like Fort Washington.

Some sixty miles outside the city, in the upstate town of Chester in Orange County, Camp LaGuardia slept approximately 950 men. This shelter was primarily intended for use by older clients. In 1983 it was undergoing extensive renovation. New dormitories were being built that would eventually house six hundred men.

There were also three main shelters for women. The Women's Shelter, which was also the principal intake center for women, was in the Lower East Side. It provided meals, showers, and social services for the women in the shelter system, and had fifty-one beds. Other sites were the Women's Shelter Annex, which held 150 women, and the Bushwick Center.

Bonnie Stone remembered what it was like then to work on homeless issues at HRA:

> It didn't take up every minute, but little by little it started to. There was a little competition for our time from some of the other programs, mostly for the home care programs. But . . . we were kind of running . . . we were flat out running all the time, 24/7. And it was great, it was exhilarating. Because we could see the product of what we were doing, we were actually housing people. Now, there was a lot of subsequent criticism about, well, they were opening these big awful places. Well yeah, we couldn't open them fast enough.
>
> And our mode was emergency. Okay, we had consented to do this, it is running us like crazy but we have to do it. So it was a little bit like, I hate to say this, but it's a little bit like war, you know . . . it was logistics, logistics, logistics. It was buying thousands of sheets and thousands of beds and hiring staff and opening up places . . . the biggest places. . . . We opened up anything we could find and any building we could get control of. So we actually got control of a couple of school buildings. The state . . . ended up giving us . . . half a dozen armories and we were just running to keep up. I think we probably opened up ten thousand beds in three years. And you can imagine. . . . I mean . . . we had a good time doing it because it was so urgent and you were doing something really, really solid.[53]

Plenty of unusual administrative challenges presented themselves as HRA struggled to abide by court orders and comply with the consent decree. One was the mystery of the short-lived sheets. The consent decree required that each client receive two clean sheets at least every week and thus HRA needed lots of sheets. Stone's procurement director found it extremely difficult to keep the shelter system in sheets. Meanwhile, her operations director never had enough. To resolve the problem, Stone found herself sitting them both down together and "having this kind of Kafkaesque discussion about the life cycle of a sheet in the New York City shelter system. And I'm just trying to keep these guys from killing each other. They only wanted to do their jobs and they were being thwarted." It was determined that the average life of a sheet was six to eight weeks, and the question now became why sheets didn't last any longer. Weeks later the mystery began to resolve itself. To achieve the necessary high-volume laundry capacity, the city at first contracted out with hotels. But once word got out that guests' laundry was being mixed with that of homeless people, the hotel would stop offering the service. After running through in this way every hotel with sufficient capacity, HRA had to use city-owned laundry facilities—those operated by the Department of Corrections at Rikers Island. Freshly cleaned sheets came out of the Rikers laundry in large bales. Guards inspected the bales to check for escaping prisoners. Their method of inspection? Running the bales through with bayonets. Once the guards' dangerous efforts were curbed, sheets started lasting longer.[54]

Clearly, the city had developed a large system and made great efforts to recognize the de facto right to shelter, and to eliminate any deterrent factors from the shelter system. The advocacy groups largely got their way, but at a high price. In early 1978, when Robert Hayes began his work, the city's operating budget for the homeless was $6.8 million; for fiscal year 1983 it was $38 million.[55]

One of the first indications of what had been wrought came with the release in May 1982 of a study conducted by HRA, "Chronic and Situational Dependency: Long Term Residents in a Shelter for Men," usually referred to as the "Keener study." This was followed up in November 1982 by "New Arrivals: First-Time Shelter Clients" (which would be revised in May 1983). These studies were conducted by the HRA Bureau of Management Systems, Planning, Research, and Evaluation under the direction of Stephen Crystal, then a newly minted sociologist who trained at Harvard. The Keener study was a study of 173 men who had been living in the Keener building for two months or more. "New Arrivals" presented the results of 687 interviews conducted with first-time clients either at the Men's Shelter or at the East New York Shelter. Both reports asked a variety of questions regarding the men's background and their reasons for coming to the shelter. The Keener study's purpose was to determine in detail who longtime users of the shelter were and why they came to need the shelters' emergency services. "New Arrivals" was principally concerned with determining where the clients were immediately before they came to the shelter.

TABLE 1.1: Keener Study—Categories of Long-Term Shelter Clients (Based on Overall Interviewer Assessments of Primary Problems)

Group	Number of Men	Percentage of Total	Mean Age
Psychiatric Only	59	34	33
Alcoholic Only	10	6	41
Economic Only	33	19	32
Drug Only	4	2	30
Physical Disability Only	6	3	49
Total	**112**	**64**	

Source: Stephen Crystal et al., "Chronic and Situational Dependency: Long Term Residents in a Shelter for Men" (New York: Human Resources Administration, May 1982), p. iv (also known as the Keener study).

The Keener study documented the heterogeneous nature of the shelter population (see table 1.1). The largest category was "psychiatric only," which accounted for 34 percent of these men. The third-largest category of the Keener study was "alcoholic only," which consisted of 6 percent of its subjects. The study also classified 2 percent of its subjects as "drug only."

This brings us to the second-largest category identified in the Keener study, and also in some respects the most interesting: those men classified as "economic only," who made up 19 percent of the subjects. The report said of such "discouraged workers" that they "had in the past been able to function at quite high levels, both occupationally and socially."

Like the Keener study, the "New Arrivals" study found that "there are substantial numbers of men seeking services at the shelters who have significant job skills and histories, and . . . many have previously been able to support themselves through employment. This further supports the need to develop employment referrals, supported work, and other means of fostering economic self-sufficiency." "New Arrivals" also found that

> the shelters are drawing from a potentially very large population pool, most of whom are not "homeless" in the sense of being undomiciled at the time of coming to the shelter. Thus future demand may be very large. It will be important to

carefully assess client needs and resources, to impose appropriate structure and make appropriate demands on clients' own efforts.

The subjects had been asked where they spent the night before they came to the shelter (see table 1.2).

TABLE 1.2: Place of Previous Night's Stay of Shelter Clients

Type of Place	Number of Men	Percent of Total
Street or Subway	256	37.6
Friends	105	15.4
Family	96	14.1
Own Apartment	80	11.7
Other Institution	57	8.4
Hospital	38	5.6
SRO	29	4.3
Jail	13	1.9
CLH (Bowery Hotel)	7	1.0
Totals	**681**	**100.0**

Source: Stephen Crystal et al., "New Arrivals: First-Time Shelter Clients" (New York: Human Resources Administration, November 198 2, Revised May 1983), p. 13, table 6.

The report found that

[t]he majority of men had not spent the previous night in the streets or subways, although this was the largest single category. Thirty-eight percent of the men had done so, while friends (15 percent), family (14 percent), and own apartment (12 percent) accounted together for slightly more. The fact that *one of seven new men had spent the previous night with family* is particularly striking. It is also significant that *12 percent had spent the previous night in their own apartment.* Institutions of various sorts, including jail, account for almost all the rest, while hotels accounted for a smaller proportion than expected, only 4 percent. Just over sixty percent of the men had not been in the streets or subways in any of their last three sleeping arrangements. (italics in the original)

Together, the Keener study and "New Arrivals" gave the city and other observers the first clear picture of what the population of the newly developed shelter system looked like. Several features stood out. The Keener study broached the possibility that limitations on the right to shelter, like work requirements or a stricter intake process, might be necessary to prevent inappropriate use of the shelters by relatively high-functioning clients. "New Arrivals" made it clear that the shelter system was being used not only by streets dwellers but also by a potentially very large population of people in a wide range of marginal housing situations. Thus was seriously broached for the first time in this context the possibility that city policy might be creating "perverse incentives" that encouraged some people to leave bad housing and enter the shelter system. At the time, I made much of this possibility and attracted a certain amount of attention in media and policy circles for doing so.[56] The theme of perverse incentives was to come up repeatedly in policy discourse and the private thinking of city policymakers even after later research—in particular Cragg and O'Flaherty's 1999 article on homeless policy under Dinkins—suggested that the concern was overblown.[57]

The early eighties was a time of very rapid expansion of the city's shelter system. Between calendar years 1980 and 1983 the single adult sheltered population more than doubled, from 2,155 to 5,061 persons, a 134 percent increase.[58] This sudden expansion of the shelter system brought about by the *Callahan* litigation had the unintended consequence of forcing the city to develop a city-operated system that relied on large public buildings such as armories rather than on smaller shelters operated by private not-for-profit organizations. Placement of new shelters required approval of the Board of Estimate, which in those days functioned as the de facto upper house of the city's legislature (the City Council functioned at that time as the lower house). The board consisted of three city-wide officials—the mayor, the comptroller, and the City Council president—each with two votes—and the five borough presidents, with one vote each. The locality-based borough presidents were very sensitive to the concerns of their neighborhoods about the placement of unwanted facilities and would typically support each other on such matters. That meant that placement of a new shelter could be blocked by the borough presidents if they could win the support of just one city-wide official, something generally not hard to do. Placement of new, private shelters under this governance system required a long negotiation process and was therefore not a practical way to expand the shelter system quickly, as the *Callahan* litigation required. The only alternative was to rely on large buildings that were already publicly owned and therefore did not need board approval, which in practice meant unused hospitals, schools, and especially armories. Smaller, private, not-for-profit-operated shelters became easier to place when the Board of Estimate was abolished in 1989 and the City Council became the city's unicameral legislature.[59] The borough presidents then lost their role in the legislative process and were no longer able to block placement of small shelters in their jurisdictions. But for the nonce, the city had to rely on armories and similar city-owned buildings.

Such available buildings often did not meet the quality standards that were laid out in appendix A of the *Callahan* consent decree. Particularly tricky was the requirement that "[t]here shall be a minimum one toilet and one lavatory for each six residents and a minimum of one tub or shower for each ten residents." These ratios were chosen because at the time they matched State Department of Social Service regulations for adult homes. Bringing a building up to that specification was expensive. For example, installing required toilets and showers (and emergency lighting) in the original Keener building in 1982 cost $700, 000.[60] The city estimated that plumbing renovations at two sites it was considering would exceed $400,000 and that bringing the Fort Washington Armory up to *Callahan* specifications would cost about $435,000.[61]

The city also found burdensome the provision in the *Callahan* decree that "[e]very facility shall have space for dining and leisure activities." Complete social services were provided at the Men's Shelter, the Charles Gay Shelter Center on Wards Island, and the Brooklyn Shelter.[62] These sites contained, the city argued, overabundant capacity for feeding clients, with the Men's Shelter being able to feed nineteen hundred men at each meal, the Wards Island complex capable of feeding four hundred men at a sitting, and the Brooklyn Shelter able to feed over one hundred men at a time.[63] Why not, the city argued, allow men to be fed and provided other services at these sites and then transported to sleeping and bathroom facilities elsewhere?

The city filed a request in New York State Supreme Court on October 8, 1982, that the specific plumbing ratios be dropped and that, instead, the city be required to provide fixtures "adequate" for all men to shower once a day and to otherwise "meet client needs."[64] The city also requested that the requirement to provide dining and leisure activities at "every facility" be construed to allow men to be fed at the large-capacity sites and then bused to other shelters for sleeping. The *New York Times* reported, without citing a source, that the requested modifications in the decree would save the city "at least $1 million on toilets and cooking facilities."[65] Besides the expense involved, the city also argued that there simply weren't enough compliant facilities available to shelter the anticipated need and that therefore "to apply these kind of unrealistic and unnecessary provisions to buildings, armories, when we need facilities to house men, would make sure that we cannot use these facilities, and that would simply exacerbate the wrong sought to be corrected."[66]

Hayes's public response to the city's request was vitriolic: "For the city to come in on the eve of winter and say 'we don't want to obey the consent decree' is not only shameless but heartless." According to him, "This is a way of keeping shelters so dangerous, dehumanizing and degrading that people will be forced to stay on the streets."[67] In court, Hayes was more measured.

At issue, for him, was not so much the plumbing ratios in themselves, but the quality of life in the shelters. Regarding the matter of the ratios, Hayes told Judge Wallach in colloquy, "It's not a major point. It's a red herring. I think it may be an intentional red herring to divert the Court's and public attention from the real issue, which is the bussing plan, the centralization and consequential injuries that the homeless suffer because of this centralization." Further, "we are opposing this massive centralization of the shelter program to the extent that it brings so many people to one location that it keeps people away from that location. It keeps them out of the system and in the street."[68] In his deposition to the court Hayes explained further:

> Of particular importance was finding means to limit the size of shelters to a humane scope. Defendant Blum, then head of the state regulatory agency for shelters, had promulgated a regulation in early 1981 prohibiting the licensing of new shelters with a capacity of more than 200 persons. The City refused to incorporate that regulation into the decree so I settled for standards for toilets, showers and lavatories which would, as a practical matter, limit the size, concentration and hence inhumanity of new shelters.[69]

Surprisingly, the *New York Times*, whose coverage of the homeless issue was followed by all parties and whose editorials had always been favorable to Hayes and the advocates, came out very emphatically on the city's side. Regarding Hayes's charges of shamelessness and heartlessness the *Times* editorialized,

> As a dedicated advocate whose tireless efforts forced the city to agree to provide shelter for any homeless person requesting it, Mr. Hayes may be forgiven a proprietary interest in the shelters. But the city's request is not heartless. It is sensible and economically prudent. . . . To oppose a sensible change in the court mandate for toilets and showers is to waste reformist energies.[70]

But the court wouldn't buy the city's arguments. On November 4, 1982, regarding the city's practice of transporting men to several facilities for needed services, Judge Wallach wrote,

> The trans-shipment by bus to and from HRA's Bowery intake facility or elsewhere of up to 1,000 destitute men on a daily basis cannot be viewed by this court as consistent with the basic structure and fundamental objectives of the decree. . . . To say these and like proposals are an honest substitute for the integrated shelter facilities originally contemplated by this decree would be to play a cruel and unacceptable hoax upon the plaintiffs and the class they represent.[71]

However, the court did take note of the fact that the State Department of Social Services, whose regulations for adult homes were the source of the decree's plumbing ratios, had, since the decree was signed, changed those regulations to require one toilet and lavatory for each ten residents and one shower or tub for each fifteen. Previously, the regulations and the decree had required one toilet and lavatory for every six clients and one shower or tub for each ten. Wallach therefore amended the decree to embody the new regulations. The city was unhappy with this small modification and had specifically urged the court against this result. In its memorandum to the court, the city wrote that "the defendants do not urge this Court to apply this new ratio since experience indicates that rigid formulas in this area cannot present predictably achievable goals, and could serve to needlessly restrict occupancy or proper use of suitable buildings."[72] Judge Wallach concluded his decision by illustrating the court's responsibility with a biblical flourish:

> The judge, engaged in separating the good people from the bad, thanks the first group for providing him with meat when he was hungry, drink when he was thirsty, clothing when he was naked and shelter when he was sick. These favored litigants seem not to understand, so the judge explains: "Inasmuch as ye have done it unto one of the least of these my brethren, ye have done it unto me" (Matthew XXV, 40).[73]

The city, apparently failing to be suitably uplifted, simply reported through an HRA spokesperson that it was "disappointed" with Wallach's decision.[74]

As can be seen, the city had developed an extensive system to comply with the first requirement of the *Callahan v. Carey* consent decree—that all applicants be given shelter. The city also made efforts to comply with the other aspect of the consent decree—the quality standards. In 1982, according to CFTH, "the shelters remain dangerous and forbidding, continuing to deter many homeless men from coming off the streets."[75] But the city disagreed. It held that it was in substantial compliance with all aspects of the quality requirements.[76] In fact, shelter conditions, with some exceptions, would continue to be bad for quite some time. Especially bad were conditions in the large armory shelters. The overnight imposition of the *Callahan* decree meant that at first the main thrust of city efforts was devoted to expanding capacity on a catch-as-catch-can basis, which made for poor-quality service. But the working principle of a right to shelter for single homeless people had been established. The entitlement phase of homeless policy had started. The city would have to learn how to manage the system better, but the learning process had begun.

2

The Development of Homelessness Policy under Koch

On March 31, 1983, the Legal Aid Society filed *McCain v. Koch*, which would turn out to be a sort of analogue to *Callahan v. Carey* in that it sought for New York City and New York State to provide shelter for homeless families. It was a class action suit brought before the New York State Supreme Court in Manhattan, with Edward Greenfield as judge. The essence of the suit was that even though the city provided shelter for single men (under the *Callahan* consent decree) and women (under *Eldredge v. Koch*), the city failed to provide housing for homeless families. Other charges claimed that city decisions on providing shelter were arbitrary and provided no written notice or opportunity for a hearing; that shelter could be terminated without notice or hearing; that the city relocated homeless families in squalid rooms far from their children's schools; that the city shuttled families among various sites; that the city failed to provide relocation benefits or transportation funds; that families in emergency shelter lost their public assistance benefits; and that families were coerced into accepting unsafe and inadequate shelter. At that time the after-business-hours entry point to the family shelter system was the Emergency Assistance Units (EAUs), of which there were four, one in each borough except Staten Island. (By 1993 there was only one EAU, located in the Bronx.)

The plaintiffs made many legal claims to support their demands. They claimed that under the Emergency Assistance to Needy Families with Children (EAF) program, the equal protection clauses of the U.S. and New York State constitutions, and article 17, section 1 of the state constitution, the city must provide sufficient shelter for all families in need, just as it provided such shelter for men under *Callahan*. Plaintiffs also argued that the due process provisions of the U.S. and New York State constitutions prohibited decision making by the EAU without notice and hearings. Finally, the plaintiffs claimed that under article 17 of the New York State Constitution, and various portions of the Social Security Act, New York State Social Service Law, and the New York State Code of Rules and Regulations (volume 18, Social Services) the city had to provide emergency housing that met minimal standards. The plaintiffs also asked the court to certify them as a class, meaning that the suit would be on behalf of not just the named plaintiffs but all similarly situated families.

The initial result of the suit was that the court issued an interim order, dated June 20, 1983, which required that "when a family is not denied emergency housing, assistance, and services," the shelter provided must meet certain minimal standards, which were spelled out by the court and were similar to those of the *Callahan* consent decree but adapted to the needs of families. Thus cribs had to be provided for infants, rooms had to have window guards, and placements had to be made with children's educational needs in mind.[1] Note that the interim order did not establish a right to shelter but only specified that when shelter was provided it had to meet certain standards. These standards were later incorporated into regulations issued by the New York State Department of Social Services (DSS).[2] This was 18 NYCRR 352.3 (g)-(h) (1983).

Susan Demers points out in an interesting article that the regulations in fact expanded considerably on the interim order.[3] Thus the interim order required a room that "has accessible to it a sanitary bathroom with hot water." The DSS regulation required that "[e]ach family must have a private bathroom. At a minimum this shall include a toilet, a sink and a shower or bathtub, all of which shall be properly maintained with hot and cold running water." Or again, the interim order required that the shelter provided be "sufficiently heated pursuant to City law." The state regulations required that

> [a] heating system shall be permanently installed and operated in accordance with applicable local law. Where local law or code does not govern the provision of heat, the system will provide heat to maintain a temperature of 69°F (20°C) in all occupied parts of the building, including corridors. Where windows do not open, proper ventilation, including but not limited to air conditioning, shall be operational.

The interim order called for "a clean mattress and pillow and . . . clean and sufficient blankets . . . [and] a sufficient number of clean towels." State regulations ordered that

> [a]ll mattresses and bedding material shall be clean. Each bed shall have at least two clean sheets, adequate clean blankets, clean pillows and pillowcases. A complete change of linens shall be made by hotel/motel staff at least once a week and more often where individual circumstances warrant or when a new family occupies the unit. Each unit shall be supplied with towels, soap and toilet tissues. A clean towel shall be provided daily to each resident.

The regulations also dealt with issues not mentioned in the interim order at all. For example, the regulations required the facility to make arrangements for

> removal of garbage; maintenance of floor coverings, draperies and furniture; repainting of the facility at least once every five years; maintenance and inspection of the electrical system; maintenance of plumbing and plumbing fixtures; maintenance and inspection of heating, ventilation and air conditioning systems; a regular vermin control program; and provision to insure that entrances, exits, steps and walkways are kept clear of garbage, ice, snow and other hazards.

Further, the interim order required that its standards be met only "so far as is practicable," while state regulations threatened that "[n]o family shall be referred to a hotel/motel, nor shall any reimbursement be made for costs incurred from such referral unless all of the requirements set forth . . . are met." Thus the required standards took a quantum leap in moving from the court interim order to the state regulations.

Part of the reason for this quantum leap was that the state was issuing the regulations with an eye to resolving the *McCain* litigation. DSS consulted with the plaintiffs and asked them what the regulations would have to contain to resolve the case. The plaintiffs wanted a set of regulations that would require hotels to meet the standards of the Henry Street Settlement, a long-established settlement house known for the quality of its accommodations. The final version of 18 NYCRR 352.3 (g)-(h) (1983) gave the plaintiffs some of what they wanted, but not all. And there remained the issue of whether the regulations would be complied with. So the litigation continued.[4]

Another fateful result of the interim order was that on September 29, 1983, DSS issued Administrative Directive 83 ADM-47, which also incorporated terms of the interim order and required that "[e]mergency housing must either be provided immediately if a homeless person is determined eligible or written notice must be given that no assistance will be provided where a homeless person is determined ineligible."[5]

The plaintiffs in the *McCain* case had input into the writing of 83 ADM-47. There was back-and-forth discussion between the DSS and the plaintiffs and words such as "delay" and "quickly" were tossed about. But the key word "immediately" came from DSS, not the plaintiffs.[6] The directive left unclear exactly what eligibility meant. It noted only that "[i]n no case, however, shall the district deny public assistance solely on the basis that a homeless person has no permanent address."[7] Eligibility standards were thus left unclear, and were not clarified with the following double negative: "when the individual is determined not to be ineligible, an emergency placement shall be made and other needs met." This lack of clarity would have far-reaching implications for policy. And a single word, "immediately," would especially turn out to have extensive consequences for the city.

In June of 1984 the *McCain* plaintiffs asked Justice Greenfield for a preliminary injunction that would finalize the interim order and require the city to provide "safe and adequate emergency housing and assistance suitable for families and dependent children."[8] The court continued to skirt the issue of whether the New York State Constitution implied a right to shelter. The court noted the language of article 17 of the constitution, which it held was "mandatory and imposes upon the State an affirmative duty to aid the needy." Nonetheless, the court acknowledged that "[n]either the Constitution nor Social Service Law . . . provide that emergency shelter shall be given to the needy in explicit terms." Then the court continued:

> However, once the defendants have undertaken to provide emergency shelter . . . the issue becomes whether the shelter provided should meet reasonable minimum standards. . . . The equitable powers of this court may be invoked to compel compliance with minimal standards. If convicted criminals have such rights, the homeless who become interim wards of a governmental entity are entitled to no less.[9]

Greenfield converted the interim order to a preliminary injunction, but he denied class certification, finding that many issues of fact and law were not common to all potential members of the class and implying that class certification was "inappropriate, and particularly where governmental operations are concerned." Both sides appealed Greenfield's decision, which was scheduled to be taken up by the state Appellate Division in the fall of 1986.

While the *McCain* litigation made its way through the court system, Legal Aid brought another action against the city. This was *Lamboy v. Gross*, which was heard by Justice Helen Freedman of the New York State Supreme Court in Manhattan. *Lamboy* was very similar to *McCain*, as it concerned homeless families that had to sleep overnight in an EAU when space in a family shelter or a motel could not be found for them. Gross was George Gross, Human Resources Administration (HRA) commissioner as of September 18, 1984. Marie Lamboy and fellow petitioner Oscar Serrano and their three children applied for emergency shelter on May 9, 1985. The city was unable immediately to find shelter for the five-member family, who therefore spent three nights at an EAU. On their first night the family was offered housing suitable for a family of four, but they turned it down and did not receive a placement on the next two nights.[10] An affidavit filed by the city indicated that Ms. Lamboy had been a challenging client. Before she applied to the EAU, she had been arrested for stealing at one shelter and banned from another for violating curfew. Another hotel had given her five hundred dollars to leave.[11] The father of the family was brain damaged as the result of a mugging and the family's six-year-old child attended special classes for emotionally handicapped children.[12] Another plaintiff was Wilma Acevedo, who had an epileptic six-year-old son. According to the *Times*, "the Acevedos spent a single night at the Bronx emergency office at 437 East 147th Street, where they slept on plastic chairs and Formica tables under fluorescent light. They were not offered beds at a group shelter because of her son's health problems."[13]

At issue was the question of whether the families had been granted shelter "immediately," as was specified in Administrative Directive 83 ADM-47. In the court's opinion, the issue at hand did not concern the state or federal constitutions but was "a much more narrowly circumscribed one, dealing simply with the question of whether the city appellants have properly complied with a State-issued administrative directive [83 ADM-47]."[14] An expedited fair hearing found that the directive had not been violated because the Lamboy-Serrano family was provided with cots and a crib and some food at the EAU. Petitioners requested a preliminary injunction preventing the respondents from denying emergency shelter for reasons other than those permitted by 83 ADM-47. Petitioners also requested to be certified as a class. Justice Freedman decided not to await a decision in the very similar *McCain* case and issued a decision on August 26, 1985.

The city argued that it had tried but simply could not find appropriate accommodations for Ms. Lamboy and her family. Judge Freedman wrote that "[t]he city seems to claim that under the circumstances it did the best it could for the Lamboy-Serrano and Acevedo families and that it attempted to comply with 83 ADM-47 but failed."[15] Below is Judge Freedman's response to this argument in full:

> The expedited fair hearing decision in the Lamboy-Serrano matter, presumably approved by the State Commissioner, suggests that the city complied with 83 ADM-47. Although there was no dispute at the fair hearing that the family was eligible for housing and was at no time informed that it was ineligible, the fair hearing officer found that it could not be determined under all of the circumstances of this case that the family was denied emergency housing assistance from May 9 through 11 because the family was furnished cots and a crib and given some food at the EAU. The officer noted that the medical condition of the

> emotionally handicapped child made referral to a family shelter inappropriate and described other problems relating to keeping the entire family together. Although the court recognizes that this family, because of its size, past history relating to other shelters and composition was difficult to place it does not agree that furnishing cots and a crib in an emergency assistance unit constitutes compliance with 83 ADM-47.[16]

In other words, no matter how difficult the task at hand, nothing justifies letting homeless families stay in the EAU. A few months later, on October 2, 1985, Freedman specifically held that "[i]n no event shall provision of overnight accommodations in the city respondents' welfare offices (including Income Maintenance Centers and Emergency Assistance Units) constitute the provision of emergency housing pursuant to the requirements of Administrative Directive 83 ADM-47 or this Order."[17] The court issued the requested preliminary injunction requiring the city to provide shelter, other than a stay in the EAU, immediately.

The city was appalled. Assistant corporation counsel Judith A. Levitt responded to Freedman's ruling as follows: "We are doing everything we possibly can right now within reason, and I think this goes beyond reason. This is the real world, not fantasy land." The city and state both appealed Judge Freedman's decision to the Appellate Division.

But was Judge Freedman correct that Administrative Directive 83 ADM-47 made no provision for the possibility that appropriate shelter could not be found and that letting a family stay in the EAU might therefore be unavoidable? She was correct, though the reason why was more complicated than her decision suggested. On June 19, 1985, the New York State Department of Social Service, which was the agency that promulgated 83 ADM-47, issued a letter to social service providers clarifying the regulation. The agency wrote,

> A *determination* [italics in the original] to place a family in an emergency assistance unit, even for one night, would be in violation of Department policy. However, there will be circumstances which make it necessary for a family to spend the night in an emergency assistance unit. Such circumstances would include emergencies arising from natural disasters (fires, floods, explosions, etc.) and isolated occasions where the local districts' good faith efforts to locate preferable alternative housing are unsuccessful. Reasonable efforts must be made by the local districts to plan for emergency needs and consistent and meaningful attempts by staff at the emergency units must have been made to locate emergency housing for the local district to meet its obligations under the ADM.[18]

The letter acknowledges that when "good faith efforts to locate preferable alternative housing are unsuccessful," families may be allowed to stay in EAUs. Demers, in "The Failures of Litigation as a Tool for the Development of Social Welfare Policy," cites this passage in her argument that the city policy of regularly placing families in EAUs should have been allowed by the court.[19] But the letter specifies that EAU placements are acceptable only during natural disasters or on "isolated occasions." At the time Judge Freedman's decision was made, scores of families were on many nights left in the EAUs. Judge Freedman, and the Appellate Division to which her decision in this case was appealed,[20] thus rightly concluded that regular use of the EAUs was not permitted under 83 ADM-47. The Appellate Division would quote the letter of June 19, 1985, and point out that "[i]t is, of course, well settled that the construction given statutes and regulations by the agency responsible for their administration, if not irrational or unreasonable, should be upheld."[21] Moreover, much to the satisfaction of Steven Banks, the plaintiffs' attorney, the decision contained "a wonderful passage . . . which says the word 'immediate' is a word of consummate clarity, it means right away, without delay."[22]

But what about a situation like the one in which the city found itself in which good faith efforts to locate preferable alternative housing are *regularly* unsuccessful? The regulation simply does not allow for such a state of affairs. Perhaps the regulators foresaw that the city would be sued for its systematic failure and that under court pressure the city would eventually improve its operation and comply. This reasoning perhaps was correct: After about twenty years of court orders and millions of dollars in fines, the city would eventually develop a system that not only did not place families in the EAUs, but did away with EAUs entirely. Whether this process was the most efficient way to reform the family-intake system is doubtful, but eventually it worked.

As the *McCain* proceedings rolled along, developments concerning the *Callahan* case continued to unfold. Robert Trobe and Bonnie Stone, who were responsible for finding shelter space, were convinced that the plumbing ratios specified in the consent decree made locating compliant buildings very hard and required adding unnecessary fixtures when otherwise suitable space was found. Stone eventually decided to try to document empirically that the ratios forced the city to build into the shelters shower and toilet capacity that was never used. Stephen Levine, executive assistant of the Bureau of Management Systems of HRA, who had a Ph.D. in history, was assigned the task of designing and implementing a study of shower and toilet use in the men's shelters. The result was "An Observational Study of Toilet and Shower Utilization at Three Men's Shelters," which was completed in early February 1985. Including an addendum and a follow-up, the study in fact looked at four large men's shelters, the Fort Washington Armory, the Franklin Armory, the Bedford-Atlantic Shelter, and the Schwarz Building at the Charles M. Gay Shelter on Ward's Island. Levine's methodology was to station observers at shelter toilets and showers during what he supposed to be peak usage periods in the morning and at dinner time. In total, fourteen peak-time periods of between seventy-five minutes and three hours were observed. At fifteen-minute intervals the observers counted the number of showers, water closets, and urinals that were being used.

The results seemed to confirm the city's position. Maximum peak-time use of water closets at a given point ranged from 70 percent to 15 percent. Maximum peak-time use of showers at a given point ranged from 72.2 percent to 7.4 percent. For urinals, maximum peak-time use at a given point ranged from 100 percent to 12 percent. (The study notes that during the one moment of 100 percent use of the urinals, there were fifteen empty water closets.) The study also reported that at no point were clients ever observed waiting to use a water closet, shower, or urinal. At all shelters the capacity of toilet and shower facilities "greatly exceeds demand, even during the peak hours of utilization."[23] The city thus moved in late 1986 for a modification of the plumbing ratios. The New York State Department of Social Services, whose regulations were consistent with those of the *Callahan* decree as they had been modified, told the court that it would grant the city a waiver of its regulations, but only if the court further modified the ratios in the decree.[24] The city proposed to the court a scheme in which the allowed plumbing ratios would rise as the population of a given shelter rose. The *Callahan* decree ratios would apply to shelters of up to two hundred clients, but, for example, for shelters of five hundred clients the ratio of water closets to clients would be one to eighteen and the ratio of showers to clients would be one to twenty-six. Such a sliding scale would, according to the city, acknowledge the "frequently demonstrated principle" that "the need for additional resources . . . does not always increase in identical proportions to an increase in the number of users."[25]

The plaintiffs felt that the debate over plumbing ratios had been definitively resolved back in 1982. They told the court,

> The only apparent difference between the City defendants' prior motions and this one is their proffer of a "study" which purportedly establishes "actual experience" with the plumbing fixtures in the shelters. However this study or survey is seriously flawed and comes nowhere near to a demonstration of "actual experience." Defendants' survey must be rejected out of hand as inherently unreliable . . . [I]t should be disregarded in its entirety.[26]

As the use of scare quotes around the word "study" suggests, the plaintiffs hardly hid their contempt for Levine's work and made a wide range of arguments against the study. They pointed out that the study itself acknowledged that one morning observation had been done while hot water was scarce; Levine himself agreed on deposition that those results ought to be discarded. They asked why observations were made at fifteen-minute intervals when continuous observation of the facilities was possible. They objected strongly to the fact that shelter clients had not been interviewed about their experience with shelter facilities. They discovered upon deposing the study's authors and implementers that one observation had been made while a movie was being shown at the shelter and another observation was conducted while a World Series game was on television. They argued that the study's results could not be "projected," that is, that it was impossible to generalize from the relatively small set of observations made to the general usage of the facilities. They questioned the qualifications of Levine, pointing out that his Ph.D. was in history and that most of his previous work for the city involved interviews or questionnaires. And they implied that the study had been done on the cheap as they got Levine to estimate that the whole project cost the city only $972. The plaintiffs concluded, "In sum, the city defendants, despite their 'study' and 'formula,' have not made the requisite showing to justify modification of the decree."[27] In his decision of October 1, 1987, Judge Sklar (who had replaced Judge Wallach) largely agreed with the plaintiffs. "[M]uch of the methodology used in conducting the surveys appears to be haphazard," he wrote. He specifically rejected "the city's premise that as population increases proportionally, fewer plumbing fixtures are needed," commenting that "[t]his assumption is not borne out by the studies." Sklar concluded that the study was "patently inadequate."[28]

The plumbing-usage study certainly had its faults, many of which the plaintiffs accurately pointed out. But the fact is that the formula the city cited and that the plaintiffs and court rejected—the formula that "the need for additional resources . . . does not always increase in identical proportions to an increase in the number of users"—is a truth cited in basic textbooks on queuing theory, which is the mathematical science of waiting in lines. For example, the queuing theory expert Robert B. Cooper acknowledges in an encyclopedia article "the important fact that large systems are more efficient than small ones."[29] At my request the queuing theory expert Prof. Kardi Technomo has calculated the optimum number of plumbing fixtures for shelters of various sizes. Some of the results are included in table 2.1:[30]

TABLE 2.1: Requirements of Various Plumbing Ratios at Various Client Populations

Clients:	200	300	350	400	450	500	600	1,000
City-proposed ratio:	1:15	1:19	1:23	1:25	1:26	1:26	1:30	1:37
# showers required by city ratio:	14	15	16	16	17	18	20	27
Optimum ratio:	1:22.2	1:23.08	1:23.33	1:23.53	1:25	1:25	1:25	1:26.32
# showers required by optimum ratio:	9	13	15	17	18	20	24	38
***Callahan* decree ratio:**	1:15	1:15	1:15	1:15	1:15	1:15	1:15	1:15
# showers required by *Callahan* decree ratio:	14	20	23	27	30	33	40	67

Sources: City-proposed ratios: *Callahan v. Carey*, Index No. 42582/79 Sup. Ct. NY County decision of Judge Stanley Sklar, October 1, 1987, p. 6; optimum ratios: personal correspondence with Kardi Technomo, 9/25/13; *Callahan* decree ratio: *Callahan v. Carey*, Index No. 42582/79 Sup. Ct. NY County, decision of Judge Richard Wallach, November 4, 1982, p. 3.

As can be seen, applying queuing theory to this problem always calls for fewer showers than the modified *Callahan* ratios would require. Optimizing showers implies that the number of clients for each shower head goes up, just as the city had proposed, although in some cases optimum ratios are higher than the city-proposed ratios and would require installing more showers than the city proposal called for.

One wishes that there were more systematic documentation of actual conditions at the shelters' plumbing facilities. In this context the plaintiffs made a fair point when they objected to the failure of the city's study to include interviews with clients. But the plaintiffs' arguments make an assumption that needs to be questioned. That assumption is that plumbing ratios are a good proxy for overall conditions in the shelters. As we saw, Robert Hayes testified that when he was rebuffed in his efforts to include a limit of two hundred on the population of a shelter, he fell back on the low plumbing ratios to limit the size and inhumanity of the shelters. But plumbing ratios were not what drove the city's decisions on shelter size. The need to accommodate large numbers of clients quickly, and the political difficulties involved in acquiring buildings that were not already owned by the city or state, were the factors that forced the city to rely on armories and other large structures. The city hardly rejected the use of large shelters because they entailed installing too much plumbing. Instead, the city went with the large shelter strategy because there were no ready alternatives and built in excess plumbing. The result was the worst of all possible worlds: big shelters (which the plaintiffs didn't want) with too much plumbing (which the city didn't want). Both sides would have been better off if the questions of plumbing ratios, shelter size, and quality of life had been disentangled and each dealt with in its own right. The debate over toilet ratios was perhaps a minor matter. It is worth focusing on, however, because through the use of queuing theory it is—unlike most controversies over shelter management—susceptible to something like an "objective" answer. In this small instance, the court seems to have allowed itself to descend unnecessarily into the minutiae of shelter operations and to have come up with a bad answer.

Meanwhile, the appeals of Greenfield's preliminary injunction in *McCain* were being considered, and on May 13, 1986, the Appellate Division of the state supreme court, in a thirty-two-page decision written by Justice Ernest H. Rosenberger, unanimously granted a preliminary injunction "barring the denial of emergency shelter to homeless families." In doing this the Appellate Division did what Justice Greenfield of the supreme court would not do, that is, "reach plaintiffs' constitutional claims"[31] and conclude that homeless families had a right to shelter under article 17 of the state constitution. Or, more exactly, the court found that "[i]t is also likely that plaintiffs will succeed on their claim that the NY Constitution article XVII obligates defendants to provide emergency shelter for homeless families."[32]

However, at the same time, the Appellate Division reversed the lower court's decision that shelter, once provided, must meet minimal standards. After reviewing what the court of appeals—New York State's highest court—had previously said about this matter, the Appellate Division held that

> the adequacy of the level of welfare benefits is a matter committed to the discretion of the Legislature. . . . In light of the broad discretion vested in the Legislature, we cannot conclude that plaintiffs are likely to prove that article XVII substantively guarantees minimal physical standards of cleanliness, warmth, space and rudimentary convenience in emergency shelter.[33]

The Appellate Division came to this conclusion "reluctantly" and hoped that when its decision was appealed, it would be "time for the Court of Appeals to reexamine and, hopefully, change its prior holdings in this area."[34] The Appellate Division thus vacated the preliminary injunction issued by Justice Greenfield in June of 1984 that required the city, when it had decided to provide shelter, to provide shelter that met minimal standards.

This finding by the Appellate Division received considerable attention. The *New York Times* ran an article on the decision entitled "Ruling Widens Shelter Rights for Homeless," which quoted a Legal Aid Society lawyer as saying, "This case is for poor families what *Brown v. Board of Education* was for discrimination."[35] This response was probably due to the Appellate Division's finding that it was likely that plaintiffs would establish a right to shelter under article 17 of the New York State Constitution. But what the Appellate Division gave with one hand it, for practical purposes took away with another when it ruled that courts could not set minimal shelter-condition requirements. The city was in any case committed to providing emergency housing to families. The most pressing policy issue was how to improve the quality of that shelter. The HRA commissioner was closer to the mark when he noted that "[w]e understand that the Appellate Division in its decision today found that homeless families have a right to this [city-provided] shelter. At the same time, the court also found that the nature of the shelter provided is up to the city."[36]

On July 3, 1986, plaintiffs obtained an order from Justice Freedman to require the city to comply with the preliminary injunction issued by the Appellate Division on May 13, 1986. The order required that the city "[p]rovide lawful emergency housing to all eligible homeless families with children, such emergency housing not to include overnight accommodations at Emergency Assistance Units or Income Maintenance Centers."[37]

However, this July 3, 1986, order added an element that was not present in the Appellate Division's preliminary injunction of May 13, 1986. That preliminary injunction said nothing that would prevent the city from housing families overnight in an EAU or IMC. The provision of the order that prevented the city from placing families overnight in the EAUs would later in the litigation turn out to be crucial when, in the nineties, 83 ADM-47 was rescinded, and the provision for "immediate" placement was then dropped and the question came before the court how long the city could leave families waiting in the EAU.

Plaintiffs appealed the vacating of the preliminary injunction about the minimum standards to the New York State Court of Appeals. In other words, McCain's lawyers asked the highest court in New York State to hold that courts do, in fact, have the power to compel shelter providers to meet minimal standards once they decide to provide shelter. On April 22, 1987, the court of appeals held that courts do indeed have that power. In reaching this decision, the court of appeals expressly said that it was not necessary to decide the question of whether there was a right to shelter. According to the court of appeals,

> the sole issue is whether the court has the power to issue a preliminary injunction requiring . . . [the state and city] . . . when they have undertaken to provide emergency housing for homeless families with children to provide housing which satisfies minimum standards of sanitation, safety and decency. We hold that the Supreme Court has such power.[38]

The court of appeals further said, "Thus to decide the narrow issue here, it is not necessary to resolve questions pertaining to the underlying obligation to furnish 'emergency shelter to eligible homeless families with children.' . . . We do not reach them."[39]

According to the decision, the New York State Supreme Court had correctly reasoned that shelter that did not meet minimal standards was no shelter at all. Since no regulations covering the quality of shelter then existed, the court had to fashion its own standards, which it developed in the interim order. When, after the state DSS commissioner issued minimal shelter standards, these were more detailed than the standards in the interim order and therefore did not conflict with them even when the interim order was finalized as a preliminary injunction. There remained, therefore, the questions of whether the city and state were meeting the standards set forth in the regulations and whether the preliminary injunction was rendered moot by the issuance of the regulations.

The court of appeals thus sent the case back to the lower Appellate Division to decide those issues. The Appellate Division found that the preliminary injunction was not moot, because the state social service regulations were binding on only Department of Social Service employees and not, therefore, on the city Department of Housing Preservation and Development, which was also involved in housing homeless families. Questions as to whether the city was meeting the requirements of the state regulations and the preliminary injunction were sent back to the lower supreme court. Thus the *McCain* case was consolidated with *Lamboy* (another case, *Slade v. Koch*, which involved accommodations of pregnant clients, was also consolidated with *Lamboy*) and ended up back before the Supreme Court of the State of New York with Helen Freedman as judge.

Where, then, did these early steps of *McCain* and *Lamboy* leave the question of whether there was a right to shelter in New York State? The Appellate Division did issue a preliminary injunction based on article 17 of the New

York State Constitution that barred the city from denying shelter to homeless families. But this finding was not considered by the court of appeals, leaving the question of a constitutional right to shelter unsettled. Nonetheless, we have in these preliminary actions an example of how a right can be created without any one person or organization explicitly creating one. We also have an example of how the American policy process, fragmented as it is and thus often held to be resistant to dramatic change because of its multiple "veto points," can, precisely because of its fragmentation, generate rapid change.[40] One political scientist described this in another context: "what is perhaps most intriguing . . . is how policy became more ambitious as it traveled from one institution to another. . . . Each institution made incremental changes that seemed small when viewed individually but that constituted major, rapid change when put together."[41]

Neither the framers of the New York State Constitution nor the courts in *Callahan*, *Lamboy*, or (finally) *McCain* nor the state regulators explicitly endorsed a right to shelter. But a combination of mutually reinforcing incremental changes produced a nonincremental change: an operational right to shelter for both singles and families, with detailed quality specifications, that would empower the advocates of the homeless to drive policy for years to come.

The obvious solution to homelessness was more permanent housing, but where would the permanent housing come from? In his useful biography of Ed Koch, Jonathan Soffer sets the background for a path-breaking housing program that would become Koch's "most enduring achievement":

> New York was facing an affordable housing crisis. Between 1978 and 1981 the number of apartments renting for $200 month declined by 43 percent, with 67 percent of renters spending more than 35 percent of their income on rent. And in Koch's first term eighty-one thousand units of housing stock, mostly at the lower end of the scale, disappeared.[42]

In his 1985 State of the City address, and then some weeks later in a more developed form, Koch announced his intention to initiate what would be called the "Ten-Year Housing Plan," which would by 1997 produce more than 150,000 units of housing for low- to middle-income families at a price of about $5 billion.[43] About 10 percent of these units would eventually be occupied by formerly homeless families.[44]

It was a daring plan. The money was city money raised with general obligation bonds. In years past, most of the money for developing urban low-cost housing came from the federal government. But under the Reagan administration, such development funds were mostly eliminated, and by 1986, as Koch said, "Federal support of housing is now just a memory."[45] Thus annual city spending on housing rose from $25 million in 1985 to more than $850 million in 1989 before tapering off to about $300 million in 1995.[46] No other city in the country would come close to matching this effort. For years after the 1975 fiscal crisis, raising such funds was impossible because bond markets were closed to the city. However, by 1986 investors had confidence in the city once again, making the Ten-Year Plan possible. The shift from federal to local dollars brought with it a major organizational challenge. The plan was to be directed by the city's Department of Housing Preservation and Development (HPD). Felice Michetti, Koch's deputy commissioner of HPD and commissioner of the department under Dinkins, noted that

> [e]ssentially HPD went from [being] at the beginning of the Koch Ten-Year Plan . . . a housing agency that historically relied on federal money and federal programs to carry out its mission . . . and really didn't do direct developments . . . to a city agency that was charged with spending $5.1 billion and spending it efficiently and free of corruption.[47]

Also making the plan possible was the fact that the city already owned thousands of potentially viable housing units. These were the *in rem* stock, buildings that the city acquired from tax-delinquent owners. In 1986, the city owned more than fifty-three thousand units of occupied *in rem* housing, and forty-nine thousands units in vacant *in rem* housing.

Koch described the development of the plan as follows:

> I think the biggest challenge [for a chief executive] is making an appropriate decision as to how to spend your money. . . . One point, I think, had a great impact on the city. I called in my deputy mayor on Operations, who was Nat Leventhal, and I said, we have to create a housing program [because] the federal people are not providing housing at all. All they do now is repair existing federal low-income housing. The state isn't providing any money.
>
> I want to have a program to create housing for low-income, middle-income, and for homeless people. A program that will provide housing and use just abandoned housing, which we have lots of. At one point we owned 8 percent of all the housing in the City of New York, which was crazy. Crazy, unless you're a communist. And there were people who said we want the city to own all the housing. I remember that very, very well. And I said, over my dead body.

> So we created 150,000 either new units or units that were new based on gutting an old building [and] rebuilding it. It cost approximately a hundred thousand dollars to create such a unit, a two-bedroom unit.
>
> I'm very proud of that program. And in that program we had units for the homeless and we also had units for people who had AIDS and we had [units for the] elderly. I mean we tried in a responsible way to address the needs of lots of people without being able to address the needs of all the people.[48]

The Ten-Year Housing Plan would be continued under the Dinkins administration, which fatefully used the apartment units it generated to rehouse the homeless, with various unintended consequences. Robert Hayes later suggested that the plan was ultimately the result of the pressure that legal advocacy had placed on the city: "The most significant thing about *Callahan* was that it convinced the Koch administration to start renovating *in rem* housing in earnest. . . . It was a radical shift—here were all these buildings in tax arrears that the city had been trying to get rid of, and now there was a use for them."[49] But this is to exaggerate the impact of homelessness on the Ten-Year Plan and of the Ten-Year Plan on homelessness. Much of the appeal of the plan to Koch was, no doubt, that it would benefit not just the homeless but also the key lower-middle-class, white constituency he was courting. Thus, while it is true that 10 percent of the families housed by the program were formerly homeless, about a third were either moderate- or middle-income families.[50]

While its shelter system had been expanding, the city also developed other services for the homeless, including street outreach programs. In October 1982 Project HELP (Homeless Emergency Liaison Project) began as a pilot program under the auspices of NYC Health and Hospitals Corporation. The project was a mobile psychiatric team, staffed with social workers, nurses, and psychiatrists, that focused on trying to convince homeless people with mental disabilities voluntarily to accept help, from offers of coffee and food to mental health services, including transportation to a shelter or emergency room. Project workers brought only twelve to fifteen homeless people to a hospital each year for the first few years of the program's operation.[51]

In 1985, in an effort to bring in more of the city's street-dwelling homeless, Sara Kellerman, commissioner of mental health in New York City, granted psychiatrists on Project HELP teams the power to designate individuals as committable. Psychiatrists thus had the power to authorize involuntary transportation of mentally impaired homeless people to emergency rooms for evaluation and admission. This designation authority was given to project psychiatrists under section 9.37 of the New York State Mental Hygiene Law and made the project into something like a mobile emergency room. However, the city continued to interpret the law as allowing involuntary transportation only in cases where danger to the client or others was "imminent."

Here's an example of Project HELP's outreach efforts:

> R.V., an elderly white man of Eastern European background, has been living in front of the United Nations for several years. Most of his time is spent shouting at the United Nations building in a language that team members were initially unable to identify. For more than a year, as various Project H.E.L.P. team members approached him, R.V. would become increasingly agitated. A team member would stand at some distance and attempt to make contact with the patient. After more than a year of such efforts, R.V. became less agitated, and team members were finally able to approach him more closely. The language in which he was shouting was determined, and a Project H.E.L.P. psychiatrist began to converse with him. R.V. has never accepted any project services, but he is assessed on a regular basis. If any significant deterioration in his condition is noted, he may be involuntarily transported to a hospital.[52]

Project HELP kept track of 1,309 street homeless people in its first thirty months, only about 3 percent of whom were involuntarily transported to an emergency room. Jane Putnam, the director of Project HELP, believed that the strict interpretation of the Mental Hygiene Law was preventing her team from assisting many people who needed care. In a coauthored article, she wrote,

> The legal procedures relating to both inpatient and outpatient care must be examined. Some patients will need "asylum" for the rest of their lives. Others may need involuntary treatment in diverse secure settings. Application of the "dangerousness" or "imminent risk" criteria is denying necessary and appropriate treatment to vast numbers of gravely disabled patients not competent to judge their needs for care and treatment.[53]

In short, according to Putnam, "We have been seeing people die with their rights on."[54]

Mayor Koch agreed with Putnam's evaluation and from 1986 to 1987 supported bills introduced in the New York State legislature that would modify the "harm to self or others" criteria and allow involuntary transportation in cases of self-neglect and grave disability. However, the bills failed to pass.[55]

As Koch considered how to organize the city's street outreach efforts, in late January of 1986, Ellen Baxter's efforts, as director of the Committee for the Heights Inwood Homeless (CHIH), to develop decent, permanent shelter for single, homeless adults was partly realized with the opening of a residence known as "The Heights" at 530 West 179th Street in the mostly Hispanic neighborhood of Washington Heights, Manhattan. The Heights was a path-breaking and highly influential project in several ways. It was the first SRO opened specifically for homeless people in New York City, and the first to develop new SRO housing of any type in the city in many years. It was the first housing project for the homeless in the nation to be syndicated, meaning that it developed a temporary network of several funding sources to make loans for its single purpose, and the first to receive a commercial bank loan. Even a set of partners at the later infamous Goldman and Sachs would eventually invest. Seven different funding sources would eventually be put together. The Heights's commitment to maintaining a mixture of different types of residents—the mentally ill, low-income people, substance abusers, people living with AIDS, as well as former shelter clients and people who had been living on the street—was also an innovation. The residents of the Heights were also protected by signing a lease, something then unknown in other forms of housing for the homeless.

Also new, and critical to the project's success, various types of services, including case management and help in gaining and maintaining entitlements residents qualified for, were provided by a separate organization, Columbia University Community Services (CUCS).[56] One of the most important features of the Heights, according to Baxter, was that residents staffed most of the residence's nonprofessional positions, including front desk management and security:

> The tenant self-management approach I think is very helpful to ensuring the quality of the housing that's delivered. I think that sometimes not-for-profit housing sponsors forget their not-for-profit mission. Being the landlord and your interest in paying your bills and serving people who have very limited income, sometimes we have to grapple with the contradictions of that. And I think that having tenants who live in the building as part of the management helps to preserve the mission. [Residents] have more of an investment in their own housing if they have a stake in it that's meaningful.[57]

Finally, in anticipation of what would be called the "New York/New York Agreements," Baxter succeeded in getting both the city and the state, who at the time were each insisting that the other move first on helping the mentally ill homeless, to cooperate on developing the fifty-five units of permanent housing at the Heights. In effect, Baxter had developed one of the first supportive housing facilities, that is, housing for a range of low-income and disabled clients who would probably otherwise be homeless that provided on-site services that made living independently in the community possible. It was a crucial innovation. Ted Houghton, in his essential account of the supportive housing movement, writes,

> The Heights . . . paved the way for all the supportive housing developers that followed, by showing how unrelated government and private funding streams could be cobbled together to build and operate housing with services. . . . CUCS staff . . . made a subtle but significant shift from clinical and treatment-oriented services to a focus on providing the supports necessary to maintain the tenants' long-term stability in housing.[58]

Eventually it would dawn on policymakers that the only way to get homeless people off the streets and out of shelters was to have some form of permanent housing where their various special needs would be met. For street dwellers and repeat shelter users, who would come to be called the "chronically homeless," supportive housing would provide that permanent base. Cynthia Stuart, chief operating officer of the Supportive Housing Network of New York—a set of nonprofit organizations that by 2015 provided about thirty thousand supportive housing units in the city—put the matter this way: "*Callahan* . . . propelled the creation of so much supportive housing because the City of New York had to provide shelter to all these people and . . . [they] weren't going to get out if they didn't have a decent apartment. So that is what supportive housing was designed around."[59]

In May 1987, Mayor Koch went out with the Project HELP team on its rounds of Manhattan and saw a number of the program's subjects. One of them was a woman who was known to Project HELP as both Ann Smith and Billie Boggs and who was later identified as one Joyce Brown. Koch described these events:

> I'd been out on the street a number of times with our HELP unit that kept in touch with people who were really out of it mentally and wouldn't go to shelters. But [HELP] kept track of them, helped to feed them, bringing them sandwiches. . . . Under the law [you] could commit them if they were in danger of injuring themselves or others, immediate danger. That was the law. But most of them were not in immediate danger [yet] they were doing things that are terrible. One for example was Billie Boggs.
>
> HELP . . . showed me Billie Boggs. She was on Second Avenue living, for long periods of time, on a grate that had some heat coming out. And she was

> sitting in her own feces and she would be yelling at passersby and when they gave her money she would burn it. It was a very sorry sight.
>
> I remember the [mental health] commissioner saying to me, people have a right to do what they want; even if it's terrible and you don't like it, they want to live on the streets. And I thought to myself, that's crazy. I think it's crazy. I said to corporation counsel, this can't go on. So the corporate counsel thought about it and . . . weeks, maybe months passed and then the corporation counsel came in to see me and . . . they said, we have found a way. . . . We think we can establish the premises that if they will be in danger to themselves or to others in the foreseeable—that's the keyword—future you could pick them up. You don't have to wait until they are going to die.[60]

This new interpretation of the Mental Hygiene Law was communicated to Project HELP and HHC psychiatrists in a memo of September 9, 1987, from HHC vice president for legal affairs John E. Linville and vice president for mental hygiene Luis Marcos. The memo urged clinicians that "*the law recognizes a concept of 'serious harm' that is significantly broader than actively suicidal conduct. Significant, passive self-neglect meets the 'serious harm' standard as well.*" The memo further urged doctors to commit those patients they believed were "in danger of serious harm within the foreseeable future."[61] Koch planned to transport up to five hundred mentally ill street dwellers in a year and dedicated twenty-eight beds in Bellevue Hospital to accommodate them.[62]

On October 28, 1987, relying on this new, broader interpretation of the Mental Hygiene Law, Project HELP involuntary transported six individuals to the psychiatric emergency room at Bellevue Hospital. One of those was Joyce Brown. Project documents described her as follows:

> Female in her 40's, known to Project HELP. She has been living against the wall of a restaurant on the Upper East Side for many months. She is dirty, disheveled and malodorous. She urinates and defecates in her location. She is delusional, withdrawn and unpredictable. Without provocation, she can get very agitated and explosive. She has a history of having assaulted passersby. She accepts coins from passersby but will tear up or burn bills. She has paranoid ideation, ideas of reference and inappropriate affect. Her judgment is grossly impaired. She has no awareness of illness or insight. Her physical condition is poor. The preliminary diagnosis is acute psychosis, possibly associated with paranoid schizophrenia. Because of her mental condition including lack of judgment, she requires hospitalization. She is also a danger to self.[63]

At Bellevue Joyce Brown was examined by a psychiatrist who diagnosed her as schizophrenic, injected her with the antipsychotic medication Haldol and a fast-acting tranquilizer, Ativan, and committed her. About a day later another psychiatrist examined Brown and confirmed her emergency admission. However, Brown chose to contest her commitment. Soon after her admission to Bellevue, she contacted the New York Civil Liberties Union and asked them to represent her in court.

On November 2, 1987, the court heard Brown's case. According to Luis R. Marcos,

> At the hearing, four psychiatrists testified consistently that she suffered from chronic schizophrenia, that she was delusional, that her thinking and judgment were seriously impaired, and that she was in need of hospitalization because of mental illness and dangerousness to herself. . . . Three psychiatrists retained by the NYCLU disputed the testimony of the hospital psychiatrists point by point, maintaining that Joyce was neither seriously mentally ill nor a danger to herself or others; they described her life-style as simply reflecting an eccentric personality, not psychopathology.[64]

For every apparently disturbed behavior of Brown's cited by the city psychiatrists, the defense psychiatrists had a response. City psychiatrists pointed to evidence gathered by Project HELP workers that Brown threw away or tore up and urinated on money that was given to her by passersby. The NYCLU's psychiatrists saw nothing problematic in this. Brown had the small amount she thought she needed, and she told passersby that she didn't want money and that she was afraid of having money on her at nightfall. Moreover, money was sometimes thrown at her by policemen who would call her a whore. So rejecting and urinating on money was appropriate. City psychiatrists thought it was delusional that Brown used aliases. NYCLU psychiatrists pointed out that Brown was trying to escape detection by her sisters, who lived in New Jersey and were looking for her and had once had her involuntarily committed. Brown defecated on the street, city psychiatrists noted. This was due to the fact, said the NYCLU psychiatrists, that local stores would not give her access to their bathrooms. Brown's clothes were dirty, tattered, malodorous, and too thin for the cold weather on the streets. NYCLU psychiatrists argued that Brown's clothes were weather appropriate because she lived on top of a steam grate and therefore heavy clothing would have been too warm. Brown reacted to a Project HELP worker by chanting meaningless rhymes that referred to her genitals, city psychiatrists noted. This was done on purpose, Brown and her psychiatrists claimed, to ignore the worker.

Justice Lippmann issued his decision on November 12, 1987. The judge found that "the psychiatric experts . . . are nearly diametrically opposed in their assessment of her [Brown's] mental condition and in their prediction as to whether she is likely to cause herself or others harm."[65] Lippmann therefore relied primarily on his impressions of Joyce Brown as she was on the stand and concluded that the city did not have the right to commit Joyce Brown. He argued,

> I am aware that her mode of existence does not conform to conventional standards, that it is an offence to aesthetic sense. [Nevertheless,] she copes, she is fit, she survives. . . . She refuses to be housed in a shelter. That may reveal more about conditions in shelters than about Joyce Brown's mental state. It might, in fact, prove she is quite sane. [Also,] there must be some civilized alternatives other than involuntary hospitalization or the streets.[66]

HHC appealed to a five-judge panel of the Appellate Division, which reversed Lippmann's decision. A three-person majority found that Joyce Brown's deteriorating condition did indeed qualify as harm to herself. Brown and her lawyers appealed the panel's decision to New York State's Court of Appeals, the state's highest court.

While Brown's case was on appeal, HHC petitioned the New York Supreme Court for permission to medicate her against her will. There were two days of hearings before Justice Kirschenbaum before the court appointed an independent psychiatrist, one Francine Cournos, to determine if Brown should be involuntarily medicated. Cournos advised against involuntarily medication. She judged that antipsychotic medication would improve Brown's condition, but that Brown had not so far harmed herself or others, and that involuntarily medication now might alienate Brown from treatment and cause her to reject medication later on when it might be more necessary. Therefore, before the court of appeals had ruled on her case, Justice Kirschenbaum ordered Brown released and HHC did so a few days later, once they had located a unit for her in a Single Room Occupancy hotel. The court of appeals then considered the Brown case moot and declined to rule on the legality of her commitment.

Sam Tsemberis, who would later be known for developing the "Housing First" model of accommodating street dwellers, began working at Project HELP in August of 1988, soon after the Joyce Brown affair. He described his time at the project, and how it led to his changed thinking about street outreach, as follows:

> I was working at the Columbia Psychiatric Institute at the time doing HIV prevention with the runaway kids. . . . When the job [at Project HELP] opened

up I was living in East Village. . . . If you remember, it was very painful to walk around the city those days—this is before Giuliani locked everybody up at Rikers—just to see the number of homeless people, especially homeless people with mental illness. So when this job [at Project HELP] opened up . . . I met with [Richard C. Surles,] who was vice-president at Health and Hospitals Corporation because the program was run by HHC out of Gouverneur and Bellevue [hospitals]. . . . I met with him in July, I guess it was, a very hot day I remember. I went there in a short-sleeve shirt. He was a little taken aback. I was like no tie, short-sleeve shirt . . . applying for the director's job. He was a very corporate kind of a person. . . .

As we're talking, I tell him . . . I'm like more of, a humanist kind of a guy, R. D. Laing was one of my heroes. I don't actually believe in involuntarily hospitalization. And, then he [said], wait—you're applying for this job and you don't believe in involuntary hospitalization? But he was intrigued by this. I don't think he knew exactly what to make of it. He called me back for a second interview [and] we had a meeting of the minds, I think he understood that deep caring didn't necessarily mean involuntary commitment. And he thought that I would be a good balance to a team that was too gung-ho to bring people to the hospital against their will. And so that's how I started working there [in] August of '88.

Well, it was intriguing. . . . The only usefulness I saw in the program was where we would bring people to the [hospital]. There were people on the street that were medically compromised. People that were coughing up blood. . . . Remember the TB epidemic at that time. There was blood in their sputum. Other people had been standing or had not slept lying down for so long that their feet had swollen and they had cellulitis of the skin that had broken through and there was pus oozing through their sneakers. And then there were people that had lost limbs from gangrene. I mean there was a lot of bad stuff going on on the street [that was] painful to see.

And we would take people to the hospital, make up a mental illness excuse because of the way they have self-neglected themselves. You know, like, their lives were at risk because of their passivity. I mean, in that sense, there were many days when we thought like we had saved somebody's leg or stopped or prevented something worse from happening to them [like] pneumonia. This was quite gratifying in a way, but there were many other days where the psychiatrists were just chasing down people just because they were delusional.

And that never had made any sense to me. Initially it would make sense to me, but it would make less sense to me when after being in Bellevue for a month they would be discharged back on to the street . . . usually carrying the same shopping bag that they had gone into Bellevue with. . . . There was

> twenty-one days of treatment, but the disposition never worked. They never got to a housing program or a residential program. And, those people, the returners—that wasn't everybody, you know, but that was like a good third or a half of the people we were bringing in—began to really, really trouble me.
>
> Because [the] cyclical aspect of . . . this intervention was not really working for them. Those people had characteristics that precluded admission . . . to housing. The kind of housing that was being built then—around '91, '92—was the first wave of New York/New York housing, and the housing strategy was basically to build mental health housing, not to build affordable housing like we actually need. They built boutique programs of twenty to thirty [units of] . . . supportive housing, [with] social workers on site, and they looked like re-institutions.
>
> Now, in order to run those places, you needed to have people coming into them that were clean and sober, and compliant with psychiatric medication. And ready to follow the rules of these SROs. That was not going to be the people we are dealing with at Project HELP, I mean, of course, when you build one of those places they would immediately fill to capacity because there was so many homeless people that you could find people that could make those requirements. But the group I was dealing [with] could not get in. They . . . didn't want to be associated with a mental health program . . . [and] stigmatized as living in a building that's solely for mentally ill people. And even if they did want to get in they couldn't stay clean long enough or agree to take medication because the medication had terrible side effects. It was not for them. Or they couldn't believe they actually had a mental illness that required medication. So, there was a real disconnect there for us and that was a very frustrating aspect of the work.[67]

Before August of 1988 the most striking battles over homelessness policy were the court confrontations of *Callahan* and *McCain* and related cases. Homeless people themselves participated in these battles by proxy, being represented by advocates like Robert Hayes and Steven Banks. Outside of the courtroom, on the streets, the role played by the homeless was a passive one: through their public presence they were seen by other New Yorkers and projected powerful images of want and suffering into the city's consciousness. I will discuss how the visibility of the homeless, and their disruption of public expectations of order, pushed their predicament onto the political agenda. But in the late summer of 1988 and off and on through the early nineties, the homeless, some of them, became the center of a more active form of disruption: the disturbances surrounding Tompkins Square Park in the Lower East Side of Manhattan.

Tompkins Square Park lies between Avenues A and B, and East Seventh and East Tenth streets, in Manhattan's Lower East Side. By the late 1980s important neighborhood groups included yuppies, who were beginning the process of gentrifying the neighborhood; squatters, mostly young and radical, who were living in abandoned buildings and trying to keep them out of the hands of speculators and the city, which was often the official owner; older, working-class residents, the last representatives of a period when most of the neighborhood was Ukrainian; and partygoers and tourists who visited the many music clubs in the area.

In June, members of Avenue A Block Association, a community group that represented the interests of local owners and renters, had gone to a meeting of Community Board 3 to call for enforcement of noise ordinances, a greater police presence, and the imposition of a curfew. Accounts differ as to whether the board accepted, or merely made note of, the call for a curfew.[68] In any case, Ninth Precinct commander Captain Gerald McNamara began enforcing a 1:00 a.m. curfew on July 11. But the curfew was enforced inconsistently, with partiers and club goers being asked to leave but the homeless generally being allowed to stay. Nonetheless, protests against the curfew began to develop. A relatively small skirmish between police and neighborhood residents took place on the evening of July 31. The big riot broke loose on August 6–7. A journalist at the park that night described the events as follows:

> It started before midnight with a ragged little rally directed at the park faithful—the unlucky, the unruly, your tired, your poor. Near the entrance at St. Marks and Avenue A a plump balding man in tie-dye exhorted about a hundred punks, politicos, and curious neighbors through a tinny speaker system: "Yuppies and real estate magnates have declared war on the people of Tompkins Square Park!" . . . The cops were going to shut the park down as they had every night that week. . . . The grim cops at the gate, the chants of "Die Yuppie scum," the M80s exploding deeper in the park—all added to the aura of latent violence.
>
> Suddenly the cops had their riot helmets on and clubs out. Someone in front of a bar threw a bottle toward the mounted police massed at 7th Avenue and the cops backed up. . . . Another bottle smashed on the pavement. And another. The mounted police backed up again. The foot patrolmen stood shoulder-to-shoulder at the park entrance. . . . By now the crowd numbered in the hundreds.
>
> About 12:55, I heard an explosion and the mounted police suddenly charged up Avenue A, scattering the knot of demonstrators still in the streets. I ducked behind a car. The police were radiating hysteria. . . . They were sweeping 9th Avenue and it didn't matter if you were press or walking

> home from the movies or sitting on your stoop to catch a breeze. You were going to move. At First Avenue, I watched two cops on horseback gallop up on the sidewalk and grab a guy by his long hair, pulling him across the street between them. Minutes later, the same guy was down on the sidewalk in front of Stromboli's, bleeding.
>
> The cops seemed bizarrely out of control, levitating with some hatred I didn't understand. They'd taken a relatively small protest and fanned it out over the neighborhood, inflaming hundreds of people who'd never gone near the park to begin with. They'd called in a chopper. And they would eventually call 450 officers.[69]

In response to the riot, Mayor Koch decided to suspend enforcement of the curfew that had been the focus of the demonstration that turned ugly.[70] There began a cycle that stretched over the next few years wherein the number of the homeless in the park would grow, the city would crack down and drive them out, but they would soon return again. With the curfew no longer being enforced, over the next few months the homeless began returning to the park, until by early July 1989 about one to two hundred people made their home in the park, and had constructed a set of makeshift lean-tos and tents for shelter.[71] On July 5, 1989, a Parks Department regulation that prohibited permanent structures in the parks was enforced by more than 250 police in riot gear who smashed down the shanties with axes and sledgehammers. Even as they did so, police acknowledged that the homeless would soon make their homes again in the park, as only the construction of permanent shelters, not living in the park, was being prohibited. And indeed, by November 1989 the homeless returned to the park again, and the Koch administration announced a final effort to clear the park. This time, it was hoped, the affair would be definitively settled as a support center would be built on the outskirts of the park to offer the homeless people living there various services and placements that were expected to remove them from the park.[72] It was not until the beginning of the Dinkins administration that those hopes would be tested.

A theory of the politics of poverty, developed by Frances Piven and Richard Cloward, holds that disruptive action by the poor is the key to the expansion of social provision.[73] The incidents surrounding Tompkins Square Park do not bear out this hypothesis. As we shall see, the upshot of these disruptions was not an expansion of rights but restrictions on the use of city parks by the homeless. The riot of August 6–7, 1988, was not so much a riot by the homeless for their rights as a riot by the police against the homeless and other occupiers of the park, so it is unsurprising that that event did not advance the cause of the homeless. But neither did the many other disruptions around the park by the homeless and their supporters contribute to the establishment or expansion of a right to shelter. In this case disruption resulted in retrogression rather than progress.

At the very end of the Koch administration, work began on an accord that would be described as a "landmark" and a "watershed" in the effort to house the homeless.[74] This was the New York/New York Agreement, signed on August 22, 1990, which was a city and state program to provide 3,314 units of supported housing for the mentally ill homeless, with a capacity to house 5,225 people, by June 30, 1992.[75] Between them the city and the state allocated $194.7 million in capital funds to build the agreement's housing.[76] This was far more money than had ever been spent on a project of this type. Years later, when the state official who negotiated the agreement, Cindy Freidmutter, presented these numbers to mental health policy makers of other states, they would be shocked at the gigantic size of the New York effort.[77]

As the name suggests, the agreement was between New York City and New York State. Years of frustration among advocates and policymakers over the lack of permanent housing for the mentally ill was one reason the agreement was widely regarded as a great breakthrough. Since, as often happens under American federalism, the two levels of government had failed to coordinate for so long, the eventual agreement came to many as a great surprise.

For years, the city had argued that the problem of the mentally ill homeless should be dealt with by the state, because mental health policy had traditionally been a state concern and because it had been the deinstitutionalization of state mental hospitals that had left many mentally ill people without a place to stay. Moreover, the city was reluctant to commit to providing housing for the homeless mentally ill because it had already undertaken to provide shelter and permanent housing for homeless families and AIDS patients and feared setting the precedent of aiding an unending string of special-needs constituencies.[78]

Meanwhile, the state argued that it was the city's failure to preserve SRO hotels and other sources of inexpensive housing that had created the crisis. Further, the state was highly defensive on the subject of the mentally ill homeless. Landmark studies by psychiatrist Elmer Struening and colleagues had shown that about one-third of the residents of the city's shelters for men were mentally ill. On that basis the city had floated proposals to have the state assume responsibility for all mentally ill shelter clients. Badly stung, the State Office of Mental Health had pronounced the studies by Struening and others as "political documents" ginned up by Koch to support his reelection efforts. Moreover, the state was faced with a lawsuit, *Klostermann v. Cuomo*, that claimed that the state's responsibility for the mentally ill extended to providing them with safe housing. The state was therefore eager to disclaim any responsibility for the homeless mentally ill.[79] As a result, well after the deinstitutionalization of the fifties and early sixties, and the low-income housing destruction of the seventies, little public-sector progress had been made on housing the homeless mentally ill.

The New York/New York Agreement was developed so late in the Koch administration that the final step of signing the agreement took place under Dinkins. However, all important negotiations and decisions were made while Koch was still in office. For the city, the process was overseen by William Grinker, HRA commissioner, and actual negotiations were done by his deputy administrator for policy and program development, Diane Baillargeon, and by Frank Lipton, a psychiatrist in charge of the department's Office of Psychiatry. For the state, discussions took place under the aegis of Richard C. Surles, commissioner of the State Office of Mental Health. His chief negotiator was Cindy Freidmutter.

As was noted earlier, many political analysts emphasize the difficulty of achieving change. What then made possible this "monumental advance"?[80] On the city's part, the tough primary challenge Koch was facing from David Dinkins, who was emphasizing the weakness of the mayor's homelessness policy, made Koch eager to achieve some progress he could claim credit for. As for the state, years of stinging criticism for its treatment finally began to have an effect. Throughout the mid- and late 1980s the state responded to critics by opening up community residences—transitional group residences for mentally ill clients waiting to be placed into permanent housing—throughout the state. Governor Mario Cuomo continued this responsive trend by appointing a progressive director to the State Office of Mental Health, Richard C. Surles, who was given a mandate to further address the issue of the homeless mentally ill. It also helped that the city and state had recently come to an agreement on the difficult issue of crowded city emergency rooms referring inpatients to state psychiatric facilities. The trust thus established encouraged progress on larger issues.[81]

Perhaps surprisingly, given the exasperation both sides had felt toward each other on the issue of homelessness, negotiations went easily. Baillargeon recalled that negotiations were not difficult. According to her, "We weren't negotiating with 'somebody's going to win, somebody's going to lose' . . . we were professionals saying this is a positive outcome all the way around."[82] That account squares with Freidmutter's:

> I think they picked two pragmatic people who—Diane and I—were problem solvers. We were there to solve the problem, not to duke each other out. We

> were two women, building a consensus rather than trying to win the fight. And we figured out pretty early that we had people behind us who had very strong ideological views and that bringing them into a room was not going to make this work. So we did agree . . . to really take our points back and try to work out this agreement point by point—going back to our principles without bringing in everybody. I'm not sure [there was] ever a meeting with everyone at the table. I don't remember one.[83]

But why did negotiations go so smoothly on this fractious issue? The negotiators agree that the key was a combination of timing, receptivity, and preparedness. In the fragmented American policymaking system, one sometimes simply has to wait for a moment of syzygy to develop when all the factors are aligned. Freidmutter remarked,

> I've been in government . . . more than thirty years, and I've been around for a lot of those moments. I've seen these kinds of change issues and have worked with government on a lot of these issues. They just come. Really . . . you could try to say it rationally, but sometimes the moment comes when you can do something transformational. And often those moments pass because people don't work fast enough or they can't reach agreements, and they let the moment pass. And the timing is off.[84]

Thus Freidmutter credits Surles because "he understood that when the moment is right for something, you don't walk away on principle, you figure out a way to do it in the best way possible."[85]

Baillargeon emphasizes the need to be prepared when the moment comes. Much has been said in recent years about the importance of ideas in public policy, but one needs to be ready with more than an idea. Baillargeon had been responsible for developing a plan for homelessness policy. Having a plan turned out to be crucial:

> My experience with this kind of stuff is that there are just these moments in time when . . . it's just the right moment. . . . And I think that part of the moment was that we were doing this plan. . . . Plans have a way of often getting put on a shelf. . . . But for the most part, when you're doing a plan and you're in government, people pay a little bit of attention. And also you don't want [to] do a plan that's boring, that has nothing new in it. And so from my point of view, I was shopping for useful, interesting, cool stuff that might get us out of the shelter business and into something better. . . . And I think the result of that was . . . a kind of openness that doesn't always happen just because one person

> has a good idea. . . . The plan had to be vetted by OMB, it had to be vetted by City Hall, it had to be vetted all over the place. And so the idea was raised to a higher level, rather than just an isolated good idea.[86]

The terms of the agreement mostly lived up to the hyperbole with which it was greeted. First, the schedule was ambitious: two years to produce more than three thousand housing units. It is true that a series of extensions resulted in the last residences not being opened until October 1998, which was still an impressive accomplishment given the parties' fiscal problems and the challenges of siting housing for disabled populations in New York City. Also, New York/New York was the first housing program targeted exclusively at the mentally ill homeless. Given the heat it had taken for so long for ignoring the deinstitutionalized and noninstitutionalized, the state was adamant that this new housing should go only to the severely mentally ill. At the time, this was ground-breaking attention to a long-neglected population, but it meant that people with substance abuse problems, people with chronic medical conditions, people living with HIV and AIDS, and people suffering from personality disorders were excluded from the agreement unless they were also severely mentally ill. (These groups would eventually be covered by a later city/state accord negotiated during the Bloomberg administration.) The city was equally insistent that, under the agreement, housing would go to the literally homeless only; people living in doubled-up or otherwise unsatisfactory situations were not eligible. Another innovative feature of the agreement designated a not-for-profit service provider, the Center for Urban Community Services, to serve as an advisor to the shelters, outreach teams, and other organizations that would refer potential clients to agreement-provided housing. The idea was to provide both large and small referral agencies with assistance in negotiating a complex bureaucracy.

Implementation of the agreement is generally thought to have been a success. Ted Houghton, in his definitive historical account, expresses the consensus opinion: "Despite some not so inconsequential delays, the NY/NY Agreement to House Homeless Mentally Ill Individuals of 1990 has been remarkably successful at achieving its promise." By December 31, 2000, a total of 7,774 persons had at one point or another been placed in housing sponsored by the first New York/New York Agreement.[87]

By the end of the Koch administration, the entitlement stage of homelessness policy had been consolidated by being extended beyond homeless individuals to homeless families. That consolidation had been achieved mostly through the efforts of advocates for the homeless in the courts. But the Koch administration, though it never succeeded in raising the quality of all shelters to an acceptable level, deserves considerable credit for creatively muddling through the necessarily challenging implementation of that entitlement. Also, during the Koch years certain limitations and dilemmas, real and apparent, of the entitlement phase began to manifest themselves. The Keener and "New Arrivals" studies suggested that certain limitations on the right to shelter might eventually be necessary. The existence of a small but salient population of street dwellers who would not take advantage of the right to shelter was addressed, unsuccessfully, in the involuntary-transportation policy of Project HELP. These and other challenges of the entitlement stage would have to be dealt with by the Dinkins administration. The policy learning process had begun and would continue.

3

Homelessness Policy under Dinkins

When David Dinkins ran for mayor in 1989, he set forth an ambitious plan to change the way the city dealt with homeless families. Homelessness, he argued, was basically a housing problem, one that could be solved by rapidly relocating families from shelters and welfare hotels into permanent housing.

The blueprint for the new administration's homelessness policy had been prepared in March 1987 by a task force that Dinkins, then Manhattan borough president, appointed. Its report, entitled *A Shelter Is Not a Home*, defined family homelessness in economic terms and argued that the solution was to provide more permanent housing.[1] Since the report's authors thought the private market incapable of supplying affordable housing, the city itself would have to do the job.

In fact, the city was already providing homeless families with permanent housing, placing them in apartments rehabilitated by the Department of Housing Preservation and Development (HPD). These were the so-called *in rem* apartments, which the city came to own as a result of tax delinquency by their owners. The number of HPD units distributed to homeless families had been rising steadily during the latter years of the Koch administration. In 1985, 2,401 such units were provided to homeless families; in 1987, 3,635. In 1988, the administration planned to increase the number to 4,042. The Dinkins task force called on the city to increase its production of rehabilitated apartments for homeless families to 8,000 per year.

The Dinkins proposal assumed that doubling the supply of city-provided permanent housing would not stimulate demand for temporary shelter. In a section of its report entitled "Myths and Facts about Homeless Families," the task force criticized what it called "*Myth 7*: Families with other housing options voluntarily enter the shelter system in order to upgrade their housing at the public's expense and get priority for rehabilitated permanent housing. *Fact*: There is little evidence that families forsake stable housing arrangements hoping to get an apartment through the city."

The report pointed out that although the number of families sheltered by the city had grown steadily during the mid-1980s (from 1,153 in January 1983 to 4,365 in September 1986), the number of families *requesting* shelter each month did not rise. "There is no indication that the availability of emergency housing has produced an increase in demand for shelter or an increase in homelessness," the report stated. The task force concluded that the growth of family homelessness resulted from too few shelter-system families moving out to permanent housing, not from too many marginally housed families moving into the shelter system.

The task force further contended that homeless families did not suffer unusually high rates of personal or behavioral problems that would impair their ability to maintain stable housing arrangements. The report pointed out that, at the time, no scientific studies had demonstrated that such dysfunctions were disproportionately common among shelter families:

> *Myth 3*: Homeless families are the "worst" of New York's welfare families. Family homelessness is the result of drug addiction, mental illness, or behavioral dysfunction. *Fact*: No facts support the belief that addiction or behavioral problems occur with more frequency in the homeless family population than in a similar socioeconomic population. Homeless families are not demographically different from other public assistance families when they enter the shelter system. . . . Family homelessness is typically a housing and income problem: the unavailability of affordable housing and the inadequacy of public assistance income.

The claim was, in effect, that since scientific research had not *proven* that the homeless were much worse in these terms than other poor people, behavioral problems were not the primary causes of homelessness, which were therefore largely structural and economic. It followed that there was no reason to expect that formerly homeless families, once they were provided with permanent housing, would not thrive and escape the shelter system permanently. "In most cases homeless families are able to manage households and can be fully integrated into ordinary permanent housing," the task force declared.

When Dinkins took office in 1990, his administration put its ideas to the test. The mayor appointed Nancy Wackstein, an advocate with the Citizens' Committee for Children who had served on the staff of his task force, to head the Mayor's Office on Homelessness and SRO Housing. Under her direction, the city vastly increased the supply of permanent housing for homeless families and continued a Koch administration initiative to give homeless families priority for vacant public housing units.

A program was already in place in 1990 to provide homeless families with permanent housing. In August 1988, in response to threats by the federal government to stop funding welfare hotels, the Koch administration had stepped up the supply of permanent housing and stopped assigning new families to the hotels. Instead, they were placed in barracks-style shelters (Tier I) or shelters with private rooms, congregate dining facilities, and stricter supervision than at hotels (Tier II). Families that had been in any part of the system for twelve months (later reduced to nine months) became eligible for permanent housing. Human Resources Administration (HRA) reports at the time showed that most homeless families greatly preferred the relative autonomy of hotel accommodations to the closely supervised Tier II shelters.[2] Thus, the Koch administration was consciously making the conditions under which shelter-system families would await apartments less attractive. As Koch himself put the matter, "we are going to, whenever we can, put people into congregate housing like the Roberto Clemente shelter—which is not something people might rush into, as opposed to seeking to go into a hotel."[3] As a result, the number of families entering the shelter system fell during the later Koch years, even though the number of permanent housing placements increased.

Dinkins, too, wanted to end the use of welfare hotels and supply permanent housing to shelter-system families. But he pursued these goals by means quite different from those of Mayor Koch. For one thing, the Dinkins administration could draw from a greater supply of permanent housing, made available by Koch's programs that were beginning to produce results. The number of units provided by the Department of Housing Preservation and Development to homeless families, which had dropped from 4,042 in 1988 to 3,201 in 1989, rose to its former level. Under a 1988 agreement between the city and the New York City Housing Authority (NYCHA), an increasing number of homeless families were moved into public housing. And other homeless families were relocated to privately owned apartments under the Emergency Assistance Rehousing Program (EARP), which paid landlords rent and gave them other substantial incentives to accept formerly homeless tenants.

The Dinkins administration hoped to take advantage of the increased supply of permanent housing to put an immediate end to the use of welfare hotels, which were already being phased out. But unlike Koch, Dinkins was unable or unwilling to move hotel families into less desirable accommodations to await permanent housing; further, in May 1990, the City Council had enacted legislation to phase out the use of Tier I shelters by June 1992. At the same time, Dinkins had to contend with the ongoing enforcement of *McCain*.

Judge Freedman's handling of *McCain* from the mid-1980s until the case was settled in 2008 has been controversial. For example, Demers argues that "[i]n several instances . . . the court essentially substituted its views of the appropriate standards to be applied for those of the executive agency officials whose responsibility it was to develop standards."[4] The conservative *City Journal* claimed that "[i]n scores of rulings since 1985, Freedman has stymied New

York's efforts to take control of its policy for homeless families."[5] Eventual city corporation counsel Michael Cardozo would claim that "the city . . . over the next twenty-five years litigated an unending barrage of motions in which the plaintiffs, relying on that initial preliminary injunction, challenged the city's evolving efforts to address homelessness. The litigation resulted in over fifty court orders touching on and regulating virtually every aspect of the city's shelter program."[6] Even the *New York Times*, which was generally supportive of Freedman's role, could take note of the "more than 40 court orders that prescribed everything from where and when homeless families could sleep to whether bottle warmers and infant formula must be available at city intake offices."[7] We can get a sense of how fair these charges are by looking at some of the court's most noted decisions.

On June 1, 1990, Justice Freedman issued a stipulation and order that required, among other things, that after July 31, 1990, the city would stop placing homeless families in housing that was not in compliance with a state regulation mentioned earlier, 18 NYCRR 352.3. The homeless families and their lawyers claimed that the city was placing families in noncompliant welfare hotels. The city argued that it was in compliance with some of the requirements of the June 1, 1990, court order and asked to be relieved from others because an unexpected increase in applicants made compliance impossible. New York State was also a defendant in the case, as we shall see. The case involved a complex web of claims and counterclaims. Many homeless families provided affidavits that the hotels did not provide basic furniture or safety features as state regulations required. City employees stationed at the hotels provided affidavits claiming that clients' basic needs were being met. Justice Freedman cited with approval the statements of the families but found the employees' statements "unconvincing" because many of the families in the hotels claimed they never received help from, or even saw, these city workers.[8] It would seem that it was necessary at this point to go beyond city and client anecdotes and make a systematic, large-scale evaluation of hotel conditions. Justice Freedman implicitly acknowledged that such a study was necessary when she declined the city's invitation to visit the hotels because "[i]t would be necessary to visit every room at every hotel and interview a large number of families in order to establish the level of compliance." Courts typically don't have the bureaucratic capacity to undertake such evaluations, which is one reason courts are ill suited to oversee complex organizations.

Nonetheless, Justice Freedman went forward. Many of the hotel rooms in which the city placed clients lacked private kitchen facilities. The city argued that such placements were in compliance with 18 NYCRR 352.3, part (e) of which read that "[h]otel/motel accommodations without cooking facilities shall be utilized only when accommodations with such facilities are not available."[9] Part (h) of the regulation, which required that the city determine whether a hotel is compliant with relevant state and local laws, referred, according to the State Department of Social Services, to fire and safety codes only. Part (g) of the regulation, which asserted, among other things, that "[p] rimary consideration shall be given to the needs of children," did not seem to be directly on point. Since interpretations of a regulation by the agency that issues them are binding, unless that interpretation is "irrational or unreasonable," it would seem that the kitchenless hotel units were compliant with the regulations.

Justice Freedman disagreed, writing,

> While the Court would ordinarily defer to an agency's own interpretation of its regulation, the City's and State's interpretation of 18 NYCRR 352.3 (h) to apply to safety and fire codes only, is not logical in view of the salutary purpose of regulations set forth in 18 NYCRR 352.2. Thus, the combined effect of 18 NYCRR 352.3 (e) . . . of 18 NYCRR 352.3 (h) . . . and 18 NYCRR352.3 (g) . . . lead[s] this court to conclude that cooking facilities are mandatory.[10]

Freedman simply isn't convincing on this matter, especially since the Appellate Division, in *Lamboy v. Gross*, had made such a point of deferring to an agency's interpretation of its own regulations.

Another famous episode in the *McCain* litigation came to a head on November 20, 1992, when Justice Freedman found the city in contempt for violating state laws and court orders and, among other penalties, required four officials of the Dinkins administration to spend a night in the EAUs. The origins of this development date back to a stipulation and order issued by Justice Freedman on June 1, 1990. That document was essentially a contract, supervised by the court, between the plaintiff homeless families and the city. Prior to the agreement, the city had often placed families in shelters or hotels that did not comply with state regulations or earlier court decisions. The agreement was complex, but essentially the city pledged to implement a detailed plan that committed them to placing families only in accommodations that complied with state regulations, including 18 NYCRR 352.3, by June 30, 1990. The city also agreed to stop placing families in barracks-style shelters for more than one night. As their part of the agreement, the plaintiffs agreed to refrain from taking action to enforce prior orders of the court while the city implemented the plan.

By January 1991 the city was failing to live up to the plan. The city continued to place families in noncompliant hotels. The city brought its failure to live up to this aspect of the June 1 stipulation and order to the attention of the court in September and October of 1990, and Justice Freedman therefore decided not to hold the city in contempt on this matter. The city invoked the perversity argument and claimed that by transferring families from emergency shelter to permanent housing, it had unintentionally created an incentive for doubled-up families to move into the system. The city shared with the judge its plans for the Alternative Pathways Program (APP), which would offer permanent apartments to doubled-up families and provide various other sorts of assistance to prevent families from moving into the shelter system. In any case, the city was continuing to place families overnight in EAUs, and welfare offices continued to place families with pregnant women and young infants in barracks-style shelters. Justice Freedman wrote that therefore "[t]he court is left with little choice but to issue contempt findings."[11] The city was found in civil contempt, and sixty-two homeless families that were housed in violation of court orders received a total of $16,500.[12]

On September 10, 1991, the parties were back before the court. The plaintiffs sought civil and criminal contempt charges against the city for 1,325 violations of court orders that they had documented since January.[13] The violations included sending pregnant women to barracks-style shelters and placing families in rooms with folding cots or other inappropriate furniture. The city admitted to the violations, and Freedman concluded that "a contempt finding is inevitable" but called for further hearings to decide which specific city officials would be found in contempt and what penalties would be imposed.

Soon thereafter Justice Freedman ordered that the city would have to stop placing families in hotel rooms without kitchenettes by September 30. Further, Local Law 18 required that the city stop using barracks-style shelters entirely by the same date. The city argued that it simply could not meet the deadline. "We can't comply with the law," First Deputy Mayor Norman Steisel confessed after a City Hall news conference. "We cannot meet the timetable. We've got to figure out what remedies are available to us while still basically fulfilling the overall intent of the law."[14] The city was in the midst of struggling to implement a new plan to deal with the influx of homeless families. This was the Alternative Pathways Program (APP), implemented in October 1990. Under APP, some of the HPD apartments that would otherwise go to shelter-system families were instead made available to families doubled up in private apartments. Much of the plan for the APP that the city had presented to the court back on January 8, 1991, had not been realized. The distribution of apartments to doubled-up families, later studies would show, had little impact on the number of families that entered the shelter system. A component of the program that provided legal services to poor families facing eviction had been delayed, and a $12.4 million program to pay rent for some thirty-two thousand families that were in arrears had not been approved by the state.

It is possible to conclude from all this delay that from 1990 through 1992 the city was simply making no progress on improving its provision for the homeless. Certainly the record that was being presented to the court was unimpressive. Steven Banks's assessment was that "the record of the past year and a half is replete with failure to stop placing families in welfare hotels, failure to comply with court orders to provide lawful shelter and failure to implement the city's own homelessness prevention program."[15] It is worth remembering, however, that between September 1991 and May 1992, the Cuomo Commission—led by Andrew Cuomo, whose task was to rethink all facets of the city's homeless policy—was being formed, was deliberating, and was ultimately embraced by the Dinkins administration. The administration was going through the enormously complicated task of rethinking homeless policy, changing direction, and developing a new organizational structure. All this, however, was happening outside the court system, which concluded that the city was simply spinning its wheels, or worse, not acting in good faith.

By November 1992, Justice Freedman had had enough. On November 13, 1992, she again found the city defendants in civil contempt, and on November 20 she issued contempt findings against four individual city officials, Barbara J. Sabol, commissioner of the Human Resources Administration; Kenneth Murphy, deputy commissioner for Crisis Intervention Services at HRA; First Deputy Mayor Norman Steisel; and Jeffrey L. Carples, assistant to Deputy Mayor Cesar A. Perales. (Sanctions against Carples would be dropped when a reassignment left him no longer responsible for EAU operations and were directed instead against his boss, Perales.) The court ordered that on a given evening, these officials would each have to stay overnight in separate EAUs and remain there until all families applying for shelter had been placed. The court also levied fines against the city that were to be paid to applicant families that had not been placed in compliant shelter between September 20, 1992, and November 20, 1992.[16] Justice Freedman commented, "I have been ordering and ordering and ordering cures of these violations for two, three, six and seven years. I just want you and everyone to know that my orders have not been effective."[17] A sense of the tension for all concerned can be gotten from a press account of the proceedings: "'What do you want us to do?' the City Corporation Counsel, O. Peter Sherwood, asked plaintively. The judge [Freedman] replied, enunciating each word like an aggravated wife instructing her dimwitted spouse: 'Do not keep them all night in welfare offices.'"[18]

In December 1992 the Dinkins administration decided to appeal the court's contempt findings.[19] On July 29, 1993, the Appellate Division issued its decision and showed little sympathy with the city: "[I]t is no defense that the municipal defendants were attempting to comply or acting in good faith. . . . The City's contention that compliance is impossible is belied by the fact that the City was able to do so in the recent past." Why it necessarily follows that what was possible in the recent past must therefore be possible in the present is not clear. The Appellate Division upheld the fines that Justice Freedman had imposed on the city. However, the order of the four officials to spend a night in EAUs was deleted because "the only purpose served by such a penalty is to punish these individuals." The Appellate Division did find that the individual officials could be fined or imprisoned and called on the lower court to "impose an appropriate sanction."[20] On December 8, 1993, Justice Freedman imposed a fine of seventy-five hundred dollars on each of the individual officials and also on Chip Raymond, then commissioner of the newly established Department of Homeless Services.

First Deputy Mayor Norman Steisel described his reaction to being held in contempt:

> Obviously, I was pissed off. I guess there are two points of view. For me, it was not a conscious effort to be in contempt. For me, it was not knowingly withholding resources or . . . in a calculated fashion preventing people from doing their job, which was to me contempt. On the other hand, to the extent that we didn't meet our plans because the bureaucratic hurdles were more formidable . . . then I guess we were in contempt. . . . I was really pissed because I felt I was trying to move the thing forward and I thought to some extent we were being undone by the very same people [who] contributed to the problems in the first place. We had this whole thing about negotiating improved agreements or adequate base agreements to get rooms in SROs and making certain of the hotels that had not been used as SROs . . . available. Obviously, that's a complicated negotiation because there was such a horrible history. If you were a hotel operator . . . you might have been economically desperate for more money, [but] you had to be careful of who comes in to these facilities given what you perceive [as] the problems and baggage they bring with them. Remember, HRA was always making commitments and saying they [had] agreements lined up and then the agreements would vaporize. At the same time, when communities got wind of the fact that we were talking to some apartment owners or some hotel, they would be distressed. They would let you know about it and my recollection is HRA either persuaded the local property owner or HRA [had] to back off. That was an enormous sense of frustration. So were we in contempt?

> From the point of view of the right people in the city, the city didn't do what it said it was going to do.[21]

Ironically, Deputy Mayor Cesar A. Perales was being held in contempt partly for being unable to comply with Administrative Directive 83 ADM-47, which he had promulgated and interpreted when he was New York State social services commissioner. He also commented on his experience before the court:

> I knew Judge Helen Freedman. . . . I'm a civil rights lawyer. I came out of that system. I was a neighborhood legal services lawyer in my youth. And so I know these people, the Legal Aid Society. I was seen as one of them. I was seen as a reformer as [New York State] Social Services Commissioner. . . . My regulations were seen as putting enormous pressure on government to do something about homeless people. So I was, in the eyes of many people, a good guy.
>
> And so it was strange to find myself in court, being told that I was not doing enough or doing it quickly enough, and those were, in essence, the reasons that were periodically brought before the court. This was a question of whether or not we could house people more quickly and meet their needs. And for me it was strange because I had always been seen as being somebody on the other side, fighting for poor people, and here I was trying to run, not run, but oversee—because I was a deputy mayor, right?—HRA. And so that was a very difficult position.
>
> I think the courts were productive. I do think that without court intervention government would have moved more slowly and would have been less responsive to the problem.[22]

Justice Freedman would eventually try other strategies to achieve city compliance but continued to impose fines up through 2006. The *New York Law Journal* reported in 2003 that the city had been fined $8 million by that point.[23]

How effective were the fines and what does this whole episode say about the effectiveness of institutional reform litigation as a mechanism for improving bureaucratic performance? Concerning the effectiveness of the fines, we have to ask what the purpose of the fines was. Steven Banks has made the fair point that the civil contempt charges against the city resulted in compensation for families that had been denied mandated services. Insofar as the fines aimed at compensation, they were effective. But the fines levied against individual administrators and the requirement that these administrators be confined, one evening, to the EAU until all applicants received shelter do not involve compensation. Instead, they aimed at getting the shelter bureaucracy to comply with court orders. Further, Judge Freedman's famous complaint when she ordered the fines—"I have been ordering and ordering and ordering cures of these violations for two, three, six and seven years . . . [and] my orders have not been effective"—suggests that the purpose of the fines was to get the court orders complied with. The bare facts of the case do not show that city administrators sprang into compliance once they faced contempt charges. The advocate-plaintiffs continued to be unhappy with city performance after the fines were levied and continued their litigation against the city for a long time. It is true that over the long term the pressure of litigation and enforcement of court decrees resulted in a vastly improved shelter system. But the present question is whether Judge Freedman's findings of contempt and the fines that went with them had a shorter-term positive impact on the system.

An early article on implementation problems in institutional reform litigation held that "defendant administrators do not always have the ability to make their institutions comply. In such cases the contempt sanction is useless and unfair; contempt should be imposed only for failings within the defendant's control."[24] But what strikes one now about the situation in which the city found itself in 1992–1993 was the complexity of the phenomena the city was struggling with and the sheer stubbornness of the problem they were attempting to solve. It is not at all clear that in this case the city administrators had control over their ability to comply with the courts' rulings. It is true that the city frustratingly presented one compliance plan after another to the court and failed to follow through on many of them; some of them that they did follow up on, like the APP, proved to be fruitless. This string of abandoned plans apparently gave the courts the impression that the city simply lacked the will to implement plans the city itself had said would work. A more plausible interpretation of this history is that as the various plans turned out to be infeasible or ineffective, the city dropped them and in the end ended up simply not knowing what to do to bring themselves into compliance.

One alternative enforcement mechanism that was not tried by the court was the use of positive incentives. Fines and contempt charges are essentially negative incentives, and psychologists have generally found positive incentives to be more effective in changing behavior. It has been suggested that "[o]ne alternative to the contempt sanction . . . is the use of positive incentives. . . . One possibility might be to have administrators award organizational prerequisites and promotions partly on the basis of compliance with the decree by unit managers within the organization."[25] Interestingly, when the city faced the problem of getting private shelter providers to comply with performance contract specifications, it relied on positive incentives in the form of bonuses for compliance. Judge Freedman never tried this positive approach and so left one alternative to contempt unused.

Under Dinkins the direct transfer of hotel and other shelter families to permanent housing began apace. One reason for this development was that in May the City Council passed a law requiring that the city stop the use of barracks-style (Tier I) shelters by June 1992, so homeless families needed to be moved elsewhere quickly. The Dinkins administration assigned large numbers of apartments to homeless families during the spring and summer of 1990. Between March and August, an average of 561 shelter families per month, or 55 percent of the shelter population, were referred to city-provided permanent housing; the average for the previous six months had been only 262, or 36 percent.[26]

By some indications, the new strategy seemed to be working. As of July 1990, only 147 families remained in the infamous welfare hotels, compared with 3,306 families when Koch committed to ending the use of the hotels in 1988.[27]

But for whatever reason, the number of entries into the system went up in short order. Immediately after the Dinkins administration began increasing the provision of permanent housing in spring 1990, new entries to the shelter system jumped from about 530 per month to about 650 per month by July. Researchers from the Bureau of Management Information Systems, a division of the city's Human Resources Administration (HRA), concluded that the number of entries into the shelter system "appears to be highly responsive to changes in housing and shelter policy. . . . It appears that 'word gets out' to the clients and community within months after a significant policy shift occurs, and that the perceived implications of the policy change affect the decision to enter the system or not."[28] Dinkins's 1987 report had, of course, argued that no such effect would occur. When entries to the shelters suddenly started going up, Wackstein recalls, "this was something pretty wild, something we hadn't contemplated."[29]

The trend created a crisis for the city, which was legally bound by the court order issued in the case of *McCain v. Koch*, to supply every applicant with shelter. "We became simply obsessed with numbers," Wackstein says. "Compliance was based on providing so many beds, so many units. There was no time for long-range planning at all."[30]

By the early fall of 1990, according to some participants, Wackstein and deputy HRA commissioners Jeffrey Carples and Kenneth Murphy and First Deputy Mayor Norman Steisel were convinced that the greater supply of permanent housing had stimulated the increased demand for shelter. Deputy Mayor Cesar A. Perales agreed. Dinkins himself came to believe this. According to Steisel, "It took a long while for him [Dinkins] to accept that [a perverse incentive] was going on."[31]

But in the end even Dinkins concluded at the time that "[u]nintentionally, an incentive for people to use welfare hotels has been created. . . . Families are frequently entering our city shelter system in order to find a permanent apartment. We do not want doubled-up families to make themselves homeless in order to find city housing."[32] In his memoirs, published twenty-three years later, Dinkins would be somewhat more equivocal but would strongly imply that he believed a perverse incentive had been created:

> When it became clear that the homeless were indeed receiving priority and that the supply of higher-quality housing was increasing, the number of people entering the shelter system began to rise dramatically. Those who had been concerned about such an eventuality were proved correct. Were there people on the edge who decided to become homeless in order to gain a better deal? Did an increased availability of housing stock, the belief that one could obtain this housing by declaring homelessness, and a national economic downturn that threw people out of their jobs and homes all conspire to create a homeless epidemic? It is entirely possible.[33]

But HRA commissioner Barbara Sabol and private homeless advocates continued to insist that family homelessness was primarily caused by a shortage of affordable housing. According to Wackstein, those officials who argued that something had to be done to discourage inappropriate use of the shelter system were "roundly denounced" by advocates for the homeless.[34]

But had the Dinkins policy really created a perverse incentive? This episode, called the "Dinkins deluge" by Cragg and O'Flaherty, is one of the most studied sets of events in the history of New York City's homelessness policy. The most extensive treatment is my own "Hard Lessons about Homelessness: The Education of David Dinkins," in the *City Journal* in summer 1993. Another detailed account is "The Failure of Liberal Homeless Policy in the Koch and Dinkins Administrations," by J. Phillip Thompson. The matter is also dealt with by Gordon Berlin and William McAllister in various forms and by Christopher Jencks.[35]

As some of their titles suggest, these authors all came to the conclusion that the policy of moving families rapidly out of shelters and hotels and into refurbished apartments or NYCHA housing created an incentive for poorly housed families to become homeless and so increased entries into the system. Cragg and O'Flaherty strikingly disagreed on the basis of an entirely different way of analyzing the situation. Dinkins administration officials who came to believe that a perverse incentive had been created based their conclusion on the historical record, personal experience, and gut instinct. As Norman Steisel put the matter, "I think there was evidence of it [a perverse incentive]. I wouldn't say it was entirely hard fact-based evidence but there was enough of it to feel that that is what happened."[36] And Cesar A. Perales based his conviction on his experience with shelter clients:

> I began, as I spent more and more time visiting Emergency Assistance Units, . . . to feel in having conversations with people that the way that people could improve their housing situation was to declare themselves homeless, go to the Emergency Assistance Unit and . . . to, in essence, skip to the front of the line and get into public housing or get some other form of housing for instance. And that began to trouble me because, obviously, that had not been my intent.[37]

Such was what Cragg and O'Flaherty described as the "conventional wisdom," and they stated that "[w]e test the conventional wisdom and reject it. Better prospects of subsidized housing increase flows into the shelter system, but this effect is not nearly large enough to offset the first-order shelter effect—taking families out of the shelters reduces the number of families in them."[38] In support of this conclusion, the authors offered a sophisticated statistical model of the market for family shelter during the Dinkins administration.

A few qualifications are in order. First, we should note that Cragg and O'Flaherty found that perverse incentives had been created. The problem was not that such incentives didn't exist; they just weren't nearly as strong as had been thought, with seven placements into permanent housing being required to entice one family into the system. Cragg and O'Flaherty acknowledged that "the lure of subsidized housing does draw a substantial number of families into shelters—not as many as the journalistic accounts suggest, but still a substantial number."[39] Further, the authors found that one policy decision did have a strong perverse incentive effect. This was increasing the percentage of families that were lodged in Tier II shelters as opposed to welfare hotels. (Cragg and O'Flaherty defined Tier II shelters as follows: "Tier II shelters, generally operated by nonprofit organizations, offer more counseling and some other amenities than hotels do, but they significantly restrict residents' freedom.")[40] Both Koch and Dinkins increased the use of Tier II shelters to reduce the number of families staying in the infamous welfare hotels. Cragg and O'Flaherty found that had the percentage of families in Tier II shelters not increased, the shelter population by December 1993 would have been only half as big as it was.[41] And finally, the authors noted that their analysis did not imply that perverse incentives may not be more important in other situations.

The Dinkins deluge theory is a classic example of a staple of conservative rhetoric that A. O. Hirschman calls the perversity thesis, which is that "*the attempt to push society in a certain direction will result in its moving all right, but in the opposite direction.*" Anyone who follows political polemics is familiar with this move: the minimum wage increases unemployment; rent control reduces the supply of affordable housing; welfare breeds poverty. What then does the Dinkins deluge episode have to tell us about the use of the perversity thesis in policy discourse? The perversity thesis ought to be applied with great caution. It is neither mere common sense, as public officials tend to believe, nor a vicious lie, as advocates usually claim. It is most useful as a springboard to a discussion of the total set of incentives that policy creates. It is positively harmful when used as a quick put-down of reformers, or as an unanswerable charge against bureaucrats. We ought to be skeptical about casual use of this thesis. The perversity argument is often an effective rhetorical strategy for defenders of the status quo as it allows them to move off the defensive and criticize reformers or advocates. But precisely for this reason it often provokes a heated reaction and beclouds rather than encourages careful thinking. But neither should we simply reject the thesis out of hand.

When, in a policy dispute that we will consider in another chapter, the Bloomberg administration appealed to the perversity argument, advocates were quick to reject the very idea as absurd; Coalition for the Homeless claimed that Bloomberg was saying "Up Is Down, Night Is Day, 2+2=5, Etc. Etc."[42] This polarizing rhetoric was unnecessary, especially given that in this particular case the plain facts told against the Bloomberg administration, as we shall see. We have seen that city bureaucrats take the reality of perverse incentives very seriously, and it is never a good idea to just dismiss the experience and wisdom of public officials, even when they seem unscientific. And there is evidence that perverse incentives might in some situations be very real. For example, while there is no evidence that those housing subsidies such as Section 8 vouchers lure homeless families into the shelter system, there is evidence that under certain conditions vouchers do have perverse incentive effects. Economists Brian A. Jacob and Jens Ludwig have found that receipt of Section 8 vouchers discourages work. Section 8 families had 6 percent higher unemployment and 15 percent higher welfare receipt than similar families that did not receive the subsidy.[43]

We ought to encourage the development of what Hirschman calls a "democracy friendly" kind of discourse, one that realizes "there are dangers and risks in both action and inaction. The risks of both should be canvassed, assessed, and guarded against to the extent possible." More often than conservatives realize, the perversity argument undermines the development of such a dialogue.

In any case, by the winter of 1990 much of the Dinkins administration concluded that they were facing perverse incentives of such a magnitude that they could not be ignored. Since the problem had supposedly been caused by an increase in the supply of permanent housing and a lessening of reliance on shelters, these trends, it was thought, had to be reversed. But the tactic the Koch administration had used—deterring demand for shelter by consciously making the system less attractive—was unpalatable to the Dinkins administration.

The result was the Alternative Pathways Program (APP), implemented in October 1990. Under APP, some of the HPD apartments that would otherwise go to shelter-system families were instead made available to families doubled up in private apartments. The city explained that the program would give doubled-up families an incentive to stay out of the shelters by convincing them that they had a chance of getting their own apartment. It was doubtful that APP was effective as a reward for doubled-up families to stay put. Because families enrolled in APP were assigned apartments by lottery, they could not be certain of getting their own apartment. By contrast, all families entering the shelter system were assured of an eventual transfer to permanent housing.

APP did, however, cut the number of HPD-produced units allotted to shelter-system families by 961 in 1991, thereby reducing the yearly supply of units available to those families to about its 1989 level. By allowing the city to cut back on the supply of permanent housing to shelter-system families, the program increased the amount of time such families would have to wait before being transferred to permanent housing. And family entries into the system did fall shortly after the implementation of APP.[44] This led some observers, including the present author, to conclude that the reduction in transfers to permanent housing caused the drop in family entries. However, Cragg and O'Flaherty convincingly contest this aspect of the Dinkins deluge theory and find that APP, in their models, had no impact on family entries into the system. APP is interesting primarily as evidence that the Dinkins administration was hitting various policy buttons in an effort to adjust incentives for entry.

In September 1991, a discouraged Wackstein resigned. In a July 1992 interview with the *New York Times*, the former point person for homelessness policy in the Dinkins administration discussed her disillusionment with the efforts to move homeless families into permanent housing. "That was our big mission," she said. "It was the mayor's campaign issue. Boy, I believed it. I approached it with energy and passion." Yet her efforts "didn't seem to be making a difference."[45] She would later say,

> I wanted to make the world better for poor people. I wanted to give them more options, more access to services, and housing and everything else and here I was . . . having meetings with HRA officials and OMB officials about what we're going to do to keep them out. . . . I know this is not what I want to be doing. And that's really why I left.

She decided she could do more for the homeless working in the private sector:

> I was just perfectly delighted when I left, I was perfectly happy to go. I went to run a settlement house . . . Lenox Hill, and I was just thrilled to be dealing with . . . three hundred homeless people rather than thirty thousand homeless people because it felt like I could make more of a difference in running a direct service agency and doing decent programs and that these people didn't try to deal with this unreal policy thing.[46]

The city's policy of placing homeless families in public housing was originally a Koch initiative, but its results would challenge the Dinkins administration's assumption that homelessness is primarily a problem of economics, rather than personal behavior. In 1988, as part of its response to the federal government's threat to cut off funding for welfare hotels, Mayor Koch persuaded NYCHA to commit to a four-year plan offering two thousand apartments a year—one in four of the authority's vacancies—to homeless families. NYCHA, which initially resisted Koch's policy, had to reorganize itself to fulfill its new obligation.

In June 1988, the authority established the Special Rental Team (SRT), whose mission was to expedite the process of determining whether homeless families were eligible to live in public housing. Those who had untreated drug, psychological, or medical problems or were suspected of criminal or disruptive behavior were supposed to be screened out.

Eligibility determinations for nonhomeless families were usually conducted in Housing Authority offices just one day a week. The SRT, by contrast, conducted daily hearings at separate offices more conveniently located for homeless families, and in some cases would send staffers out to shelters to conduct interviews. Homeless families, therefore, got through the eligibility process in an average of two to three months, with perhaps one in three declared eligible immediately after the interview. Meanwhile, nonhomeless families faced an average six-month wait and were almost always subjected to further investigation before their eligibility was determined. Because the screening process for homeless families was thus less rigorous than for nonhomeless ones, some Housing Authority officials suspected that SRT was interpreting eligibility criteria rather loosely. SRT staff, however, hotly denied that they were failing to weed out dysfunctional homeless families.

In 1990, the authority further stepped up its efforts to place homeless families by establishing the Command Center, a centralized unit that aimed to speed up the process of matching eligible homeless families with vacant apartments. Normally, when a housing project had a vacancy, it would be reported up through the regular chain of command: the local project manager would inform the Housing Authority's district office, and the district office would inform the central office, whose application department maintained the authority's waiting list. Under the new regime, vacancies were first reported to the Command Center, which would immediately match a new vacancy with an eligible homeless family. Early on, the Command Center interpreted its mission as ensuring that the Housing Authority filled its yearly quota of apartments for the homeless before any vacant units were made available to nonhomeless families on the waiting list. Accordingly, the Command Center would "warehouse" vacancies; that is, if a homeless family were not immediately available for a given apartment, the Command Center waited until one became available, rather than release the apartment to a waiting nonhomeless family. Only if a homeless family declined a particular vacancy, which was its prerogative, would an apartment be offered to a waiting-list family. With the establishment of the Command Center, placement of homeless families picked up sharply. In all of fiscal 1990, 2,418 homeless families received apartments, but the majority of them—1,318, or 55 percent—were placed in the final quarter of that year alone (April through June 1990), just after the Command Center had been established.[47]

The mission of accommodating homeless families, however, conflicted with the Housing Authority's institutional interests, as well as the interests of its tenants. The city's public housing managers had held "an article of faith for many years that the New York City Housing Authority maintains its reputation as the very best of the large public housing authorities in the nation because of its deliberate policy of an 'economic mix,'" as Sally Hernandez-Piñero, who became the authority's chair in February 1992, explained.[48] In order to maintain social stability, the authority tried to balance the population in its roughly 179,000 apartments at about one-third elderly, one-third working poor, and one-third very low income (families on public assistance). But between 1985 and 1991, the mix of entrants into the authority changed drastically. Very low-income families increased from 32 to 54 percent of total yearly entrants, while the elderly decreased from 49 to 35 percent and the working poor dropped from 19 to 12 percent. Housing Authority officials came to see the homeless referrals as a threat to their longstanding policy of "economic mix."[49]

Public-housing tenants resented the preferential treatment accorded to homeless families. In 1990, Housing Authority projects were home to some one hundred thousand members of families doubled up in Housing Authority units, in addition to their 470,000 authorized residents. These doubled-up residents were eager to apply for public housing vacancies but found that none would be available until SRT had filled its quota for homeless referrals. Housing Authority tenants did not take kindly to seeing their own "internal homeless" pushed to the back of the line.

By 1990, tenants had become so frustrated that they held public demonstrations protesting the expedited placement of homeless families in public housing. City Hall dispatched First Deputy Mayor Norman Steisel and HRA commissioner Barbara Sabol to soothe tempers at a public meeting with Housing Authority tenants. Steisel later reflected that

> [t]here was even a point in time where Barbara Sabol advocated very strongly to . . . put people into the Housing Authority. It creates all sorts of problems. The Housing Authority, for whatever they are, they have their own sets of problems. They are pretty stable communities and it was clear that there was information available that happened to show that the homeless people got other kinds of support. It made problems in the community, both real and perceived, so that many of the Housing Authority [families] . . . resisted. . . . There was high resistance to it and some with good cause.[50]

Steisel and Sabol promised to transfer some one million dollars from HRA to the authority in order to cover costs associated with integrating the formerly homeless families. The situation was helped not at all when these promised funds were eventually cut from the HRA budget and therefore were never transferred to the Housing Authority.

It was only a matter of time before Housing Authority officials would side with their tenants, partially as a means of strengthening their own hand in the inter-bureaucratic struggles over responsibility for the homeless. "I can't have any moral authority if I have to say to our people that they have to do something that I know is undermining our housing," explained NYCHA chair Hernandez-Piñero. "That just goes to the core of the relationship I'm trying to develop with the tenants. The stories of some of the people on our waiting lists would break your heart too."[51]

The resistance to homeless families among public-housing tenants probably came as a surprise to the Dinkins administration. *A Shelter Is Not a Home* had attacked "*Myth 13*: No community wants housing for the homeless in its own backyard. *Fact*: . . . Communities have accepted housing for the homeless when the facilities are small-scale and well-supervised by an accountable non-profit organization, priority is given to homeless people from the same area, and advance planning includes local input."[52] Public-housing tenants certainly would have been more receptive to the policy if it had given priority to "homeless people from the same area"—that is, to doubled-up families in public housing. But this is as much as to say that the Housing Authority should not have accepted outside homeless families in the first place, since its own internal homeless could have filled most, if not all, of the available vacancies.

Even if the homeless families referred to public housing had possessed the social skills of diplomats, regular tenants would probably have resented a policy that put them at a disadvantage in getting vacant apartments. But were the tenants' doubts about the functioning capabilities of the homeless justified, or were they, as Dinkins's task force had argued in 1987, the result of "stereotypes of homeless people which have aroused unfounded fear and prejudice"?[53] In September 1989, New York University's Health Research Program published a scientific study that could be interpreted as supporting the tenants' view.[54] The control-group study compared 704 homeless families requesting shelter at one of the city's Emergency Assistance Units with 542 nonhomeless families on public assistance interviewed at welfare offices.

The findings of the study contradicted several of the assertions made in Dinkins's 1987 report. For one thing, homeless families were in fact demographically different from other public-assistance clients. They were more likely to be black, less likely to be Hispanic, and much younger on average than nonhomeless poor families. Further, homeless families have consistently higher rates of behavioral problems than their housed counterparts. "On almost every measure of 'well-offness' or ability to function independently," the authors remarked, "homeless families are in somewhat worse shape than the housed public assistance population."[55]

It is true that reported substance-abuse and mental health problems involved only a minority of homeless families. One should not conclude, however, that the higher reported rates of behavioral problems among homeless families are too small for such problems to play a role in causing homelessness. A combination of such "small" differentials can have a powerful impact.

"Although the differences in the two groups are not dramatic for many of the individual measures, the cumulative effects of the higher incidence of numerous problems may be the major cause of many families' homelessness," the study noted.[56]

However, follow-up research to the initial Knickman and Weitzman study suggested that the differences between homeless and nonhomeless poor families are less dramatic than their initial work indicated. From 1990 to1996, the National Institute of Mental Health supported a long-term follow-up study, in which 70 percent of those families in the initial study who had not used shelter prior to the 1988 interview were re-interviewed. One study based on these new interviews found that the problems of homeless families did not prevent them from achieving housing stability once they received some form of housing subsidy.[57] Another follow-up study found that, five years after entering a shelter, formerly homeless children and continuously housed children exhibited few differences, although such differences as there were favored the continuously housed children.[58] It has also been found that there are few differences in the social networks of homeless and housed families.[59] This follow-up research suggests that however risky homeless families might have seemed at first, they would have successfully stabilized themselves once they got access to NYCHA apartments. But in 1990 Housing Authority families and staff seemed to have reason to worry, and they resisted accordingly.

Therefore the Housing Authority reduced its efforts to place homeless families. In the summer of 1991, the Command Center abandoned its practice of "warehousing" vacant apartments for the homeless. In June 1992, Hernandez-Piñero abolished the SRT. Homeless families applying for vacancies in public housing were once again subject to the same eligibility review as everyone else. And Hernandez-Piñero renegotiated the 1988 agreement, so that the authority was obliged to accept only about fourteen hundred homeless families a year.

Even before he became mayor, Dinkins's interest in the homeless had especially focused on homeless families. Thus the document that would become the guide to administration homeless policy, *A Shelter Is Not a Home*, focused exclusively on homeless families. Looking back from 1992, the Cuomo Commission would hold that homeless single adults had been treated like "a forgotten population."[60] Wackstein confirmed this judgment by noting that "in our administration, like in many others, subsequent and before, the family issue tended to overwhelm everything else."[61]

But, as mayor, Dinkins would have to address that ongoing problem as well. For singles, his administration had relied, as Koch's had, on former armories that had been converted to mass barracks-style shelters, with perhaps hundreds of beds filling up the buildings' large open spaces.

Converted armories provided protection from the elements but were otherwise not satisfactory. One researcher provided a vivid picture of the huge Fort Washington Armory as it was in the early nineties:

> The low-ceilinged donut-shaped first-floor corridor that ran the length of the block was crowded with African American and Latino men in every state of dress and undress. . . . In the distance rats scurried under ancient standing metal radiators in the empty eastern end of the long hallway.
>
> A dark room off the hall revealed dozens of men dozing under the faint blue light radiating from an aging nineteen-inch color television mounted high up in a corner. Past the TV room, the hallway curved around to the other side of the building where ropes marked off the cafeteria line and its conflicts over stale bologna sandwiches and mealy apples. Even the air was different in "the Fort." Industrial disinfectant mingled with the smell of human sweat, cafeteria food and residual radiator moisture. Not unbearable, the smell was unpleasant and just nauseating enough to put one a little on edge. . . .
>
> Ascending the broad open staircase at the end of the first floor corridor, the third-world bazaar of used small electronics, hair cutting, drug deals, and other petty commerce gave way to the vast drill floor where nearly seven hundred beds stretched out in long rows spaced two feet apart. The wooden floor was larger than a football field, and was enclosed high above by a cavernous sloping, domed ceiling. This main room was like something between an indoor sports arena and one of the orphans' work houses in *Oliver Twist*. Residents were forbidden to go up into the bleachers that ringed the room about twenty-five feet above the floor, where the director of the shelter had his office.
>
> At one end of the drill floor was a giant steel shutter door that was raised electronically every morning, including in winter, "in order to air this smelly place out," as shelter workers put it. This was also seen as a way of getting residents out of bed and making it too cold to comfortably stay there during the day. . . .
>
> The men near the center of the drill floor, who continued to sleep through the noise, cold air, and movement of a late winter mid-morning, lay on metal cots with spindly iron legs stuck into tennis shoes, oxfords, boots, and all variety of other footwear. . . . Despite the common precaution of putting the legs of one's bed into shoes and tying the shoes to bed frames with tight knots, some shelter residents told me that they had actually lost shoes to thieves who lifted up their bed while they slept.[62]

A description from the *Times* in 1992 confirms the above account of the Fort Washington Armory shelter:

> After the lights go down at night at the Fort Washington Armory in upper Manhattan, paranoid schizophrenics lie nervously next to ex-convicts they rightfully fear. Noises arise in the darkness: the moans of men having sex with men, the cries of the helpless being robbed, the hacking coughs of the sick, the pounding of feet running through a maze of 700 cots packed into one vast room.[63]

Wackstein's deputy director at the Mayor's Office was Anne Teicher, who was in charge of policy for singles. Teicher's focus became eliminating the armory shelters and replacing them with many smaller shelters dispersed throughout the city. She described the administration's singles policy as follows:

> So actually the policy was pretty progressive. It just crashed and burned. The concept was to create smaller [shelters], to get away from these huge armory-style shelters. At that time there was still the Fort Washington Armory and these huge shelters. . . . I think there were at that time still hundreds of beds. But to create these smaller shelters around the city that would be more like transitional housing. Because at that time it was still like three hots and a cot theory. There weren't a lot of . . . on-site services to really help them while they were in the shelter. So the concept was to create program-rich, smaller shelters. That was the intention.[64]

A City Council law required the administration to come up with a five-year plan for sheltering the homeless and so the focus of that plan became developing a blueprint for building a network of smaller, program-providing shelters that would allow the large armory shelters to be closed. By late 1990, work on the scheme had begun, which would be released in October 1991 as the *New York City Five-Year Plan for Housing and Assisting Homeless Adults*, and which addressed policy for single persons exclusively.

The plan had two main thrusts. The first, "primary," goal was "to transform the service system for homeless adults from one that merely provides shelter to one that provides homeless people with the training, rehabilitation and other services that would enable them to participate as fully and independently as possible in the life of the city."[65] The idea that homeless individuals needed "rehabilitation" was an important development and reflected the belief that Wackstein and others in the administration had come to that homelessness frequently was the result of some disability or "underlying cause" that policy had to address. Wackstein described the crystallization of this controversial idea as follows:

> There was a belief that I had and that others had that the people who ended up in the shelter system needed things other than shelter. And that . . . engendered some controversy with groups like Housing Works, which was an advocacy group for people with AIDS, and the Coalition for the Homeless, because there was a real ideological rift, saying that homeless people, all they needed was a home, all they needed was a place to stay. And I did not agree and I still don't agree. . . . People, whether it's families or individuals, they don't end up in the shelter system, generally, unless there are other needs that need to be addressed.[66]

Wackstein's belief that the homeless had other problems beside a lack of housing proved so unpopular with Housing Works that the group pasted posters on Wackstein's block that showed her photo with an "X" through it. This notion that homelessness was usually rooted in some underlying disability was the beginning of the paternalistic understanding of homelessness, and would be picked up and developed in detail by the Cuomo Commission, as we shall see.

The five-year plan described its other thrust, which would have more infelicitous consequences, as follows: "The cornerstone of this Plan is a five-year, $200 million development program to create 2,500 new beds in model transitional housing facilities to replace an equal number of beds in existing shelters."[67] To accomplish this goal, the city committed itself to a process of building about twenty-four shelters throughout the city. The process of finding appropriate sites, according to the plan, was to involve "*Early and Meaningful Community Involvement*," "*Fair Distribution of New Facilities around the City*," and "*Undertaking a Comprehensive Approach to Siting*" (italics in the original).[68] For the first time the Fair Share provision of the city's new charter, which called for a fair distribution of "burdens and benefits associated with city facilities," would be implemented to ensure the distributive justice of the process. The *New York Times* described the planning process:

> Meet the 1990's incarnation of the political machine: an I.B.M. 3090 computer. It was enlisted by the city to help formulate its proposed dispersal of the homeless from barracks-style dormitories to two dozen smaller shelters scattered in every borough. . . .
>
> The computer spewed out 490 locations after exempting 20 community districts deemed to be oversaturated. Its human handlers ruled out 252 and visited the remaining 238, eventually culling 35—a third of them in commercial or industrial settings—from which 24 are to be selected.
>
> From the beginning, the Dinkins administration sought to enlist other elected officials in the process and is doing so again. Except for Ruth W.

Messinger, the Manhattan Borough President, many preferred the political cover of the computer.[69]

In short, the plan was to be everything such processes are supposed to be: rational, comprehensive, transparent, consultative, and fair. The administration was optimistic; *A Shelter Is Not a Home* had rejected the "myth" that "[n]o community wants housing for the homeless in its own backyard" and asserted that "[c]ommunities have accepted housing for the homeless when the facilities are small-scale and well-supervised by an accountable non-profit organization, priority is given to homeless people from the same area and advance planning includes local input."[70]

But when the five-year plan was released and a ninety-day public comment period began, things didn't go as planned. Things got off on the wrong foot when a copy of the plan was leaked to a Staten Island newspaper, which reported that shelters were to be located in that borough. Anne Teicher reported that "[w]hen we went to a meeting in Staten Island I was afraid. They were horrible. I was afraid I was going to come out and find flat tires." Things got no better in the rest of the city, Teicher found:

> After the plan came out we went to a lot of community meetings. . . . They were brutal. They were really brutal. It was really painful. Because of the way things came out. It just hit the fan. We were going to put these shelters all over the city. They were going to be horrible; you know what shelters are like, blah, blah, blah. And we don't want these people. And NIMBY. It just activated the NIMBY response all over. . . .
>
> We knew that that was a major issue. There's always opposition to siting anything. I think we might have been a little naïve. We were trying to do it comprehensively. Instead of dribbling out these sites over a period of time, we would identify all the sites at one time and we could then show the Fair Share aspects of it. And it was very rational. But it was a little naïve that you could do this and not have this uprising of NIMBYism.[71]

Wackstein had the same experience:

> I probably still have the scars on my back from going to Community Board meetings. They didn't want homeless family facilities but even more they didn't want facilities for single adults. Because there was this very widespread perception that they were either addicts, crazy, or like people with AIDS. And remember this was back in the late eighties, early nineties, everybody was up in arms about people with AIDS in their communities. So there was that sense

> that these were people who were going to bring disruption to neighborhoods. So it was very hard to get anything sited.[72]

Almost no one outside the administration stepped forward to defend the siting process. City council speaker Peter F. Vallone summed up the general public reaction when he said, "You're unnecessarily frightening all the people of the city, and it doesn't make any sense. . . . It's spreading homelessness and hopelessness throughout. It's almost as if you're saying we have a serious disease and we'll spread it so everybody will suffer from it."[73]

Clearly, the high-profile planning process had served not to defuse opposition with its obvious fairness but to offer unpersuaded community leaders a target for their fire. A crucial mistake had been the decision to have the proposed shelters, which were to be managed by nonprofits, actually built by the city. With the city in charge of the building process, a very visible, centralized siting plan seemed to the Dinkins administration to be the only way to avoid the "unfairness" of the Koch administration's nonconsultative practices. But visibility resulted in vulnerability without viability. Much more workable would have been a plan to have nonprofits not only manage but build the shelters. Then individual nonprofits could have, piecemeal, entered into individual negotiations with given neighborhoods, which would have lowered the profile of the process and avoided the concentrated fire of the whole city at once. This was the approach that was in fact ultimately followed at the advice of the outside advisor, Andrew Cuomo, whom the Dinkins administration brought in.

Early on, key members of the Dinkins administration concluded that their approach to homelessness was not working. As a response, in September 1991, Mayor Dinkins farmed out the job of rethinking homeless policy to a Commission on the Homeless, headed by Andrew Cuomo, the governor's son and eventually governor himself. In February 1992, the commission released its report, *The Way Home: A New Direction in Social Policy*, which challenged the assumptions that had guided the early Dinkins policy.[74]

The commission endorsed the Dinkins deluge hypothesis and argued that placing thousands of homeless families into permanent housing contributed to an enormous surge of families entering the shelter system:

> After inheriting a system with approximately 1,500 families in hotels at the end of 1989, Mayor Dinkins was able to dramatically reduce the number of families in hotels to about 150 in August 1990. Placing thousands of homeless families, many of whom had only recently entered the shelter system, into permanent housing appears to have contributed to an enormous surge of families entering

> the system in the later part of 1990. By 1991, the City was forced to return, to a lesser but still substantial degree, to hotels. Today, there are almost 1,000 homeless families. It is unfortunate that hotels are once again a significant source of emergency shelter for the City's homeless.[75]

The Way Home also claimed that behavioral problems were an important cause of homelessness. It conducted its own extensive survey of homeless individuals and families in the city:

> The results were enlightening. The commission found that homelessness is frequently a symptom of some underlying problem, such as lack of job skills or education, a substance-abuse problem, or mental illness. It results when one or more of these problems interact with a number of social and economic factors, including a shortage of affordable housing.

The commission's findings were striking: 42 percent of the families surveyed seemed to have either a mental health or drug problem, and no less than 29 percent of adults in shelter families tested positive for illegal drugs.[76]

The commission went even further, arguing that the sociological reality of homelessness in New York was incompatible with a policy of unconditional right to shelter. The advocacy groups that had won recognition in various ways of a right to shelter pursued such an approach in the belief, shared by Dinkins in his 1987 report, that homelessness was primarily an economic problem. The "basic thrust" of this strategy, according to the Community Service Society, was "to shift the focus from rehabilitation, the attempt to return the disabled to normalcy, to welfare." Hard experience forced the Cuomo Commission to insist again that shelter regimes had to emphasize rehabilitation at least as much as welfare or shelter:

> The disabilities suffered by homeless single adults have been ignored for too long by administrations as well as some advocates. It is not enough to provide only shelter to these vulnerable and troubled individuals. Many of them need significant social services and medical attention. . . . Society's honest acknowledgment of the problem is the first step toward a solution.[77]

The commission articulated what might be called the "underlying problem" approach to homelessness, which focused on determining and addressing the reasons why a particular person or family is homeless: "Homelessness is often a symptom of one or more underlying problems for which the answer is not simply access to housing, but also access to social and related services, including job training and assistance, independent living programs, substance abuse treatment, and mental health care."[78]

Another crucial conclusion of the commission was the need for what might be called the "mutual obligation" approach to providing shelter. Potential clients had some kind of an underlying problem that contributed to their homelessness. Therefore they had to address that problem as a condition of receiving aid. This was especially important because not every request for aid could be answered. "Government should not, and cannot, be expected to provide housing to everyone who asks for it," the commission stated. "A determination of need must be made so that government's limited resources can be targeted to the most needy."[79] Those in need had to address the reason why they were in need. Thus the homeless had a responsibility as well as a right. *The Way Home* put the matter as follows: "The emergency shelter system must incorporate a balance of rights and responsibilities. A social contract and a mutuality of obligation must exist between those receiving help and society-at-large."[80]

Eventually the Giuliani administration would give administrative substance to this call for "mutuality of obligation" by developing a shelter system that, insofar as was consistent with the city's legal obligations, would be structured to strongly nudge clients to enroll in rehabilitative services in return for being provided with shelter. The general call for mutual obligation was thus the germ of what would be an enforced quid pro quo: shelter in return for compliance.

In other words, the Cuomo Commission articulated for the first time in detail the paternalistic paradigm of homeless policy. The two key assumptions of this philosophy would be, first, the belief that there was "something wrong" with homeless people, an "underlying cause" that was crucial to their being homeless. The second assumption was that this underlying cause must be addressed through a quid pro quo of shelter for self-help in the form of enrollment in some form of rehabilitation. Other policy recommendations of the Cuomo Commission included the creation of a new "small, entrepreneurially styled" city agency that would coordinate efforts to deal with homelessness; provision of rent vouchers to homeless families; increased reliance on nonprofit organizations, rather than city agencies, to provide services to the homeless; and establishment of requirements that homeless families undergo screening and treatment before being assigned to permanent housing.

The Dinkins administration's response was ambivalent. When the report was released in February 1992, the mayor would only say, "I'm fully committed to examining whether we can go forward."[81] Perales and Sabol criticized the proposal to develop a new agency.[82] As the *Times* noted, "The controversy left the Mayor in the awkward position of deciding whether to take the advice of his staff or the commission he appointed in September."[83] Dinkins quickly created another panel to explore the practicality and political viability of the commission's proposals.

Several factors may explain the initial apparent lack of official enthusiasm for the commission's recommendations. In objecting to the proposed new agency, for example, Sabol may simply have been trying to protect her own bureaucratic turf. The same may have been true of HPD commissioner Felice Michetti, who questioned the use of rent subsidies. It is also possible that some of the commission's positions—such as the claims that perverse incentives to enter the system had been created, that dysfunctionality was widespread among the homeless, and that homelessness was more than a housing problem—may have been difficult for liberals in the administration to absorb.

Nonetheless, by September 1992, Dinkins embraced the commission's recommendations. Besides possible ideological problems, the administration's initial coolness towards implementing the Cuomo Commission's recommendations may have reflected an appreciation of the practical problems that remained to be resolved. That task was thrust upon Charles, or Chip, Raymond, who would eventually become the first Department of Homeless Services commissioner, but who was before that appointed to a small entity within the mayor's office to study the commission's recommendations and create a detailed implementation plan. That office was called the Mayor's Office of Homeless Facilities and Service Development. This represented, at last, the clear decision to go ahead with the new agency. On December 2, 1992, Raymond became director of that office.[84] One of his first moves was to bring in as his assistant chief of staff Muzzy Rosenblatt from the Mayor's Office of Construction. Rosenblatt remembered some of the issues that remained to be worked out:

> Does a new municipal agency need to have, because of its new mandate, new functions, that didn't exist as part of HRA? For example, its procurement activity as designed was going to be and became much more robust than the procurement activity that was going on at HRA, [which] wasn't in the business of outsource. So how do we . . . embrace the notion of privatization, [of] outsourcing everyone? How do we do it? The notion was going to be we were going to take [a] municipally run system with municipal employees and contract out to private entities, not for profits. What happens to the workers? Now the Cuomo Commission didn't answer that question. It didn't ask that question. And so that question needed to be asked and needed to be answered and done in a way that was thoughtful. . . .

> So, that was a major issue. Another issue was the budget. Was this agency going to wind up spending more . . . without getting anything more? A big mantra at the time . . . that the editorial boards began to embrace was cost mentality. Can't cost any more or less. Now when [you're] decentralized, you create certain diseconomies. You may get greater effectiveness, you may get greater results, but the cost of achieving those results may also be greater even though the cost benefit may be positive. . . . But the City Council said, no more—we cannot cost more. . . . So it was much easier said than done to create a new agency. In the end we did it, but those are some of the major issues at the time.[85]

Among Raymond's first tasks was drafting legislation to create his department and then guiding the bill through the City Council. But rather than the streamlined, entrepreneurial agency suggested by the Cuomo report, the proposed Department of Homeless Services had a staff of nearly three thousand, most of whom transferred from HRA. Legislative approval was necessary to establish the new department, but by mid-May 1993, the proposal was stymied in the City Council. Speaker Peter Vallone, who had enthusiastically endorsed the Cuomo Commission recommendations when they were released, objected to the size of the proposed agency and argued that the mayor had not specified how the revamped shelter system would deal with such matters as drug treatment, mental health care, and job training. Raymond testified before the council that the administration had been so occupied with the logistics of establishing the agency that it had not had time to "present that kind of gigantic plan."[86] The City Council would finally pass the legislation creating DHS on July 1, 1993. However, in order to retain City Council power over the department, City Council speaker Peter Vallone insisted on having the power to vote it out of existence after two years.[87] The legislation also stipulated that the department would have to cease the use of welfare hotels in order to be continued.

Raymond was in some ways an unusual choice to be the first commissioner of the new Department of Homeless Services (DHS). Most observers were struck, not always positively, by the fact that during the 1980s he had managed ballet companies, including the New York City Ballet and the Joffrey Ballet. Asked how his experience with managing ballet companies qualified him to run the shelter system, Raymond replied that "he wasn't responsible for what went on the stage, but that the lights went on. . . . What we don't have now is somebody selling the vision of what goes on the stage."[88] But Raymond also had extensive managerial experience that was less unusual. He had worked in the Lindsay administration for four years, first in the Human Resources Administration, then as assistant commissioner of the Department of Sanitation, and later for a task force on SRO housing. He had also worked as deputy commissioner of the Department of Mental Health, Retardation, and Alcoholism, and during the Koch administration, as deputy commissioner for housing, he had been in charge of the city's extensive holdings of *in rem* apartments. He had even been a part, early in his career, of a consulting company that had been responsible for implementing various reforms at the infamous Willowbrook institution. In that effort Raymond worked with Norman Steisel, who would become Dinkins's first deputy mayor and was a strong supporter of the Cuomo Commission's recommendations.

Raymond described his career as follows:

> In my career it's very easy to pick out a few things that are disconnected, but the thing I always try to do is carry, you know, a kit bag of very good management tools. I rely very heavily on other people. I don't have to be expert in any field because I'd feel that you could find people who are experts. And learning about, you know, homelessness, and learning about *in rem* housing, and learning about mental health, that's the easy part. The tough part is managing a system and that's what I felt I was pretty good at.[89]

In short, Raymond was a manager, not an advocate. That was his appeal. His appointment represented a victory for Steisel, who was skeptical of the call of the advocates for more resources, and who felt that better management could make a real difference. Steisel had clashed with Sabol at HRA who, like the housing and homeless advocates, called for an increase in the housing allowance of the state welfare grant and who was skeptical of the value of a new agency. According to Steisel,

> HRA . . . didn't have the managerial talent or focus to drive through some of these questions about expanding or improving the facilities. . . . So when we created the agency [DHS], it's the reason we hired Chip. He wasn't out of that world. He wasn't a social service advocate or activist. . . . He was a real generalist. . . . He was a very skillful manager and the idea was we wanted to give the impression to the world as well as to our agencies that we were going to work with them, we now had someone in there who was a manager. . . . So that was the shift in emphasis we were trying to demonstrate by bringing him in.[90]

The eventual embrace of the Cuomo Commission's recommendations, the creation of DHS, and the appointment of Steisel's "protégé,"[91] Raymond, all represented the at least temporary victory in New York City of what may be called the "managerial" as opposed to the "structural" approach to the homelessness problem. In his classic article entitled "The Quandaries of Shelter Reform: An Appraisal of Efforts to 'Manage' Homelessness," which was contemporaneous with *The Way Home*, Dennis P. Culhane argued that

> the ability of shelters to serve as homeless management agencies is constrained by the structural causes of the homeless problem. Without renewed commitments from public agencies responsible for the treatment of mental illness and substance abuse, for reintegrating recently paroled persons in the community and for promoting child welfare, affordable housing, and income maintenance, the shelter system will remain overburdened and unmanageable.[92]

New York City was in effect embracing the idea that shelters could be managed effectively, and make a substantial contribution to solving the homelessness problem, even in a situation that did not promise much immediate improvement in the social welfare system. It was an approach that was to dominate city policy through the Giuliani and Bloomberg years.

By his own account, Raymond was never very successful at what he identified as "the department's biggest problem . . . through-put, getting people in and out the back door." Throughout his tenure, the EAU continued to be terribly overcrowded, with so many families sleeping in chairs and on the floors that "there were periods of time when you could hardly get in the door." "I think that my biggest disappointment was that we couldn't . . . solve the problem and the problem to me was always bringing people in and getting people out and at that we were never terribly successful."[93] Neither did Judge Freedman find Raymond's efforts satisfactory. On December 8, 1993, two days before his resignation, Freedman imposed contempt findings on Raymond because "he was the official whose decisions about emergency shelter placements from EAU's most flagrantly violated Court orders."[94]

To be fair to Raymond, he had, from the very first day of his appointment, expressed doubt that he could relieve crowding at the EAU. "I'm not sure that in reality we will be able to reach the point where we won't have people sleeping in EAU's," he said on being appointed. "I'm not sure we will. I just don't think the system can deal with it."[95] And indeed, the city's first efforts to manage homelessness were not successful.

Contemporaneous with the publication of *The Way Home* was a development that would eventually, under the Bloomberg administration, usher in a new era in homelessness policy, one that would challenge the paternalist paradigm that was first completely articulated by the Cuomo Commission. This was the founding by Sam Tsemberis in 1992 of Pathways to Housing, an organization that would revolutionize outreach to street dwellers by implementing the Housing First approach. Pathways to Housing and Housing First grew out of Tsemberis's increasing frustration at the city's Health and Hospitals Corporation, where he ran the outreach program Project HELP, infamous for its ultimately frustrated effort to involuntarily transfer Joyce Brown, aka Billie Boggs, and other mentally ill homeless people, off the streets and into the hospital psychiatric wards. Tsemberis described what he saw as the limited results of this approach:

> We had realized at that time—this is like four years into the Project Help experience—that taking people to the hospital, even if they may have been a danger to themselves or others, was not resulting in any good outcomes, other than to get them out of the immediate danger for a short time. They kept returning to the street, a vicious cycle of making this terrible anguished decision about do we need to hospitalize this person, should we take them now or not. And then after a lot of debate we would take them. Three weeks later or four they were back out on the street. . . . I was desperate to try something new.[96]

The approach Tsemberis and his collaborators—who included psychologists William Anthony, David Shern, and Mikal Cohen—decided to apply was psychiatric rehabilitation, or psych rehab, whose "major focus . . . is on achievement of individually defined goals."[97] William Anthony, who had developed the psych rehab approach at Boston University, described it as "an intervention that essentially . . . helped people figure out what they wanted, then helped them figure out what they needed to have or do to get what they wanted, and then teach them the skills and provide them the supports to get what they wanted."[98] In the context of Project HELP's street outreach work, implementing the psychiatric rehabilitation model implied that instead of being told that they would be transported to psychiatric services, street dwellers would be *asked* what they wanted and the outreach team's job would be to accomplish that request. To implement and evaluate this approach among Project HELP clients, Tsemberis and Shern received a grant in 1990 from the National Institutes of Mental Health entitled "Taking Psych Rehab to the Streets." The insistence on client choice in the psych rehab model was so radical that Tsemberis himself had trouble sticking to it consistently, although in the end that commitment prevailed. Tsemberis recalled,

> We had a big debate when we got that psych rehab grant. Bill Anthony and Mikal Cohen were like, no you have to ask people. I thought like, we just take people off the street and bring them into housing. That was the whole point of doing something different. I sort of knew they wanted housing. And [Anthony

> and Cohen] said, no, you have to ask them what they want. And if it's not housing, then you'll give them what they want. If it's haircuts, that's what you're going to be doing. [I said] I can't believe that we went through all this trouble and we're giving people haircuts! And I had to appreciate the importance of the principle of what choice really means. Choice really means you're offering support for whatever it is the client needs.[99]

The results of the "Taking Psych Rehab to the Streets" experiment were striking. When Tsemberis and company compared the outcomes for clients who received the experimental, psychiatric rehabilitation outreach to the outcomes of clients who received the standard Project HELP approach, they found that

> [c]ompared with persons in standard treatment (n=77), members of the experimental group were more likely to attend a day program (53% vs 27%), had less difficulty in meeting their basic needs, spent less time on the streets (55% vs 28% reduction) and spent more time in community housing [as opposed to shelters and the streets]. They showed greater improvement in life satisfaction and experienced a greater reduction in psychiatric symptoms.[100]

But what did street dwellers want when they were asked? According to Tsemberis,

> People were quite articulate. . . . People knew exactly what they wanted and the terms that they wanted it on. Everybody wanted a place to live first and then maybe they would consider treatment. Even though we were finding that using psych rehab we could engage people much more quickly, we had a much more therapeutic alliance, we were able to meet their demands in the sequence they wanted them, like food or shelter or like that, but they, what they wanted was a place to live and the program was really an outreach program, not a housing program, so we couldn't deliver on what they most urgently needed. And I could not persuade the Health and Hospitals Corporation to start a housing program. . . . out of Bellevue. . . . They were like, we're a hospital, we don't do housing, it's not our mission, it's not our mandate. So I left the Health and Hospitals Corporation in 1992 and I started . . . Pathways to Housing.[101]

According to the homeless mentally ill themselves, the key to getting them off the streets was to offer them housing first, and then, possibly, treatment for their illness, rather than forcing them into treatment first with the expectation that treatment of the underlying cause of their homelessness would eventually make them fit for housing. What was lacking in the psych rehab model as Tsemberis was implementing it at Project HELP was the offer of permanent, independent housing that did not require sobriety or compliance with treatment. Such then were the prerequisites for moving from a shelter or similar community residence to supported housing, that is, a permanent apartment where psychiatric and other services were provided. At the inauguration of his not-for-profit Pathways to Housing, Tsemberis received a five hundred thousand dollar grant from the New York State Office of Mental Health to add this housing component to his outreach efforts. Tsemberis described the results:

> [Other] contracts for supported housing were already in place, we didn't invent that. All we had to do was serve fifty people and provide services for them. Everybody else in the city was basically doing this kind of a program but they were doing it as a graduation out of community residences.
>
> So, if you lived in a community residence for a long time, were compliant, and were clean and sober, you'd be put into an apartment usually shared by one or two other people. We took that same contract and gave an independent apartment to a person, no treatment, no sobriety. Just like they wanted. . . . and they wanted the housing first, that's what people wanted. And then we did the case management support after they were housed.
>
> . . . We started around November '92 and so at the end of '93 we reported to the Board of Directors at Pathways. . . . So, our report after that first year was 84 percent of the people we had taken from the streets—these Project HELP people—and brought in to apartments, delusions, addiction, and all, were still housed after that first year.
>
> And we thought, "Oh, my God, we're on to something new." Who knew that people were so capable? Who knew that these people who seemed so disorganized, actually, when you think about it, they had such incredible skills on the street. They knew where to eat, they knew where it's safe to sleep, they knew where soup kitchens are open or not, they knew how to not get arrested, and they knew who to trust with their stuff. All that stuff. All these skills, not really visible, initially, clearly manifest once the person was housed. Living a life in an apartment was a piece of cake compared to living a life on the street. They did spectacularly well and the program has been growing ever since.[102]

Thus was born Housing First, which in time would develop into a paradigm that would begin to displace the paternalistic philosophy developed in *The Way Home*. But first the immediate future would see the city develop the paternalistic shelter system that the Cuomo Commission was calling for.

Dinkins's slow grasp of the Cuomo Commission's agenda created an opening for Rudolph Giuliani in the mayoral election of 1993. Owing to some complicated sparring over exactly who should be included in the mayoral debates of 1993, it ended up that the only forum in which Dinkins and Giuliani confronted each other directly was one sponsored by the Citizens Housing and Planning Council and devoted to housing issues. Giuliani thus had maximum opportunity to step into the breach. The *New York Times* reported that

> Mr. Giuliani, who had avoided in-depth discussions of these issues until last night, mocked the Democratic Mayor for naming a panel to study the study of his own commission on homelessness, rather than moving immediately to carry out its recommendations. "Give me a break—make a decision," said Mr. Giuliani, the Republican-Liberal candidate for mayor.[103]

Giuliani, of course, won that election. How important his campaign promises to reshape homelessness policy were in his victory is not known. Some of his specific proposals—such as the unrealistic suggestion of imposing a ninety-day limit on the length of shelter stays—may even have hurt him, although probably more by mobilizing the homelessness-policy community against him than by their lack of popular appeal. Giuliani appointed Joan Malin, a former Dinkins administration official, to head the new Department of Homeless Services. How Giuliani reshaped city homelessness policy is the subject of the next chapter.

Mayor Dinkins and some of his top administrators deserved considerable credit for facing up to the truth that they had pursued a wrongheaded policy. They accepted what became the conventional wisdom apparently based on recent experience that perverse incentives and behavioral problems are central to the problem of family homelessness, and the Cuomo Commission has developed a detailed plan for reform. But the administration was not vigorous enough in translating its own hard-won insights into policy. Whether because of ideological reservations or because of bureaucratic turf wars, the administration was slow to embrace unequivocally, much less to implement effectively, the recommendations of the Cuomo Commission report. Implementing the plan would become a priority for the incoming Giuliani administration.

During the Dinkins administration, the first moment in the development of shelter as a right came to a close; this was the moment of entitlement. Throughout the Koch and most of the Dinkins administrations, policy spun around, first, establishing that there was indeed a right to shelter and, then, making good on that right by in fact providing shelter largely on demand. Two characteristics of this stage of the development of shelter as a right stand out. First, court intervention was a necessary, *but not sufficient*, condition of establishing the right to shelter. It is conceivable that a right to shelter could have been established by legislative means, but in fact the movement to establish that right focused on a court-oriented strategy from the beginning. Legislation by the City Council came after the right had been established and focused on regulating the provision of shelter.

However, it is important to understand exactly how the courts helped establish a right to shelter. There was not a single landmark decision that created the right. It is an error to think that the courts simply discovered a right to shelter in New York State's constitution and issued a *Brown*-like decision that so found. The fact that article 17 of the state constitution famously mandated the "aid, care and support of the needy" undoubtedly created a legal environment in which litigation demanding a right to shelter was at least colorable. But the constitution left the implementation of the mandate to aid the needy to the discretion of the legislature and was never interpreted by the courts as clearly establishing a right to shelter. The courts' role in helping to establish a right to shelter lay in creating a complex web of findings and decisions in the *Callahan, Lamboy, McCain*, and other cases that relied on a various legislative and constitutional provisions.

Second, other features and actors of state and city politics were necessary to consolidate the right. As we saw, through the Koch and Dinkins administrations, the courts never established a right to shelter in so many words. Courts held that *if* the city undertook to provide shelter, it would have to do so on certain terms and provide housing of a certain quality. The fact that the city was already providing shelter—albeit in the form of the old Men's Shelter at 8 East Third Street and the infamous welfare hotels—was crucial. The city itself was thus an important actor in establishing the right to shelter because the court mandates all assumed that the city was, as a matter of contingent fact, providing shelter. The city was also a crucial actor insofar as it voluntarily decided to sign the *Callahan* consent decree. This is true despite the fact that the city was undoubtedly under strong legal pressure without which it would not have established a right to shelter on its own. For as we saw, in the end the city thought that, given the circumstances, signing the consent decree was the right thing to do, admittedly in part because they underestimated the size of the commitment they were taking on.

During the Dinkins administration, the limitations, or perceived limitations, of the entitlement stage of homeless policy became apparent. A response to those limitations, that of paternalism, was also articulated under Dinkins. Implementing that response would be the challenge of the Giuliani administration. The policy learning process continued.

4

Homelessness Policy under Giuliani

Giuliani was sworn in as mayor on January 1, 1994. Joan Malin was appointed commissioner of DHS on February 24, 1994, with Muzzy Rosenblatt staying on to become first deputy commissioner. Before she became DHS commissioner, Malin had worked as deputy commissioner under Dinkins and had helped develop the Tier II shelters under Koch.

According to Malin, "in the Koch years . . . it was totally crisis management . . . how we get through the day, how we get through the night. . . . It is like headline avoidance policy . . . how do we do things that are just not in the press all the time?"[1] During the Dinkins years, the city at last developed, through the Cuomo Commission, a vision of what homelessness policy should look like. Again according to Malin, "The Giuliani folks when they came in, basically said we don't disagree with that policy, we want to continue the work of the Cuomo Commission. . . . But they also put more emphasis on operations, in terms of how to manage numbers."[2]

Just the existence of DHS as its own agency and not part of HRA revolutionized homelessness policy from what it had been earlier. For Malin, being independent

> [a]llowed us to focus in the way that we would not [have] been able to do at HRA and I say that because I was at both places. You know, as a commissioner, you're at the table with the deputy mayors and when they're making changes in the budget, or they're thinking about allocation of resources, or vacancy control or whatever, you can advocate for your organization. When you were within HRA, HRA had to advocate for you along with five other mini-organizations and you never get the priority unless there was something so urgent and so crisis-driven that you had to be able to do it. And so to me it made a huge difference . . . your ability to negotiate with NYCHA, with HPD, and from commissioner to commissioner. And that was significant.[3]

Nonetheless, the department's existence remained tenuous. In September 1995, as provided for in the original enabling legislation, the City Council revisited the question of whether the department should continue to exist. By a vote of thirty-two to thirteen, with one abstention, the council voted to extend the life of the department to October 1996. A condition of further renewal was that the department end its use of large hotels without kitchens in each unit. A 1993 law allowed the department to house families in hotels for up to sixty days as it looked for permanent housing for them. For stays of longer than sixty days, the law held that only hotels of one hundred units or less could be used and that each unit had to have a kitchen. As of September 1995, the department was still using hotels that violated both provisions. Another sore point for the council was the department's continued practice of having families sleep in the EAU as shelter was sought for them. Despite these shortcomings, the council voted to reapprove the department for a year. One observer's comments, those of Gretchen Buchenholtz, executive director of the Association to Benefit Children, captured the general sentiment: "There are serious problems with the hotels and the EAU. But given the limitations, I think that any day I would prefer to have the agency continue in its independence than see it go back into a bureaucracy like the Human Resources Administration."[4] But bitter disputes over the existence of the department, and over the terms of its existence, would resurface later in the Giuliani administration.

Early on in her tenure, Malin had a big impact on policy. Only about a month after Malin's appointment, a mayoral spokeswoman acknowledged that "the Mayor is relying on his new Commissioner for Homeless Services, Joan Malin, to help formulate the policy that will guide this administration."[5] For example, Malin reported to Giuliani that some of the positions he had taken during the recent campaign were untenable. Giuliani had proposed that stays at the shelters would be limited to ninety days. Malin pointed out that this was simply illegal: "With the court mandates and the whole regulatory framework from the state . . . one really couldn't do ninety days and out."[6] Giuliani had also proposed to challenge the court decisions that established a right to shelter. Malin advised otherwise. "The public doesn't want us to walk away from the right to shelter. They just want us to do it better," she argued.[7]

The big question then became, How could the city legally impose some kind of limits on the use of the shelters? The administration wanted to be able to say to clients,

> We do our part, they do their part, but there's some point in which we can say this is a limited resource for people very, very much in need and then when we're done with our part, we're done. And we can ask people to leave. A lot of the policy was trying to figure out how to do that, recognizing the constraints of the mandates that we were under and the state regulations we were under.[8]

As we saw, the Cuomo Commission had already developed the public idea through which such limits would be achieved. This was the concept of "a mutuality of obligation" or "a balance of rights and responsibilities."

This public idea was not likely to be ignored because in the highly competitive political environment of New York at that time, all parties had strong incentives to "claim" a potentially popular idea.[9] Who would take it up? Though he himself had organized the Cuomo Commission, Dinkins chose not to emphasize its main idea, probably because he had been a prominent supporter of the strictly rights-based approach the commission was implicitly criticizing. And so a political opportunity was handed to Giuliani, who pounced on the ideas developed in *The Way Home*. Giuliani campaigned on a platform of introducing a "mutual responsibility" model in the shelter system.

In short, Giuliani can be thought of as a political entrepreneur, marketing the public idea of "balancing rights and responsibilities" and winning electoral support with it. This conception of social policy reform came with Giuliani into City Hall, where it shaped the particular outline Giuliani's social welfare policy in general was to take. Thus welfare reform under Giuliani took the form of imposing work requirements as a way in which welfare clients could "give something back." Giuliani hoped to impose similar requirements on shelter clients, and throughout his term he would struggle against courts, state regulations, and advocates to do so.

In May 1994, DHS released the document "Reforming New York City's System of Homeless Services," which explicitly embraced the Cuomo report and its concept of mutual obligation, which would become a primary reform objective of the department:

> Eligibility rules ensure that those most in need of assistance and services have access to them. . . . Mutual responsibility will be established through an agreement known as an independent living plan, signed by both the provider and recipient, which indicates the homeless persons' acceptance of the responsibility to participate in programs provided to assist them in resolving their crises and in moving toward independent living, mutual responsibility.[10]

A policy of mutual responsibility could also be described as paternalistic, though the Giuliani administration did not use that term. But how to enforce paternalism? In late 1994 it seemed the city might be able to enforce paternalism through a strong eligibility process. On December 29, 1994, the outgoing Cuomo administration rescinded the state regulation 83 ADM-47, which had required that "[e]mergency housing must be provided immediately if a homeless person is determined eligible."[11] The new regulation, 94 ADM-20, instead stipulated that "[i]t is the expectation that assistance will be provided within 48 hours of application for such [temporary housing] assistance." The regulation also encouraged policymakers who believed in tightening the eligibility process, for it required that the city "must make reasonable efforts to determine the applicant's eligibility prior to providing temporary housing assistance."[12] Malin felt that new regulations might make possible a strong eligibility process. "Rather than having to house everyone immediately, having forty-eight hours potentially gave you the opportunity to do more eligibility or to do more of what I would call preventive services in the hopes that would help them stabilize where they are."[13]

Thus the administration thought that paternalism could be enforced by having clients sign an independent living plan as part of a stronger eligibility process. In the wake of the *Callahan* consent decree, no process for determining eligibility for the shelters had been developed because the language of the decree seemed to establish eligibility criteria so broad that any shelter applicant was likely to meet them. The mechanism through which the new mayor planned to enforce paternalism was to "implement a comprehensive eligibility determination process and ensure that scarce resources will be available to those most in need."[14] The administration reasoned that however poor an applicant might be, there was still at least a formal question of whether he or she qualified for home relief or was physically, mentally, or socially dysfunctional. And if upon investigation applicants turned out to meet these criteria, was it not reasonable that they be "expected to cooperate with staff and not-for-profit providers to identify the resources to which they may be entitled, and the assistance and services they need"? If so, and given that the consent decree reserved the right of the state to promulgate regulations for the shelters, couldn't this expectation be expressed in a written and signed "independent living plan," as DHS's reform plan called for? The Giuliani administration asked Governor George Pataki to have the New York State Department of Social Services promulgate the regulations necessary to establish eligibility determinations and the independent living plans.[15]

At first, the city was not able to persuade the courts of the validity of this approach. Shortly after the new state regulations were promulgated on an emergency basis, New York State Supreme Court justice Helen E. Freedman temporarily barred the city from implementing them as far as homeless families were concerned.[16] The Coalition for the Homeless (CFTH) similarly requested of Judge Stanley L. Sklar, who oversaw the implementation of the *Callahan* decree, to declare the state regulations null and void. CFTH argued that the decree "established minimal eligibility criteria for the purpose of avoiding the disqualification of needy individuals from assistance who were unable to navigate bureaucratic requirements. It is just such requirements that the emergency regulations seek to impose on Plaintiffs now."[17] By 1997, Judge Sklar had not ruled on the permissibility of eligibility requirements and independent living plans under *Callahan*. The city agreed not to implement the regulations and to notify the court should it decide to do so. While all parties awaited Justice Freedman's decision regarding families, the city developed an implementation strategy that would pass muster under *Callahan*.

If overt paternalism in city-run shelters was stalled in court, the city found another strategy to achieve the same end: privatization. Before the late 1980s, contracting out for shelter provision had not been a major city policy. Both Manhattan borough president David Dinkins and the City Council criticized what they believed was the city's underuse of nonprofits as shelter providers.[18] Perhaps in response to these criticisms, in its 1987 final report Mayor Koch's Advisory Task Force on the Homeless signaled a change in direction by recommending that the city "increase participation by nonprofit service providers and other private sector groups in developing and operating temporary housing."[19] Despite his earlier support for the direction, however, when Dinkins became mayor in 1989 no dramatic privatizations took place, partly because other policy developments, especially the crisis in homeless families, distracted his attention. When the Cuomo Commission reported, it also recommended that the city "not-for-profitize" the shelter system. The city should "refer individuals in need of service out of the shelters and into appropriate, existing not-for-profit residential service programs."[20] Although this recommendation really only restated Dinkins's earlier support for nonprofits, the commission's suggestion that the increased supply of apartments available to shelter families had caused the surge in new entries divided the administration and prevented action. In May 1994, Malin's plan for reforming New York City's system of homelessness services made the development of "small, community-based programs, provided by not-for-profits," one of its ten primary objectives. "The not-for-profit community has been at the forefront of identifying and providing for the needs of homeless people. An even greater reliance will be placed on it to deliver these services."[21]

Switching from a mostly city-operated system to a privatized or not-for-profitized system was a daunting managerial challenge. Malin described the task as follows:

> [Coming] out of HRA, then trying to create a new agency and with a new mindset and . . . thinking about things in a new, different way . . . that's a very challenging thing to do from an organizational perspective in any event. [It's] particularly challenging to do when many of the same people are coming over

> and there was not a lot of latitude to bring in new people. Resources were tight, the civil service rules, and all that kind of stuff. That is just huge. At the same time you're trying to manage a very large budget, you want to make policy changes. Shifting to a nonprofit-based system requires a whole different way of thinking of the way you do work. I mean you had people for the last ten years—and I will say there were some wonderful people that I worked with, whose hearts were in the right place and they really worked very hard to get the three hots and a cot, the whole thing—that's not the same thing as managing a contract.
>
> Once you're contracted to a nonprofit, how do you work with that nonprofit? How do you not micromanage and yet assure accountability of public resources? [How do] you know the city is getting what it's asking for in terms of quality services and how do you think about quality services? This is a whole different way of thinking about the delivery of care and that was a big challenge, to get the same people who were doing the other stuff to think about it a different way and [do] different jobs. [And] at the same time you are managing.[22]

Despite the challenges, privatization advanced under the Giuliani administration as never before. In 1988, 73.1 percent of single men's shelters were operated by the city, and 26.8 percent were privately operated. By 1996, 45.7 percent were city run and 54.3 were privately run.[23] Family shelters were also privatized. By 1996, 72 percent of homeless families were sheltered in private, not-for-profit shelters.[24] By the end of 1998, most of the eighty family shelters had been turned over to not-for-profit organizations.[25] What, then, were the consequences of the privatization, or, more accurately, the not-for-profitization, policy? Consider the fate of the Men's Shelter at 8 East Third Street as it was in 1997.

A revisit to the Men's Shelter at 8 East Third Street in the late 1990s revealed an institution seemingly transformed as thoroughly as any pumpkin ever was by a fairy godmother. The building had been completely cleaned, repainted, and redecorated. The stale smell was gone, not to be found even in the facility's washrooms and kitchen. (To accomplish this it was necessary to tear up the sidewalk outside the building and lay new concrete.) The men themselves were clean and better clothed.

But as striking as the improved quality of life was the change in practices at the new 8 East Third Street. No clients were to be seen on the street. The men were issued laminated ID cards, and everybody wore them, visible for all to see. There was no pointless waiting or wandering. All the men one saw were either obviously doing something—attending a meeting, providing security, doing clerical or cleaning work—or seemed to be on their way to do something. Nothing untoward was said or done to me during my visit. Indeed, when I entered one dormitory, a man who was also a sort of watchman got up from his desk, shook my hand, and bade me welcome. It turned out he thought I was a new client, who should be greeted in this fashion as standard operating procedure.

Besides the obviously improved levels of amenity and order, 8 East Third Street's program—the set of distinct services, procedures, and achievements that clients are expected to complete in some specific sequence—had also been revitalized. Fourteen years previously, as the intake point of the men's system, the facility had not had a program beyond the interview with the "5 x 8 staff." A small infirmary that slept some dozen men was the only on-site service available. For everything else, including shelter and food, men were referred elsewhere in the system, or to commercial flophouses in the neighborhood, where the city paid for their stay.

In 1997, 8 East Third Street no longer served as a general intake point but as a program shelter to which men elsewhere were referred. Prospective clients had to already be in the shelter system, suffer from substance abuse problems, and be willing to participate in the facility's highly structured six-month therapeutic program. Incoming clients signed a contract specifying the cardinal rules they must obey, which included prohibitions on violence, substance abuse, and sexual activity. Clients also agreed to shower daily, keep a neat appearance, and provide urine for drug testing on staff request.

Once they were accepted, residents were assigned a case manager, with whom they worked out a treatment plan that specified attending at least three program meetings a week, perhaps including on-site GED classes or substance abuse meetings. As they completed their plan, they moved through three stages, indicated by the color of a sticker they were given to wear on their identification. Compliance with the treatment plan was monitored by the case manager and enforced through various disciplinary actions. Residents were supposed to complete their plan in six months. If they did not, their stay might be extended for up to nine months. A resident who had not completed his program by then was referred out of the facility to another shelter with a less demanding or more appropriate program. Thus the changes at 8 East Third were, first, an improved quality of life and degree of order and, second, the development of a strong, mandatory program.

Privatization of the shelters made possible the development of a more paternalistic system. Whereas the courts did not allow the city to levy requirements on clients in city-run shelters, they allowed this in the nonprofit-run facilities to which public shelters referred clients. The *Callahan* decree required the city to provide *some* shelter to every applicant and that such shelter be of a specified *quality*. But the decree had nothing to say about where or how shelter was to be provided. When the issue came up as to whether the Borden Avenue Veterans Shelter (BAVS), a Salvation Army shelter under contract to the city, could require its residents to undergo drug testing, the city successfully argued that it could:

> The Salvation Army, if it were a state actor, would not be violating shelter residents' due process rights by refusing to allow them to stay at BAVS since there is no right to stay in a shelter of one's choice and since the City will provide alternate shelter to residents who do not wish to subscribe to the BAVS program. . . . The consent decree in *Callahan* wherein New York City agreed to minimum standards for homeless men's shelters does not [affect] this issue.

Under privatization, the shelter system developed two tracks. Clients who requested shelter from the city without requirements could get it in such city-run general shelters as the Thirtieth Street Shelter at Bellevue Hospital, which, besides serving as the intake point to the single men's system, was a general population shelter for some 520 residents. Another city-run general shelter then available was the upstate Camp LaGuardia Shelter with approximately 1,000 clients. These facilities offered little in the way of services and programs. They did not enjoy the best reputation, but they were subject to the quality and access specifications of the *Callahan* decree, and in providing them the city fulfilled its legal responsibilities.

To get better programs and services, shelter residents had to volunteer to enter the so-called program shelters, those that offer a set of services aimed at the needs of some particular type of client. Most program shelters are run by private nonprofits. This is so not because public shelters are incapable of offering programs; for example, the Greenpoint Shelter with its program for substance abusers is city run. But since the state will only approve and subsidize those private shelters that offer some specific program, desirable programs tend to be in the private rather than the public shelters.

And the private shelters have the power to enforce rules that the city lacks. Because clients have no right to a particular shelter, private shelters may require and enforce participation in their program as long as noncompliant clients are free to return to a general shelter. The two-track system gives clients a degree of choice that is not available in an all city-run systems. It also makes possible an exercise of authority that is less drastic, but perhaps more effective, than the impermissible denial of city shelters. Indeed, the provision of choice and the existence of a useable sanction go hand in hand. It is because clients make a voluntary choice to go to a certain program shelter that the shelters can reasonably expect clients to adhere to their program. For what sense does it make to volunteer for a program of which one wants no part?

To get a sense of how the private nonprofits operate, it is useful to look at one of the oldest of these shelters, the Borden Avenue Veterans Residence (BAVR or, less commonly, BAVS). This shelter illustrates how the system has taken advantage of its de facto two-tier structure to become more paternalistic. It is also one of the best-documented shelters because of the work of anthropologist Janice M. Hirota.[26] BAVR's program material makes clear its authoritative philosophy:

> To create an atmosphere where staff and veterans know how to proceed, BAVR has developed a two-part contract that "obligates" the new arrival to a social service plan that will lead to "mutual goals" agreed to by the man and the administrators of the residence.
>
> Part A of the contract is the price and ticket of admission. The man must be a veteran, and he must come from one of the more than twenty shelters in the city's system. The A Contract outlines the rules and regulations the veteran will be living by at BAVR. It leads to the signing of the B Contract. The B Contract calls for the man to "establish and comply" with a service program tailored to his individual needs. If the man fails to comply or breaks the rules after admission, the Borden Avenue Residence has the authority through the contract to put him out. Other shelters in the city, not nonprofit agencies, have a hard time imposing that kind of discipline. Because of the contract, BAVR stands as a beacon that guides its residents toward the ultimate goal of independent living, dignity, and self-confidence through job placement and work.[27]

It should not be thought, however, that the threat of dismissal from the program shelter and the fear of returning to a general shelter are the sole or primary means by which the two-tier system exerts authority. These concerns are real, but cannot regularly serve as the main source of discipline. Many clients, despite their having chosen to apply to BAVR, see their signing of the contract as involuntary or as an empty prerequisite. Indeed, a past director of the shelter has acknowledged that the contracts are primarily management tools rather than sources of realistic sanctions.[28] The force of the contract comes not so much from formal sanctions as from the tie it helps establish between the client and the institution. Thus Hirota writes, "The contract system is emblematic of what is, from a social service point of view, the ideal relationship between worker and resident. Within such a system a client's problems are recognized and resolved by worker and resident working together in an individualized relationship of mutual respect and reciprocal accountability."[29]

Thus the contract represents written recognition by the client that he has certain problems (often some form of disability, but always at least the need to search for permanent shelter). It therefore establishes a basis for social service staff to periodically review the client's efforts to deal with those problems. In this way they may prompt him to fulfill the program.

The BAVR program is clearly paternalistic. It assumes that clients have some kind of "problem." They need help to "do the right thing" about it, and such help will be "good for" them. These assumptions are expressed more or less subtly. Al Peck, former director of BAVR and now director of homeless services for the New York City Salvation Army, expresses them bluntly:

> Many of the veterans suffer from multiple dysfunctions. Most prominently, drug and alcohol addictions, exacerbated by post-traumatic stress disorder (PTSD) and other mental illnesses, with resulting physical health problems. These must be treated before a veteran can make a successful transition to independent living. "We can find them jobs and a place to live, but if they don't address their real problems, it's only a matter of time before they lose the job and end up back on the streets, or in some other shelter," said a social worker in the early days of the shelter. Since jobs were not the only answer, a system was set up to encourage those veterans who wished to change their lives from homelessness to be contributing members of the community.[30]

But clients do not face only clear-cut disabilities. Many display a set of behavioral and attitudinal stances that Hirota termed "drift," which "means a basic lack of self-direction. . . . Drift seems extensive among BAVR residents; in particular, it marks their approaches to important personal decisions, including whether to stay or leave the shelter, what to do all day, and how to handle money."[31] Whether in fact most BAVR residents, or shelter clients generally, tend to drift is a question, and Hirota herself acknowledges that this trait "tends not to be captured in the available statistics."

The BAVR program, however, clearly assumes that left to themselves, clients will tend to drift, and that therefore "structures and programs [must] help clients make choices that will break the pattern of drift and thus encourage them to take control of their own lives."[32] The key aspect of the BAVR that Hirota identifies as encouraging clients to take control of their own lives is the nine-month review.

This process follows up on the A and B contracts clients signed earlier. After 270 days in the shelter (consecutive or not), the client and his case worker meet with a review board consisting of the director of the shelter, the supervisor of social services, the head housemaster, and sometimes representatives from other shelter services. The case worker has prepared a file on the client that includes a brief evaluative summary, an updated confidential medical report, the amount in the client's savings account, and a status report from the shelter employment programs. The board reviews the client's activities for the past months and his present and future plans, including his plans for leaving. The client makes a statement and the staff asks questions, which typically focus on substance abuse problems, emotional issues, and the search for permanent shelter. Out of this discussion the board generally makes specific service recommendations that are then drawn up in the form of a new B contract, which is scheduled for review in thirty to ninety days.

The review reinforces the shelter's paternalistic regime. First, reviews are a low-key method of enforcing the obligations clients enter into in their A and B contracts. They are performed not so much because clients might fail to "pass" the review and end up being sanctioned (most reviews end with the redrafting of the contracts) but because reviews provide the shelter administration and staff with an opportunity to concentrate their informal authority. The highest representatives of the shelter administration—the shelter director and the director of social services—take part in drawing up a new contract, which "puts teeth into whatever recommendations are made." Further, a review presents the client with a unified voice from the shelter administration and staff, and thus "limits chances for the client to play any end against the middle." Finally, without threatening to immediately eject a client, the review reasserts the temporary nature of shelter stays and thus focuses a client's attention on the need to search for a permanent situation.[33]

The other program shelters of the city system display the same directive orientation as BAVR. Project Renewal employs the referral-contract program-monitoring model, as does the Ready, Willing, and Able shelter operated by the Doe Fund in Brooklyn. In general the trend toward privatization has made possible the development of a paternalistic shelter regime that could not have been achieved through other means. However, as we shall see, the paternalistic regimes of the program shelters had their limits. In particular, the question of what to do with the clients who for various reasons would not volunteer to enter a program shelter was unresolved and would eventually force the city to consider significant modifications in the paternalistic philosophy. In short, shelter quality and management improved dramatically during the process of not-for-profitization. Another example of this trend involved the transition of a facility, not from public to not-for-profit management but from for-profit to not-for-profit management. The transformation of the Times Square Hotel from a dilapidated, infamous welfare hotel in the late eighties to, in 1994, a multipurpose residence stunningly renovated to recapture the faded beauty of its heyday from the twenties through the sixties was remarkable. An account in the *New York Times* from 1989 paints a picture of how bad things had become:

> There are only two single beds in the room at the Times Square Hotel where Kimberly Andrews, her husband and their 5-year-old son, who are homeless, have been living since September. The paint is peeling so badly from the walls onto the stained carpeting that Ms. Andrews routinely sweeps twice daily. The family's room, on the 12th floor, does not have window guards or a smoke detector.
>
> The elevators break down constantly, the rates are exorbitant ($2,640-a-month for Ms. Andrews's room), children play in hallways where drugs are sold and many muggings have occurred. . . .
>
> City officials acknowledge the conditions at the Times Square—hundreds of violations are documented in their own inspection reports—but say they have nowhere else to place the families.[34]

A later account documents the change:

> Visitors to New York sometimes try to check into the Times Square Hotel, not realizing it is a supportive housing facility.
>
> It is an understandable mistake. The 15-storey art deco building is attractive, well-maintained and stylishly furnished. Its vaulting lobby and marble staircase bespeak the elegance of a bygone era.
>
> [In the late eighties,] the hotel was a dump. Its ceilings were caving in. Its halls were dark and dangerous. Its tenants—drug addicts, homeless families and elderly people with no place else to go—shared the premises with rats and maggots.
>
> In 1994, the beautifully restored Times Square Hotel emerged from its scaffolding. . . . Today, the hotel is home to 652 proud, stable, well-cared-for residents.[35]

The Times Square was the largest of what was to become the most common form of supportive housing, that is, a supportive SRO (single room occupancy), which provides various types of apartments with on-site supportive services. At the Times Square those services were offered by the Center for Urban Community Services (CUCS), the same provider that worked at Ellen Baxter's pioneer supportive housing facility, the Heights. A striking feature of the Times Square was the diversity of the populations it served: 130 clients were in rooms built and supported under the New York/New York Agreement for housing the mentally ill. Fifty-three units were devoted to formerly homeless people who did not suffer from mental illness, fifty units were devoted to people living with AIDS, and the remainder of the units were for elderly and low-income workers, including many artists from the local cultural scene.

Rosanne Haggerty was the policy entrepreneur behind the renovation of the Times Square. She was a recent graduate of Amherst College, and had been working on housing-related issues for Catholic Charities, where she became familiar with the then new and little understood Low Income Housing Tax Credit (LIHTC), which would become a key part of the financing of the Times Square renewal. In 1991, barely thirty years old, she got the seemingly unlikely idea to turn the decrepit old building, then in bankruptcy, into the world's largest supportive housing project. Though a neophyte, she displayed a knack for formulating plans and communicating them to diverse interested stakeholders. A key early supporter was the local Community Board 5, chaired by Nicholas Fish, who reported, "she won over Board 5 by disclosing not only her general plans but also detailed financial data, including the formal prospectus for bank lenders."[36] Crucial support also came from Mayor Dinkins, who arranged for city acquisition and reconstruction financing. Haggerty described the process of selling her idea and getting it realized:

> What was so remarkable about the experience was I didn't have the backing of an organization, but just the idea of there was a way to save this building by taking basically smart ideas from other places, around mixed-income housing, around integrating jobs, around creating the robust supports that people would need to get back on their feet, and that it was actually highly efficient economically to do this. And that there were other populations besides individuals who were homeless who were seeking and would benefit from affordable housing in the Times Square area. Those were basic ideas that were all true in themselves but connected. There were examples around the country of good-quality mixed-income housing. There were good examples on a smaller scale of supportive housing, like Ellen Baxter's work. . . . I had learned in my work at Brooklyn Catholic Charities how important it was to also deal with linkages to jobs and good access to transportation and that all these things really mattered in terms of the success of any community. And that there were other groups whose needs could be complementary to those of the homeless. For instance, low-wage workers seeking affordable housing in the arts, or in the hotel industry, who were part of the Times Square economic ecosystem.

> So anyway, putting these ideas together struck so many people as obvious. . . . Really these ideas are logical, have been proven somewhere else, and the trick would be to integrate them. And what was so compelling was I immediately got support to keep going with this idea from what would seem to be unlikely places. Like the business community in Times Square. Like the Community Board. Unions that wanted housing for their members like the hotel industry and the actors' and related unions. And that there were so many groups who typically wouldn't be in the same room together who actually saw themselves as having a stake in having a solution to a policy challenge or a couple of policy challenges: big bankrupt buildings, needing better solutions to homelessness, wanting to spur positive community development in Times Square. And so this notion that very unusual coalitions can come together even around really edgy challenges the city faces is something that is the big takeaway for me from the whole Times Square experience.[37]

Alongside these breakthroughs in developing and managing facilities for the homeless, the legal machinery of *McCain* continued to operate and act as a driver of policy. By the time of the Giuliani administration in 1994, Justice Freedman herself would observe that "[t]he purpose of the fines was to secure compliance with legal requirements, but that does not appear to be happening."[38] Freedman deployed her new approach on November 22, 1994, when she appointed as special master one Kenneth Feinberg, who was well known for his work as a settlement master and referee in asbestos litigation against New York City and would later serve as head of the U.S. government's September 11th Victim Compensation Fund. Soon after, lawyer Barbara Cutler would become his assistant. On February 1, 1995, through a consent order overseen by the court, the parties agreed to a plan that had been negotiated by the special master and that, among other provisions, suspended the prospective fine mechanism for a period of six months. Feinberg described his role as a special master as follows:

> What we did was, whenever there was a crisis—overcrowding, failure to provide appropriate services, procedural roadblocks at the intake offices, eligibility criteria— . . . instead of these problems becoming a major confrontation in the court room, we would attempt, with success sometimes, to at least avert a legal crisis by working something out. . . . We periodically avoided situations in the courtroom by having what we called Band-Aid reforms that would alleviate the immediate crisis. . . . Everybody wanted to keep it out of the court. "Let's not go before Judge Freedman, let's not force her to act." And that's what we did for a number of years.[39]

Feinberg entertained some opinions that were perhaps surprising for someone in the middle of an intense institutional reform litigation. He believed that "the courts are a poor arm of government for imposing structural reform on public policy issues like homelessness." And he subscribed to the perversity argument, saying, "I was always skeptical that the bulk of the individuals who were in the intake center claiming homelessness were homeless. . . . My experience in New York City . . . was that much of the homeless problem was self-generated." But given the situation, Feinberg saw no alternative to dealing with the problem through the courts. Feinberg felt that the criticism directed at Justice Freedman was

> [v]ery unfair. What do those critics want Justice Freedman to do? In the abdication of ultimate responsibility of other branches of government to solve the problem, why is Justice Freedman a target? . . . I always said to critics . . . "You have a better way? What's the solution? Will you come up with a solution that will permit Justice Freedman to bow out? She'll bow out. I'll bow out. I'm not very comfortable micromanaging the homeless system in New York City." And that sort of quieted the critics.[40]

The February 1995 plan outlined the role of the special master and called on the city to take a wide range of "immediate actions." These included increasing the staffing at the EAU and at welfare hotels; establishing procedures for providing families with brokers' fees and other expenses to help them relocate in permanent housing; ceasing referring families to congregate shelters where there were active contagious illnesses; distributing at the EAU a wide range of products for small children, including diapers, cribs, formula, baby food, and Pedialyte (a treatment for diarrhea); maintaining security, sanitation, and proper heating and air conditioning at the EAU; and referring domestic violence victims expeditiously to appropriate services.

The provision in this plan that the city EAUs provide Pedialyte—the brand name was specified—soon became a standard piece of evidence in the claim that Justice Freedman had descended into micromanagement of the complex homelessness bureaucracy. The *Times* noted that "[c]ity lawyers . . . say that Judge Freedman has used her power to manage shelter operations down to the last detail. She has, for instance, ordered that the city make infant formula, bottle warmers and Pedialyte available to homeless families."[41] Also in the *Times*, Joyce Purnick claimed that "[i]n the last 22 years the court has stipulated almost every detail of the city's treatment of homeless families—from how quickly families must be placed in shelters to the availability of a particular brand of anti-diarrhea medication."[42]

It turns out, however, that the specification of Pedialyte came not from Justice Freedman or the plaintiffs, but from the city. At this point, February 1995, the Giuliani administration was in power and was desperately trying to avoid the contempt charges that had so damaged the Dinkins administration. The city lawyers therefore drew up a plan that was elaborate and detailed enough to get the plaintiffs to hold off on contempt charges. And so Pedialyte was included. The city felt it had no alternative. According to Thomas Crane, then chief of general litigation in the city corporation counsel's office: "We offered to make it available because we had our backs against the wall and . . . we had no leverage. So we sort of offered up all sorts of things because we had no ammunition. . . . She [Justice Freedman] memorialized something we had offered . . . under duress."[43] Ken Feinberg's skills as a mediator got Steven Banks to go along.[44]

The February 1995 plan also required the city to develop and implement within six months a plan for promptly providing families with shelter that met court and regulatory requirements. But the proposed six-month grace period during which fines were supposed to be suspended did not last that long. On June 16, 1995, Legal Aid was back in court calling for new fines against the city for having allowed more than three thousand families to stay overnight in the EAU since January.[45] Legal Aid submitted documents showing that conditions in the EAU continued to be horrific. One affidavit of Sanford Friedman, M.D., a professor of pediatrics at Albert Einstein College of Medicine who had experience with animal research, found conditions in the EAU in September 1995 to be "worse than any animal housing I have ever witnessed."[46] Reports from the special masters and a visit to the EAU by Justice Freedman confirmed that many families continued to spend days in the EAU and that conditions were very bad.

On March 15, 1996, a little more than a year after the first set of recommendations of the special masters was presented to the court, the special masters presented a new plan. Not much progress had been accomplished in the past year. After acknowledging the fiscal constraints the city faced, the new plan continued,

> The plight of the homeless families [sic] shelter system in New York City has been further impacted by bureaucratic inefficiencies and delays. The outlook is grim.
>
> Although progress has been made in some areas, over the past few months the mediation process has been unable to resolve effectively several conflicts relating to conditions and the overnight housing of homeless families with children at the EAU.[47]

In other words, the mediation of the special masters had resulted in little progress in improving the shelter system. Much of the new plan simply repeated many suggestions from the old plan that had not been implemented. As Justice Freedman would write in a May 1996 memorandum decision, "In fact over the last year and a half, in spite of the hard work of the Special Masters, the issuance of interim orders, and repeatedly providing additional time, non-compliance has grown."[48] With the special masters not being as effective as had been hoped, Justice Freedman went back to fining the city, even though earlier experience suggested that approach had not worked either.

Representatives of the city and the plaintiffs disagree sharply on the value of Feinberg and Cutler's special mastership. As Thomas Crane, a lawyer for the city's corporation counsel, saw the matter,

> Freedman, I think, realized that . . . litigation driving the program may not [have] been the best way to do things; she appointed Ken Feinberg as special master and he had—one of his colleagues was really doing the day-to-day stuff, Barbara Cutler. That was not a fruitful special mastership. . . . I think Barbara tended to agree with everything that the plaintiffs wanted.[49]

Steven Banks, of Legal Aid, while acknowledging that the special masters were not able to resolve big problems with the shelter system, was nonetheless much more positive about their accomplishments:

> I think that was a good model, because there were a lot of problems that were able to be resolved with his [Feinberg's] intervention, and Barbara Cutler's intervention on his behalf, that would have required court, judicial resources. And from our perspective resolving things outside the courtroom and getting relief for our clients more quickly was a very important thing. And so that period of time between 1995 and 2001 or at the end of 2001 was an important period where having a special master in place who understood the legal requirements and would agree with the city if our articulation of the legal standard was wrong or would agree with us if our articulation was right and our clients were greatly helped and the court was helped because there wasn't constant litigation. . . . I think on the macro level the progress that was needed was not made. On a micro level a lot of individual families were helped and a lot of problems were solved that would have [gone to court].[50]

Another set of controversial decisions that Justice Freedman made concerned the requirement that the city place families in legal shelter "immediately." As we have seen, this requirement originated in the state social service regulation 83 ADM-47, which resulted in repeated sanctions against the city. Effective December 29, 1994, the city got relief from this requirement when the state Office of Temporary and Disability Assistance (OTDA, formerly the Department of Social Services) issued a new administrative directive, 94 ADM-20, which stated that "[i]t is the expectation that assistance will be provided within 48 hours of application."[51] It was widely considered that the new regulation, issued on almost the last day of Mario Cuomo's administration as governor, was a favor to Giuliani in return for his support of Cuomo during the governor's losing campaign for reelection. Such was the opinion of Steven Banks, who called the change "a political payoff" and commented, "The governor in his last act is cavalierly saying that families with children can be left to sleep on tables, chairs and floors, This, evidently, is the real Mario Cuomo."[52] Michael J. Dowling, the Cuomo administration's commissioner of social services, explained the governor's action differently: "His basic comment is that we've got to operate the shelter system so that services are provided to people as quickly as possible, but that our standards have to reflect the reality of the situation."[53]

In May 1996 the city returned to court, confident that it now had a longer time period in which to act. But Justice Freedman disagreed. She wrote,

> Contrary to the position taken by defendant City . . . I do not believe that the provision of 94 ADM-20 that "[i]t is the expectation that [temporary housing] assistance will be provided within 48 hours of application for such assistance" permits the defendants to leave vulnerable families sleeping crowded together on office floors for two full days. That interpretation of 94 ADM-20 contravenes its provision that "each district is required to comply with all court decisions which apply to the district's policies related to homeless persons and families." . . . The overnight housing of homeless families at EAUs or IMCs (now called ISCs) is explicitly prohibited under the July 1986 *McCain* order, which has never been modified or vacated on appeal. Accordingly, the July 1986 order must be obeyed.

Freedman went on to argue that the ban on overnight stays in offices had many different bases besides 83 ADM-47. She cited various court decisions, the Emergency Assistance Program, state and federal equal protection guarantees, and article 17 of the New York State constitution.[54] It turned out that the favor that Governor Mario Cuomo had supposedly done for Mayor Giuliani was much less of a favor than it seemed to be.

The incoming Republican governor, George Pataki, proved to be more helpful. On December 27, 1996, 94 ADM-20 was amended. The provision that districts must comply with all applicable court decisions was dropped. New language that shifted the burden of proving homelessness to the applicant families was substituted. Below is a sample of that language:

> The considerable resources now devoted by some districts to temporary housing assistance necessitates that the obligation placed upon districts to assist homeless persons better reflect the balance between the needs of those seeking assistance and the desire of the Department and districts to provide this assistance in a rational, cost-effective manner.
>
> While it is a matter of critical importance to the Department that districts have the means for providing necessary assistance to the truly homeless, *the general principle that individuals and families have primary responsibility for securing their own housing remains.* (italics added)[55]

To make the point clear about how the primary responsibility to find shelter was now on the applicants' shoulders, the city presented the court with an affidavit of John E. Robitzek, acting general counsel of the OTDA (the promulgating agency of the revised administrative directive). The court summarized Robitzek's interpretation of the revised regulation as follows:

> [T]he presumptions and burden of proving homelessness has shifted to the families seeking shelter in that they must demonstrate clearly and convincingly that any previously available housing, whether their own or shared, is no longer available and that they are unable to access any other temporary or permanent housing. He notes that the portions of the ADM's requiring verification of homelessness have been strengthened and the presumptions favoring homeless families have been weakened or deleted.[56]

By March 1998 the parties were back before Justice Freedman with the plaintiffs again requesting, among other things, that the city stop leaving families overnight in the EAU. Justice Freedman wrote that

> [d]espite the changes in 94 ADM-20 the Court believes that previous appellate holdings in *McCain v. Koch*, *McCain v. Dinkins*, *McCain v. Giuliani* and *Robinson v. Grinker* mandate enjoining City defendants from finding families who clearly do not have appropriate alternative housing, or who cannot produce all of the documentation required but cannot return to previous housing, ineligible for temporary shelter.[57]

But the question to be determined here was, After the repeal of 83 ADM-47 and the promulgation of the revised version of 94 ADM-20 on December

27, 1996, how long did the city have to find shelter for applicant families? How long could the city allow such families to stay in the EAU? Did the city in fact have forty-eight hours to determine whether a family was eligible for shelter, during which time a family might stay in an EAU? To answer this question requires some recapitulation. Recall that in 1985,

> The city had been required by 83 ADM-47 to provide shelter "immediately." In *Lamboy* [Order, Freedman, J., Oct. 2, 1985, at 5, *Lamboy* (Index No. 41108/85], Justice Freedman held that having a family sleep overnight in an EAU did not constitute providing shelter, and hence families that stayed overnight in an EAU had not been provided shelter immediately.

Then, on December 29, 1994, the city had seemed to get relief from the "immediately" requirement when OTDA had issued a new administrative directive, 94 ADM-20, which stated that "[i]t is the expectation that assistance will be provided within 48 hours of application."[58] The city had therefore believed that it could leave families sleeping in the EAU for two days. But Justice Freedman had disagreed. She had pointed out that 94 ADM-20 also provided that each district was required to comply with all court decisions that applied to the district's policies related to homeless persons and families.[59] On July 3, 1986, Freedman had issued an order that said emergency housing was "not to include overnight accommodations at Emergency Assistance Units." So, according to Freedman, despite the new regulation 94 ADM-20, the city still couldn't keep families overnight in the EAU, much less for forty-eight hours.

On December 27, 1996, as mentioned above, the Pataki administration revised 94 ADM-20, which had been promulgated by the outgoing Cuomo administration. Again, the provision that districts must comply with all applicable court decisions was dropped. New language that shifted the burden of proving homelessness to the applicant families was substituted. So now the city concluded that finally it really did have forty-eight hours to find a family shelter and that it could leave a family waiting for that period of time in the EAU.

Steven Banks disagreed. When the Cuomo regulation was issued, it was reported in the *Times* that "Mr. Banks has argued that rulings based on the state constitution still prohibit the city from keeping families at the office overnight."[60] And after the revised Pataki regulation, Banks continued to argue that the state constitution disallowed having families stay overnight in the EAU and disallowed the city having forty-eight hours to place a family. According to Banks,

> So now we're in '95. And we go to court because we've got this directive with the city saying "we can leave people sleep there for forty-eight hours." And we say "you can't do that." . . . Now it's what does the constitution require. . . . The '86 decision actually said there is a right to shelter and you can't let people sleep in the Emergency Assistance Unit.[61]

The '86 decision that Banks was referring to is *McCain v. Koch*, 502 N.Y.S.2d 720 (N.Y. App. Div. 1986), May 13, 1986. There the Appellate Division of the state supreme court found that "[i]t is also likely that plaintiffs will succeed on their claim that the NY Constitution article XVII obligates defendants to provide emergency shelter for homeless families." Thus the Appellate Division granted the plaintiffs' request for a preliminary injunction that would bar the state and the city from denying emergency shelter to homeless families.

The court noted that if this preliminary injunction, requiring the city to provide emergency shelter, were not granted, families would end up staying in the EAUs because the city was not providing them with emergency shelter. EAUs did not constitute emergency shelter but were only offices where applying families waited to be placed in emergency shelter. Thus, unless families were given emergency shelter, they would end up staying in EAUs. The Appellate Division noted that "in the event a preliminary injunction is not granted, they [the applying families] will be forced to sleep on the floors, desks, and counter tops of IMCs and EAUs."[62]

Nonetheless, what the preliminary injunction forbade was the denial of emergency shelter; it did *not* prohibit allowing families to stay in EAUs while their applications were being processed, however long that might take. The issue of how quickly the city must provide emergency shelter had been determined by the "immediately" requirement of 83 ADM-47 and by Justice Freedman's decision in *Lamboy* that staying in an EAU did not constitute emergency shelter. But 83 ADM-47 was repealed, and there remained no requirement in the Appellate Division's 1986 *McCain* decision that, because of state constitutional requirements, the city could not keep families in an EAU. Staying in an EAU overnight might be unfortunate, but it was not forbidden by the Appellate Division as long as that stay was part of a process of determining the eligibility of a family and providing them appropriate emergency shelter.

In fact, this decision (*McCain v. Koch*, 502 N.Y.S.2d 720 [N.Y. App. Div. 1986], May 13, 1986) concludes that while it is likely that there is a right to shelter, the courts can't regulate the quality of that shelter. Thus the decision reads in part,

> [T]he adequacy of the level of welfare benefits is a matter committed to the discretion of the Legislature. . . . In light of the broad discretion vested in the Legislature, we cannot conclude that plaintiffs are likely to prove that article XVII substantively guarantees minimal physical standards of cleanliness, warmth, space and rudimentary convenience in emergency shelter.[63]

So even if one assumes that the Appellate Division of the state supreme court recognized in this decision that there was a right to shelter in the state constitution—in fact, the decision only says, "It is also likely that plaintiffs will succeed on their claim" that such a right exists—it seems the decision doesn't say anything against letting families stay in the EAU.

In fact, the linking of the Appellate Division '86 decision with the prohibition of leaving families in the EAU comes in an order by Justice Freedman dated July 3, 1986. At the beginning of this order, Justice Freedman explained what kind of an order the plaintiffs were asking for:

> Plaintiffs herein having sought an order requiring defendants to take adequate steps to comply with the preliminary injunction issued herein by the Appellate Division, First Department on May 13, 1986, which would include providing emergency housing to all eligible families with children but would not include overnight accommodations at Emergency Assistance Units or Income Maintenance Centers.[64]

Note that this formulation of the plaintiffs' request does *not* imply that the Appellate Division's preliminary injunction forbids overnight stays in the EAU. It implies that the plaintiffs want an *order* that forbids such stays. Now, Justice Freedman did grant such as order, as follows: "Now, it is hereby ordered and adjudged that city defendants . . . provide lawful emergency housing to all eligible families with children, such emergency housing not to include overnight accommodations at Emergency Assistance Units or Income Maintenance Centers."[65]

But the point is that the source of the ban on overnight stays in the EAU is *not* the Appellate Division's decision that found likely the state constitutional right to emergency shelter. The source of that ban is Justice Freedman's order of July 3, 1986. In other words, there is no link between the constitutional right recognized by the Appellate Division and the ban on EAU sleepovers. Or in still other words, the ban on EAU stays is based on a court decision, Judge Freedman's order of July 3, 1986, and not on the state constitution. But the Pataki revision on December 27, 1996, of 94 ADM-20 removed the language that required the city to comply with court decisions. So in fact that regulation's provision that the city had forty-eight hours to provide assistance was good.

It is important to note that Justice Freedman sometimes found against the *McCain* plaintiffs in cases that the Legal Aid lawyers considered essential. Such was the case concerning the promulgation, on January 16, 1996, under New York State Social Service law, of a new section 352.35 to18 NYCRR, which was entitled "Eligibility for Temporary Housing Assistance for Homeless Persons." The new section provided that homeless individuals and families must cooperate in the development of an independent living plan, which is a strategy developed by the applicant and the city to, among other things, get the applicant out of emergency shelter and into permanent housing. Failure to cooperate in the development of such a plan or to abide by it could result in sanctions, including termination of shelter. Homeless applicants were also required to comply with public assistance requirements, which could include "looking for work, engaging in training, accepting jobs and work assignments."[66] This provision would turn out to be very controversial once the city implemented a large-scale workfare program, the Work Experience Program (WEP), that became the largest welfare-work program in the country. The most striking part of the new section provided that "[p]rior to denying or discontinuing temporary housing assistance . . . the social service district [i.e., the city] must evaluate the individual's or the family's need for . . . preventative services for children and protective services for children and, if necessary, make an appropriate referral."[67] In other words, if a family with children had its shelter discontinued due to failure to live up to its independent living plan, its children could be placed in foster care. The plaintiffs argued that this provision was invalid on its face in that it attempted to overrule administratively the May 13, 1986, *McCain* decision of the Appellate Division that implied a state constitutional right to shelter. Plaintiffs further claimed that "a regulation suggesting a foster care alternative for the children of families who have been expelled to the streets is shocking."[68]

On November 16, 1995, Freedman had issued a temporary restraining order enjoining the city from implementing that portion of the regulation that authorized termination of shelter to families with children that fail to abide by their independent living plan. But on December 30, 1996, she denied the plaintiffs' request to make the ban on enforcing those provisions of 18 NYCRR 352.35 permanent. Freedman wrote,

> While this Court seriously doubts the wisdom of a regulation that potentially causes small children or infants to be consigned to the streets for their parents' or caretakers' infractions or perceived non-compliance or noncooperation with DSS directives, such a regulation is not on its face so irrational or beyond the

> scope of DSS' authority under Social Services Law §20 as to warrant the continuance of the temporary stay. . . . Although valid on its face, the regulation of course cannot be arbitrarily or irrationally applied or applied in such a way as to violate constitutional, statutory or case law.[69]

Upon a grant of reargument, Justice Freedman still declined to agree with the plaintiffs concerning 18 NYCRR 352.35 and wrote on May 27, 1997, that "the Court remains satisfied that the sanction provisions of the regulation do not on their face violate either the New York State Constitution or the Social Services Law nor do they directly contravene any appellate decision."[70] This decision was upheld on appeal to the Appellate Division on July 30, 1998.[71] Thomas Crane of the city's Law Department believed that these decisions represented a "milestone" in that they allowed the city to begin developing an effective eligibility-determination process.[72]

On January 12, 1999, Justice Freedman issued an order that again had the Giuliani administration complaining of judicial micromanagement of DHS. By 1996 it had become city policy to find ineligible families applying for shelter who had been living doubled up with other residents immediately before requesting shelter. Indeed, in an interdepartmental memo entitled "Guidelines for Determining Eligibility of Doubled-up Families for Temporary Housing Assistance," dated August 23, 1996, city policy in such cases was described as follows:

> People who resided in doubled-up housing immediately prior to requesting temporary housing assistance are presumed to be ineligible for assistance.
>
> If the family resided doubled-up with a relative, and claims the relative will not permit them to return, the family is determined to be ineligible. It is not necessary to make a field visit in these cases. However . . . a field visit may be conducted.

Application of this policy resulted in scores of families being "booted," as the *New York Daily News* put it, from the EAU. But Giuliani defended the practice, saying, "The fact is that we're far better to force many of these solutions back to families, so that family units resolve these issues before it becomes the responsibility of the entire city."[73]

But this policy seemed to be in violation of state welfare Administrative Directive 86 ADM-7, which provided that

> [c]ommunity resources, including friends and relatives, which are actually available to the client must be used before an immediate need can be met by

> the local district. Local districts must not provide assistance to applicants who refuse to utilize such resources.
>
> However, the local district must be sure that the resource is actually available. Unless the client volunteers to use family and friends, the agency must check with such people to see if they are willing and able to help.[74]

The regulation also provided that applicants found ineligible must be provided with written notice explaining the reason for their ineligibility.

On December 6, 1996, Justice Freedman issued an order that the city comply with the relevant portions of 86 ADM-7 and "make sure that the [other housing] resource is actually available" (brackets Freedman's) to a formerly doubled-up family before finding them ineligible.

On January 12, 1999, Freedman issued an order that seemed to do no more than restate that the city did indeed have to make sure that alternative housing really was available to families found ineligible because they had been doubled up. The city objected vigorously. Deputy Mayor Joseph Lhota complained that "the advocates want us to diminish eligibility requirements, to shelter people who aren't homeless but don't want to go back to their family, and that's not right." Lhota's analysis of the politics of the situation was that "[t]he tug of war is from a desire on the part of City Council and advocates to micromanage the department of homeless services."[75]

In October 1999 it turned out that what was at stake was far more than simply requiring DHS to make sure it had its facts right in eligibility determinations. The *New York Times* reported that

> [f]or the first time since the turn of the century, homeless people in New York City will be required to work as a condition of shelter, under a Giuliani administration policy to be put into effect before the end of the year, an administration official said yesterday. . . . The homeless who are able to work and who fail to comply with the rules will be refused shelter, and in the case of families, the children could be put in foster care, said Anthony P. Coles, the senior advisor to Mayor Rudolph W. Giuliani.[76]

Once the courts had declined to strike down 18 NYCRR 352.35—the state regulations that contemplated denial of shelter to clients who failed to comply with their independent living plan, which could include work assignments—the question was, When and how would the city implement those requirements? City officials had announced that they were getting ready to implement that policy but announced no specific starting date. As of October 1999 most homeless advocates and shelter providers believed that implementation of the policy would be put off at least until warmer weather arrived.[77] Thus the decision to move ahead, in the winter, with work requirements and the possible placement of children of noncompliant parents in foster care came as a shock. Steven Banks remarked,

> It's extraordinarily callous, with the cold weather coming now, that the city wants to put vulnerable New Yorkers on the streets. The track record of workfare programs in the city hasn't been one in which significant numbers were placed in jobs that allowed them to pay prevailing rents. It has been essentially a tool to reduce the caseload through sanctions.[78]

Legal Aid lawyers asked Justice Freedman for a temporary restraining order preventing the city from implementing the workfare and foster care policies. They also wanted to prevent the implementation of workfare requirements in the singles shelter system and therefore applied also for a temporary restraining order (TRO) from Justice Wilk, who was presiding over the *Callahan* case. The result was an unusual emergency hearing presided over by both judges. Leonard Koerner, a lawyer for the city, argued that the Appellate Division had already found that the relevant state regulation, 18 NYCRR 352.35, was valid on its face and could now only be challenged on a case-by-case basis after the regulation was implemented. Only the state's top court, the court of appeals, Koerner argued, could stop the implementation of the regulation. "You may be right," Justice Wilk conceded, but decided "in the spirit of the season" to grant the plaintiffs' request for a TRO delaying implementation of the regulation through January 14.

The city was outraged. Michael D. Hess, then the city's corporation counsel, exclaimed, "The decision is an emotional one, not a legal one. They talked about the Christmas season. That's not how you decide cases, based on what month it is or what temperature it is outside."[79] The administration appealed the granting of the TRO to the Appellate Division (First Department) of the state supreme court. But in March 2000 the Appellate Division denied the city's appeal. Giuliani announced that it would appeal the Appellate Division's decision but took no action for the last two years of his administration.

On June 26, 1996, Joan Malin stepped down as DHS commissioner. Her greatest success, she felt, was the not-for-profitization of the department's services. Her greatest disappointment "was the Emergency Assistance Unit and the whole front end of the system .We [were] never able to figure out a more effective way of trying to help and work with families." Relations with the courts had continued to be a difficult point throughout her tenure. According to Malin,

It was a highly tense relationship. I think Helen [Freedman], her heart was in the right place, attempting to do the right thing. . . . I think [I made] an effort to try and get around it or develop some kind of working relationship where there was some acknowledgment . . . of how much the city had done or could do and what we could not do and what . . . Legal Aid was asking of us.

We could go in with reams of data showing what we've done and yet Steve [Banks] could walk in with three or four . . . compelling stories that would break your heart and we would completely lose. There was like no way around it.

Relations with advocacy groups such as Coalition for the Homeless and Legal Aid also remained difficult: It's still frustrating because I don't think they wanted to appreciate how difficult it was and what stresses and strains we were under. I never felt like that they were a partner that understood and I felt I was as good as the last headline. But the relationships with the nonprofit organizations felt much more like an alliance."

Apparently court relations, being necessarily adversarial, made for an adversarial relationship with the advocates, but relations with nonprofits, being contractual, were more along the lines of working agreements. As for managing under court supervision, Malin said,

There were some elements of it which you basically did not manage. You took what resources you had and responded to what was being asked of you as opposed to trying to think through a different or more creative or more effective way of doing it.

If you stepped back and actually looked at the homeless system in the City of New York, no one would plan it to look the way it did. It's ridiculous. And yet we were sort of boxed into that because each increment had been mandated by different courts, at different points in the courts' engagement. That really created a system that's almost impossible to manage well.[80]

In July 1996, Gordon J. Campbell was appointed DHS commissioner. At the time Campbell was chief of staff to Peter J. Powers, Giuliani's first deputy mayor. Campbell had been in city government since 1986, having worked for a while at the Human Resources Administration under Koch and for a short stint at the Department of Education, where he dealt with another challenging case of institutional reform litigation, *Jose P. v. Board of Education*. Before taking the DHS position, Campbell was asked by Thomas Crane, chief of the General Litigation Division of the Corporation Counsel's Office, "Are you sure you want to do it because you're going to be named in over seventy lawsuits?" However, Campbell was a lawyer and a former prosecutor who felt very comfortable with litigation.[81]

It turned out that Campbell had as many problems dealing with the City Council as he did dealing with the courts. In 1995 the council had extended the life of DHS until October 1996 with the requirement that the department discontinue the use of hotels with more than one hundred units and without kitchens in each unit. As the deadline approached, the department and the administration struggled to find ways to comply. At one point, Campbell argued to the City Council that the 1995 law was overridden by a judicial order that mandated the end of chronic overcrowding in the EAU. The "stunned" council did not agree and characterized the department's continuing use of noncompliant facilities at the Kennedy Inn in Jamaica, Queens, as illegal.[82]

When the October deadline came and the Kennedy Inn was still being used, the city decided to move its residents to other hotels or Tier II shelters. The families protested. According to one press report,

> Residents of a Jamaica hotel for homeless women and children blocked traffic briefly yesterday to protest the city's plan to oust them from the premises by the end of the month.
>
> Holding signs that read, "We won't go," several Kennedy Inn residents stood outside in the rain along Baisley Blvd. to call attention to the decision by the city's Department of Homeless Services to discontinue use of the for-profit hotel. Marlene Barnes, thirty-one, mother of two sons, ages five and eleven, said that the Kennedy Inn has been her safe haven for the past sixteen months: "'It makes me feel depressed. This place is nice,' Barnes said. 'We take GED classes, we have a church downstairs and a medical van.'"[83]

The department managed to achieve compliance by December 1996. Eventually the Kennedy Inn would be bought by Hampshire Hotels and Suites, which gutted the entire facility and reopened it as a luxury hotel servicing nearby Kennedy Airport.[84]

The department's existence came up for renewal once again on June 30, 1998. The City Council continued to have concerns. Families continued to stay overnight in the EAU. Councilman Stephen DiBrienza, chairman of the council's general welfare committee, which oversaw the department, wanted to require as a condition of making the department permanent that the EAU be equipped with cots and cribs for families waiting to be placed. Campbell's argument that these accessories were unnecessary as waiting time in the EAU had been reduced to no more than twenty hours did not convince DiBrienza. Also of concern was the fact that ongoing privatization brought with it a reduction in the ranks of the department's workers, as many of their jobs were now being performed by nonprofit staff. Thus agency staff, which had been 3,000 in 1994, had been reduced to 2,170 by the summer of 1998.[85]

On June 24, the council passed a bill to make DHS an independent agency. The vote was forty-one to six. But the bill included several conditions, and the mayor announced that he would veto it. Among the conditions were a requirement that beds, cribs, and self-contained, lockable sleeping rooms be made available in the EAU; a limitation on the number of beds in new adult shelters to two hundred; a provision that mandated submission of reports to the council on sanitation, fire, and health conditions; and more supervisory staff at certain shelters. Giuliani supported making the department permanent but rejected the conditions, saying, "What they tried to do is load it down with so many terms, conditions and burdens that they would have destroyed it." He threatened to veto the bill, which he did on July 24.[86] DHS then existed by executive order and thus completely under the mayor's control.[87]

The council responded by passing a bill to impose the conditions Giuliani had objected to. The mayor vetoed that bill on December 7.[88] Giuliani made much of the bill's provision to limit new shelters to two hundred beds maximum, which he claimed would have to be applied retroactively to existing shelters of over two hundred beds, thus creating a need for up to twenty-five new shelters. These the mayor threatened to open in the districts of council members who might vote to override the veto. The council denied that the bill's size requirements would be retroactive, and moved to include an amendment to emphasize that point. Giuliani conceded that an amendment would reduce to no more than five the needed new shelters, which he still promised to open in the districts of recalcitrant council members. Nonetheless, the council overrode the mayor's veto on December 17 by a vote of thirty-six to eight and passed Local Law 57 of 1998, which retained the provisions objectionable to Giuliani.[89] Besides limiting the size of shelters to two hundred beds, the bill also tried to address the issue of families staying overnight at the EAU, which was a continuing problem. The bill required that while families were waiting to have their eligibility for shelter determined, they had to be kept, not on an office floor but in a self-contained and lockable room with a bed or crib as appropriate. The bill also required the city to provide applying families with help in gathering the official documents that they needed to produce to get their applications approved.

At the passage of Local Law 57, the mayor made preparations to open a shelter in the district of his opposition's leader, chairman of the General Welfare Committee, Stephen DiBrienza. When no other facilities turned out to be available in DiBrienza's district, the city served eviction papers on a psychiatric center that had been serving hundreds of mentally ill people for twenty-five years. Eventually four other programs offered at the building would be threatened with eviction to make way for the shelter that was to punish DiBrienza.

The City Council would again make homeless policy with Local Law 019, passed on May 18, 1999. This was an attempt to deal with some of the consequences of the repeal of the "immediately" provision of 83 ADM-47. With the end of that requirement, Justice Freedman had found that the city could not be fined for allowing a family to wait in the EAU for twenty-four hours while an eligibility determination was made. To prevent DHS from doing so, Local Law 019 provided that "[a]ny family with children seeking shelter who is still in the process of applying as of ten o'clock in the evening on the day such family sought shelter shall be provided temporary shelter placement for that night."

Why such furious opposition on the mayor's part to the council's initiatives, given that both sides supported the underlying objective of making DHS a permanent agency? Sources indicated that more important than the two-hundred-bed limitation were provisions for reporting to the council and regulating the activities of the EAU.[90] The real debate was over who could control the department and what policy should be. Provisions to improve conditions in the EAU in effect put legislative teeth into court orders made by Justice Freedman and were thus seen as encroachments on mayoral power. Requirements to maintain staffing levels at shelters expressed skepticism about the ongoing privatization of the department's services, and the reduced personnel needs it entailed.

Of course from the mayor's point of view what needed explaining was the council's insistence on involving itself in the management—or even micromanagement—of DHS. Martin Oesterreich, who would become the department's commissioner in March 1999 after the interbranch warfare quieted down, believes, "It was designed to extract the maximum possible damage on the mayor."[91] During that period, Giuliani was widely thought to be contemplating a run for the U.S. Senate seat that would eventually be occupied by Hillary Clinton. Giuliani looked to be a formidable candidate who would be able to claim credit for the city's improved economic climate and lower crime rate. A potential weakness of the mayor's was his controversial efforts to reform the city's social services. According to this theory, a Democratic City Council hoped to hurt the Republican mayor's Senate chances by highlighting the shortcomings of his homelessness policy.

Eventually a compromise was reached. Plans to evict the community groups and develop a shelter in DiBrienza's district were dropped. Legislation to make DHS independent of HRA was passed. The mayor agreed to provide job security for two thousand people at the department. And Martin Oesterreich, the commissioner of the Department of Youth and Community Development, emerged as the administration's choice to head DHS.

Fortunately, given the stormy political environment that had just surrounded the department, Oesterreich turned out to be a conciliator. *City Limits*, a magazine that covered the city's advocacy and service professions, described the new commissioner in an article entitled "My Favorite Martin":

> Shhh. The mayor's newest commissioner, Department of Homeless Services boss Martin Oesterreich, is getting a reputation as an accessible, open, honest guy. In fact, one advocate worried that if the mayor hears how popular the guy is, he'll get the axe. . . .
>
> Says Coalition [for the Homeless] executive director Mary Brosnahan: "In contrast to [former commissioners] Joan Malin and Gordon Campbell, he doesn't take things personally."[92]

Oesterreich made a point of maintaining good relations with the court and Steven Banks:

> I certainly think that Steve Banks was not happy to see me go because he got to trust me. I mean I never lied to the guy. If I said I would do something I did it. And if didn't think I could do it I told him straight out.
>
> And you know we tried to come to a mutually agreeable point on those issues. [I] understood very well that this was in some ways a money maker for Legal Aid Society and I don't mean that from the fees, I mean that from the fact that . . . this was part of their overall mission, that [it] was part of their fund raising appeal.[93]

In other respects, Oesterreich was more like his predecessors. He was a manager, not an advocate or an expert: "I wasn't brought in because of theory. I wasn't brought in because of policy and stuff. I was brought in because . . . with twenty-some years of city experience I knew how to handle the internal city activities." He also subscribed to the "underlying cause" account of homelessness, and to the belief in the heterogeneity of the population that had been articulated by the Cuomo Commission and institutionalized under earlier commissioners:

> My greatest challenge was devoting myself to the fact that homelessness was the presenting condition but it wasn't the underlying condition. . . . I think my

> greatest challenge was to try to explain to people that the homeless are not all alike. They are all alike in that they present as homeless. But the reasons for presenting are much different.

Steven Banks, asked to identify the best DHS commissioner he had worked with, would later say,

> Marty Oesterreich. And it would have been against type because he was commissioner under Giuliani, and . . . one would have thought we would have a contentious relationship. Marty Oesterreich was about solving problems. He wasn't about ideology, philosophy. He was about trying to solve problems. And he also understood our role in the litigation. Our role is to represent flesh and blood people who have problems. And sometimes that collides with what the administration wants to do or not do. And ultimately the issue is, is it legal and therefore they would win if they went to court? Or is it likely to be found unlawful and therefore we're going to win if we go to court? Or, alternatively, is there some middle ground that is just going to be a better result? He was always very willing to listen. That doesn't mean we didn't have litigation. It doesn't mean that there weren't disagreements. But he was oriented toward problem solving. I think that's what makes a great public servant . . . problem solving. As opposed to, "I'm right because we're the government and therefore we get to form policy and we don't have to consider the fact that it may have an impact on individuals that could be unlawful and therefore you can stop it."[94]

During Oesterreich's tenure the census in the shelter system rose above twenty-five thousand, higher than it had been since the late 1980s. This, despite the administration's finally successful efforts to develop a strict eligibility-determination process. Oesterreich famously commented, "I can't screw the front door any tighter," a remark, he would ruefully acknowledge, that "was probably the thing that they are going to put on my fucking tombstone."[95]

Other indications of the limits of the Giuliani overhaul of the shelter system began to present themselves. In particular, the program shelters that had been developed with so much effort turned out not to be effective in dealing with all clients. This problem became apparent to Mark Hurwitz, who began at DHS as an assistant commissioner with a particular interest in single adult clients. Hurwitz was a lawyer who had been the first director of the Urban Justice Center's Mental Health Project, which helped patients released from psychiatric facilities make the transition from hospitalization to community living. Eventually he became concerned that the paternalistically oriented shelter system was not addressing the problem of the considerable number of clients who declined to participate in a rehabilitative regime of one of the program shelters. Hurwitz described the problem as follows:

> The system had really been designed as a series of program shelters to meet the specific needs of individual types of clients. So there were employment shelters, there were substance abuse shelters, there were mental health shelters. And then, because of the *Callahan* consent decree, which required that the city give shelter to anyone, there were general shelters [for] people who didn't want to go into a program.
>
> So while I was assistant and deputy commissioner one of the things I realized was these program shelters were operated the same way that those providers operated their programs that were not shelters. They were residential treatment programs for people with addiction problems. They were mental health community residences. At the time those kinds of programs required you to, if you were there for substance abuse treatment, to be clean and sober and to be committed to sobriety. If there were a mental health program you had to have insight into your mental illness, be willing to take medication. And so the program shelters, rather than being designed to serve anyone who had a mental illness or anyone who had an addiction problem, they were designed to serve those who were most, in the words of the providers, were most amenable to treatment or who were likely to respond well to treatment. That created this problem of the people with the worst problems got stuck in the general shelters and never left. And so I began a push to require just the shelter providers to take anyone regardless of their willingness to accept treatment.
>
> That was a big change just in the shelter system. And then that actually started causing pressure on the housing system because now these nonprofit providers that were running shelters were being expected to place people out into housing. And [the shelter providers] were saying, the housing providers are requiring six months of sobriety; who in the shelter system can stay clean and sober for six months? And they . . . don't take anyone on methadone. There were all these restrictions.[96]

In other words, Hurwitz was beginning to realize the limitation of a system that required clients to accept treatment before they would be eligible for permanent housing. This was the same realization that Sam Tsemberis had come to in his operation of the Project Help street-outreach program back during the late Koch years. Eventually, Hurwitz became aware of Tsemberis, who had moved on to found Pathways to Housing, a provider of housing to street people that, as we saw, would become famous for developing the Housing First strategy.

Evidence supporting the Housing First model had continued to accumulate. In 1997 Pathways to Housing had become part of the New York Housing Study (NYHS), which was a federally funded experimental comparison of the outcomes for street-dwelling homeless people of the Pathways housing-first, treatment-(possibly)-later model of providing permanent housing and the then traditional practice of providing permanent housing only to subjects who were sober and complying with psychiatric treatment. After five years, 88 percent of clients who participated in the Housing First model provided by Pathways remained housed, compared to only 47 percent of those who participated in the traditional, treatment-first approach.[97]

By 1999, Hurwitz had become aware of Tsemberis's success and interested in incorporating a Housing First philosophy into the city's shelter system. According to Hurwitz,

> I started educating the shelter providers and we actually invited Sam Tsemberis to one of the shelter director meetings. And he came. At the time we were using overhead projectors. He asked to have an overhead projector available. And he put one slide on the projector. And it was a diagram showing a box that was labeled "treatment" with an arrow to a box that's labeled "housing." This is the current system. If you want to get housing you have to first go to treatment and agree to treatment. Then he said we have this philosophy of Housing First and we see it a little differently. And then he proceeded to do a headstand and looked at the slide upside down. [He said] we think if you get into housing, if you give people housing first they are much more likely to get the treatment that they need.[98]

During the coming Bloomberg administration, Hurwitz would be promoted to deputy commissioner at DHS, where, as we shall see, he continued to push to incorporate the Housing First approach into city practice.

On April 22, 1999, Mayor Giuliani and Governor Pataki announced a second "New York/New York Agreement" to create an additional fifteen hundred supported housing units for the homeless mentally ill over five years. Capital costs were split, with the city putting up $85 million and the state $45.7 million, while the state agreed to cover all operating and service expenses.[99] New York/New York II was a follow-up to the first New York/New York Agreement negotiated under Koch and signed in 1990 by Governor Mario Cuomo and Mayor Dinkins, but the second agreement was widely considered a disappointment. According to Shelly Nortz, the long-time Albany lobbyist for

Coalition for the Homeless, advocates had been pushing for an agreement to produce ten thousand units of supported housing.[100] More modestly, the Giuliani administration had been asking for twenty-five hundred units and committed the city to contributing $85 million in capital costs, which it asked the state to match. But for months Governor Pataki refused to commit more than $40 million.[101] According to Nortz, during his first term Pataki "really didn't have an interest in putting any additional resources in. . . . They just literally didn't seem to comprehend the value of it. I think what happened is that the city just decided to take what they could get and move on."[102]

Advocates for the homeless were greatly discouraged. Mary Brosnahan, the executive director of the Coalition for the Homeless, was quoted as saying that the agreement "falls far short of what is needed."[103] Eventually Shelly Nortz would be able to put the matter in perspective: "I wouldn't say II was a failure. I would say it was a disappointment. And that we turned right around and said, not good enough, and then really brought out the troops for the protests."[104] The second agreement turned out not to be the end of the New York/New York process. A combination of advocate-organized protests, more research, a better understanding of the success of supportive housing, and shrewd political maneuvering by Pataki would result in the governor ultimately making a 180-degree turn and agreeing to a much larger and truly path-breaking New York/New York III Agreement before the end of his tenure in Albany.

During the Giuliani administration, the paternalistic moment of homelessness policy crystallized. The political demand that clients needed to "give something back" and take responsibility for their situation—a demand that expressed itself nationally at the federal level by the reform of welfare in 1996—was addressed. Better services were provided, system management improved, and shelter conditions got better. But the homelessness problem showed no sign of ending and would eventually rise to new heights. Developing a strategy that promised an eventual resolution of that crisis would fall to the Bloomberg administration. Policy still had plenty to learn.

5

Homelessness Policy under Bloomberg

The Bloomberg administration claimed to have accomplished what one source describes as "a philosophical U-turn" at the Department of Homeless Services (DHS).[1] The essence of the attempted change can be seen in the department's rewritten mission statement. At the beginning of the Bloomberg administration, in January 2002, the statement read, "The Department of Homeless Services, in partnership with public and private agencies, provides temporary emergency shelter for eligible homeless people in a safe, supportive environment. In an atmosphere of cooperation and respect, we deliver services through a continuum of care, where the client assumes responsibility for achieving the goal of independent living."[2] A new statement of June 2012 read, "The mission of the Department of Homeless Services is to overcome homelessness in New York City. DHS prevents homelessness wherever possible and provides short-term emergency shelter and re-housing support whenever needed. These goals are best achieved through partnerships with those we serve, public agencies, and the business and nonprofit communities."[3]

The two key changes are that in the new statement, DHS proposes to "overcome," as opposed to manage, homelessness, and that prevention has been added as part of the mission on a level with sheltering the homeless. Such a shift in mission, if achieved, would certainly count as a striking change. This is so because, as J. Q. Wilson discusses in his classic account of public organizations, *Bureaucracy*, the mission of a public agency is rooted in its critical tasks, that is, in the behavior of the front-line operators without which the organization ceases to function. And these critical tasks are determined not so much by the orders of executives but by the situational imperatives and naturally occurring incentives that the front-line operators face. If policymakers wish to change the critical task of a public agency, they must change the immediate situation faced by its operators as they perform their duties.[4]

Thus to change the critical tasks for police departments from fighting crime to community problem solving, officers had to be taken out of patrol cars and made once again to walk beats. To change the critical tasks of welfare-office clerks from determining eligibility to finding jobs, the positions of the eligibility technicians and job developers had to be merged and the policy incentives that favored eligibility determination over job development had to be changed.[5] Similarly, shifting the mission of DHS from just sheltering the already homeless to doing both that and preventing homelessness would require major changes in the situational imperatives and incentives faced by its front-line operators. The questions are, then, Did this shift of mission actually take place, and if so, how was it accomplished and what does it imply about the nature of change in an urban bureaucracy? But to understand homelessness policy under Bloomberg it is necessary to review changes in thinking about homelessness that developed during the 1990s.

Some of the earliest research on the rise of homelessness in the 1980s suggested that homelessness might be a temporary problem that would diminish with the end of that decade's recession.[6] But very soon research began to paint a less optimistic picture. Thus in a widely cited article of 1987, Richard Freeman and Brian Hall reported that

> our research demonstrates that the perception of homelessness as a temporary blemish on the American scene is seriously in error. Despite the substantial recovery from the 1982–83 recession, the number of homeless persons appears to be increasing. . . . In the absence of major economic and social changes or a new housing policy for the extremely disadvantaged, the United States is thus likely to be plagued by a long-term problem of homelessness of a sizeable magnitude.[7]

Similarly, in 1984 homeless advocates and researchers Kim Hopper and Jill Hamberg wrote that "[t]he present crisis will endure . . . a permanently dislocated class of the absolutely shelter-poor, forced to resort to emergency accommodations or to double up for periods of indefinite duration, seems the probable prospect." They insisted on "the necessity of far-reaching structural reform if present misery is to be abated and the forces which generate it are to be contained."[8] And in 1987 I pessimistically wrote, "The first thing that has to be said about the homelessness problem is that solving it is going to take time. There are no quick fixes."[9]

This pessimism had two causes. Those writers, such as Hopper and Hamberg and Freedman and Hall, who emphasized social-structural factors as causes of homelessness did not see any likelihood that such factors would soon markedly change and thus concluded that homelessness would be with us for the foreseeable future. Writers such as the present author who emphasized the role of dysfunctional personal traits and behaviors believed that helping such a population would be very difficult and that therefore homelessness would prove to be an intractable problem. But research done in the 1990s would require alterations in our understanding of the structure of homelessness and of the homeless population.

First of all, research from the late 1990s challenged explanations of homelessness that emphasized individual traits and behaviors by showing that homeless families, at least, were not so different from similar, poor but housed families and that such differences as did exist did not prevent homeless families from being rehoused. Thus, according to one such study,

> Homelessness was a stage families passed through, not a permanent state: Four-fifths of families who entered shelter had their own apartments 5 years later, and three-fifths were stably housed, having been in their own residence at least 1 year and an average of nearly 3 years. Individual characteristics associated with shelter entry did not prevent most families from becoming rehoused.[10]

Another study found that of its sample of 233 homeless families, years later 80 percent were in their own apartments and only 3 percent were in shelters. Moreover, for most families the most successful intervention is simply to provide housing. Homeless families who received permanent housing were generally able to stay housed, but among homeless families who did not receive such housing about half ended up back in the shelter. Provide housing and homelessness is, generally, cured—for families.[11] A stay in the shelter to obtain services was not the key to ending homelessness. Formerly homeless families who obtained permanent housing without returning to the shelters also stayed stably housed. Thus ending homelessness for most families was easier than writers who emphasized personal disabilities thought it would be. Indeed, these findings held out the hope that homelessness might be prevented altogether because "families living under untenable circumstances can obtain and remain in conventional housing even without ever entering shelter when affordable housing is made available."[12] In short, research raised the possibility that family homelessness might be ended or even prevented altogether.

Other research provided still more reasons to be optimistic. Particularly important was the work by Randall Kuhn and Dennis Culhane in which they developed a typology of the homeless.[13] Using factor analysis on longitudinal administrative data from the shelter system for individuals of New York and Philadelphia, these researchers were able to distinguish three categories among the homeless. They write,

> We find a cluster consisting of those who used the shelter for a short time, presumably as a time to recover from a temporary emergency; a cluster of episodic clients who move in and out of the shelters frequently, possibly alternating shelter stays with bouts of street homelessness, hospitalization, and incarceration; and a cluster of chronic stayers who rarely leave the shelter for long periods.[14]

These clusters of transitional, episodic, and chronic clients were distinct demographically, with transitional clients being the whitest, and least disabled, of the clusters; with chronic clients being the oldest, blackest, and most disabled; and with episodic clients generally in between. (See table 5.1.)

TABLE 5.1: Client Characteristics by Cluster: Percent of Cluster in Category: New York

	Transitional	Episodic	Chronic
DEMOGRAPHIC			
Black	83.6	90.5	92.9
<30 Years	36.1	37.7	23.2
>50 Years	8.3	6.3	13.9
DISABILITIES			
Mental Illness	6.5	11.8	15.1
Medical Disability	14.2	19.8	24.0
Substance Abuse	28.2	40.0	37.9
Any of Three	38.4	52.3	55.4
All Three	1.3	3.0	3.3

Source: Randall Kuhn and Dennis P. Culhane, "Applying Cluster Analysis to Test a Typology of Homelessness by Pattern of Shelter Utilization: Results from the Analysis of Administrative Data," *American Journal of Community Psychology* 26, no. 2 (1998): table VI.

Transitional clients made up 80 percent of shelter users, with episodic and chronic users each making up 10 percent. But perhaps the key finding of this work concerned the shelter usage patterns of these three clusters of shelter users. For these researchers found that "[t]he chronic shelter users, although a relatively small and finite population, consume nearly half of the shelter days and therefore, targeted programming seems both potentially beneficial to the clients and effective in reducing shelter cost."[15]

In other words, research that came out in the mid- through late 1990s suggested a way out of the corner into which analysts of homelessness seemed to have painted themselves. Dealing with family homelessness did not have to await resolution of intractable behavioral problems. Indeed, with early enough intervention, much family homelessness might be prevented. As for homeless individuals, if policy focused on the chronically homeless, which is the population that counts for the most shelter days, then a solution of the problem might not have to await a complete restructuring of the American economy or welfare state. Ending chronic homelessness turned out to be a problem that might be accomplished with not much more expenditure than is currently, but inefficiently, being spent.

It has been argued that nonincremental policy changes are preceded by the development of a professional consensus among experts and by the dilution of that expertise into an easily disseminated public idea.[16] In the case of homelessness policy, the public ideas that developed out of the work of Culhane and Marybeth Shinn and others were "end chronic homelessness" and "prevent homelessness." What was needed now was for policy entrepreneurs to spread the word about these new public ideas.

By the late 1990s a number of organizations and activists began redefining their work in light of the findings of the latest research on homelessness. So important was this work that Philip F. Mangano, executive director of the United States Interagency Council on Homelessness (USICH) and among the first advocates to rethink homelessness, said that "research is the new advocacy."[17] Also among this new breed of activists was Nan Roman, president of the National Alliance to End Homelessness (NAEH), which had been founded by, among others, Susan Baker, wife of the influential Republican operator James Baker. Roman believed that advocacy for the homeless had changed considerably since its beginnings in the late 1970s and early 1980s. Advocacy had become institutionalized in a whole homelessness industry. Earlier, the movement had been led by what Roman calls "social entrepreneurs." By the late 1990s the leaders were professional nonprofit managers, which makes for a very different type of advocacy.[18] Mangano sums up the change in worldview as follows:

> In the past we have looked at the private sector primarily as a source of resources. We wanted the business community and corporations to kick in some dollars to help create new programs. What we've done with our national partnership in terms of the inclusion of the private sector with the public sector is not only to get resources. That's important because there are a lot more resources in the private sector than there are in the public sector for sure. But we have looked at the mindset of the private sector, of the business community, of the downtown business association, of the chamber of commerce, of philanthropy. We want their mindset focused on the issue of homelessness. And their mindset drives our efforts towards business solutions, not simply the management of a problem. Business is not content, for the most part, simply to manage problems. They are interested in solving it.[19]

Ending chronic homelessness partly by preventing homelessness was one of the public ideas that was developed out of recent research by new advocates such as Roman and Mangano.

Culhane's research also played a vital role in legitimating another approach to reducing homelessness, supportive housing. We have seen how this strategy of placing disabled homeless people in high-quality, permanent housing that provided on-site support services to make independent living possible had been developed in New York City by Ellen Baxter, Rosanne Haggerty, and other activists and policy entrepreneurs. In 1990, the first New York/New York Agreement was an important policy breakthrough in which the city and the state collaborated to create 3,314 units of such housing for the homeless mentally ill by 1992. In 1999 a second New York/New York Agreement was widely considered a disappointment when the city and state agreed to create far fewer supported housing units, 1,500, over five years. Part of the problem was that state officials were reluctant to deeply invest in a solution they considered unproven.

The needed evidence was provided in an influential 2002 study by Culhane, Stephen Metraux, and Trevor Hadley that found that placement of a homeless person into New York/New York I housing resulted in a savings in the use of such services as shelters, hospitals, and jails to the amount of $16,282 per housing unit per year.[20] This study had been commissioned by the advocacy organization Campaign for Supportive Housing (CSH) with the specific intent to disseminate information documenting the positive impacts of the first New York/New York Agreement. Connie Temple of the New York office of CSH describes the research and its impact as follows:

> After New York/New York I . . . we were pushing for more supportive housing. Our chair of the board, Richard Ravitch, met with the governor's office. And they said, prove to us that it's cost efficient. And so from that I was charged with finding the money and a researcher. . . . And after the study was released, Dr. Culhane and I went to Albany and met . . . with the key people in the Budget Office and explained it to them. All the agencies understood this study. It really changed the dialogue.[21]

Culhane's research on supported housing dovetailed nicely with his analytical focus on chronic homelessness, for once the chronically homeless are identified, where other than the shelters are they supposed to go? Supportive housing turned out to be a cost-effective answer.

Another crucial, research-based public idea that would have wide effect on homelessness policy was Housing First. We have already seen how this idea developed out of the work of Sam Tsemberis, first at Project HELP and then at Pathways to Housing, both based in New York. Throughout the first decade of the twenty-first century, a critical mass of research developed pointing to the effectiveness of Housing First strategies in improving housing retention and decreasing time spent on the streets. For example, an analysis based on the previously discussed New York Housing Study, using a randomized control experimental design and published in the *American Journal of Public Health* in 2004, found that "participants in the experimental condition (Housing First) had significantly faster decreases in homeless status and increases in stably-housed status relative to participants in the control condition (treatment first or continuum of care) . . . with the experimental group reporting less time spent homeless and more time spent stably housed compared with the control group."[22] Subsequent nation-wide studies converged around the finding that over terms ranging from one year to as long as five years, Housing Frist programs achieved a housing retention rate of about 85 percent for their clients, far larger than treatment-first control group programs.[23] The Housing First strategy was thus another area of professional consensus in homelessness research that had crystallized by the early 2000s.

The question was how to disseminate and implement these ideas. As executive director of the federal Interagency Council, Mangano seemed to be in a weak position to get anything done. Such task forces are notoriously ineffective.[24] Indeed, the Interagency Council, which was established in 1983, at first achieved little success and was allowed to fall dormant when its first director resigned in 1986. The revival of the council with the naming of Mangano as executive director in 2002 was one of the few concrete manifestations of the Bush administration's philosophy of compassionate conservatism. Finding that cooperation from federal agencies was hard to get, Mangano decided to concentrate on involving states and localities. Thus was developed a strategy of getting state and local governments to develop ten-year plans to eliminate chronic homelessness. This effort has been successful in the sense that more than two hundred cities and counties have developed such plans. One of the localities that developed such a plan, with certain changes, was New York City.

On June 23, 2004, Mayor Bloomberg announced his plans to "make the condition of chronic homelessness effectively extinct in New York."[25] In saying this, Bloomberg was making the goal of ending chronic homelessness, which had been developed by the NAEH and disseminated by the USICH, his own. In New York that policy has been articulated by a coordinating committee that was formed in November 2003 and was cochaired by Bloomberg's chief of staff and two distinguished nonprofit leaders. According to one of the cochairs, Lilliam Barrios-Paoli, then of the United Way, the New York coordinating committee was aware of the work of the USICH but came to many of the same conclusions on its own. Barrios-Paoli felt that one purpose of the coordinating committee, which involved representatives from more than 125 concerned organizations, was to try to develop a consensus around a plan to end chronic homelessness that would not be contested and so not end up in court.[26]

Early on in his administration, Bloomberg said of homelessness policy that "[e]very single thing we do, we seem to wind up in court."[27] Indeed, in part, the coordinating council, along with other measures we will discuss, was an element in Bloomberg's efforts to avoid litigation and keep the courts out of managing the shelter system. Making policy through the courts limited the parties involved to essentially two, the city and the advocates of Legal Aid Society. But part of the new direction in homelessness that Mangano and USICH were disseminating was an emphasis on including the private sector in planning, and adopting a businesslike mindset in policymaking. Hence the use of a coordinating committee rather than courts, for, as city officials said, "advocates for the homeless would be included in the planning process, but . . . the main considerations in developing the steering committee were to involve people from the private and nonprofit sectors to work with the government."[28] However, in some respects the plan development process in New York was different from what went on in other cities influenced by USICH. For example, the usual ten-year plan was recast as a five-year plan because, as Bloomberg reportedly said, "'I know it's ten years but I've only got five.'"[29] And the New York plan, given the city's extensive family shelter system, placed much greater emphasis on dealing with homeless families than did the plans of most other cities.

The five-year plan called for a major change in homelessness policy and was elaborated in a document entitled *Uniting for Solutions beyond Shelter*. "In many ways," wrote the *New York Times*, "the draft reveals a philosophical U-turn for the city, which over several administrations became oriented toward providing emergency shelter to homeless people, rather than considering ways to prevent homelessness."[30] Besides a focus on prevention, another prong of the plan was an embrace of supportive housing. Part of the five-year plan was a commitment to develop twelve thousand units of supportive housing for homeless families. This promise represented "a landmark commitment" in the eyes of some advocate groups who had previously been critical of the city.[31] It also reflected the influence of Culhane's evaluation of the impact of the New York/New York I Agreement.

Another key strategy embraced by the five-year plan was Housing First. *Uniting for Solutions beyond Shelter* promised to "[e]xpand 'Housing First' options for those on the street."[32] Related to Housing First was the idea that upon admission of a family or individual to the shelter system, "planning for permanent housing should begin immediately" rather than wait until rehabilitative services had rendered the client housing ready.[33] Also emphasized was the strategy of focusing on chronic homelessness, with *Uniting for Solutions beyond Shelter* stating that "New York City embraces the goal of ending chronic homelessness."[34]

These, then, were the main elements to the Bloomberg administration's early vision of dealing with homelessness: prevention, supportive housing, Housing First, and ending chronic homelessness. It was an impressive agenda, one that involved focusing on policy options that were strongly supported by sophisticated research. It was an approach that will be termed here "post-paternalistic" because it involved an end to the paternalistic concern of diagnosing "underlying causes" of homelessness and—in cases where prevention was unsuccessful—a focus on rehousing rather than rehabilitating shelter clients. The Bloomberg administration's embrace, in its early years, of this post-paternalistic agenda would mark the most promising moment in homelessness policy in the billionaire mayor's term. Very interestingly, *Uniting for Solutions beyond Shelter* saw rental assistance for shelter families to speed their exit from the system to be consistent with this post-paternalistic agenda. The plan stressed that "[t]ax dollars earmarked for homelessness should support solutions like prevention, rental assistance, and supportive housing" and asserted that "[r]ental assistance resources must continue to be available in shelters to re-house chronically homeless individuals and families."[35] As we shall see, when the administration decided to end rental assistance and other subsidies to homeless families, the promise of its early years would come to a sad end.

The five-year plan amounted to a commitment in 2004 to reduce the city's shelter population—which was 36,399 people in June of 2004[36]—by two-thirds by the end of 2009. Thus the *Times* reported, "Mayor Michael R. Bloomberg unveiled an ambitious plan yesterday to reduce the number of homeless people in the city by two-thirds over the next five years, proposing to build thousands of units of new housing and put new restrictions on city shelters."[37] This pledge implied that the shelter census would have to drop to about twelve thousand persons by 2009.

Perhaps the most striking measure endorsed by the administration to stay out of the courts was the Family Homelessness Special Master Panel (SMP). The SMP was created by the city and the Legal Aid Society, who were the parties to the main lawsuits that had dictated family homelessness policy since the first suit was brought back in 1983. By 2003, according to the agreement dated January 17, 2003, that created the SMP, the parties were "desirous of achieving the goal of ending the current cycle of litigation and reaching the point where the problems of homelessness can be dealt with by government and the larger society without the necessity for the intervention of the judiciary."[38] To that end, both parties agreed to a two-year hiatus on litigation during which time the SMP would study the situation, make recommendations for change, and decide whether and on what terms to recommend the settlement of the lawsuits.

The two parties had different motivations for wanting the SMP. For the Bloomberg administration, the two-year hiatus on litigation was a way of achieving the freedom from court supervision that it had wanted. Of course, in a certain sense, there already was a mechanism in place to avoid litigation. This was the two special masters, Ken Feinberg and Barbara Cutler, who had been appointed in November 1994. The plaintiffs were in general pleased with the work of Feinberg and Cutler, but the city was unhappy. By the end of the Giuliani administration, Feinberg had become less involved with the homelessness litigation and Barbara Cutler's role had expanded. But the city felt Cutler was biased against them. For example, Corporation Counsel Michael A. Cardozo asserted that the city "no longer had confidence" in Cutler and that the plaintiffs were getting "two bites at the apple," once before Cutler and once before Justice Freedman.[39] So the city welcomed the new, three-person SMP as a way of bringing in mediators who, in its opinion, were less biased. Thomas Crane, chief of general litigation in the city corporation counsel's office, was particularly pleased with one of the SMP's members, John D. Feerick, former dean of the Fordham School of Law, whom he felt "was much more neutral" than Cutler.[40]

Legal Aid had been much happier with the Feinberg-Cutler special mastership than the city had been. They believed the special masters were effective at resolving day-to-day problems facing homeless families without having to go to court. When Feinberg had largely bowed out and the city would not work with Cutler, Steven Banks was willing to see another special master mechanism put in place. As for the two-year hiatus in litigation, which the city made much of as a mechanism for getting out from under the courts, Legal Aid saw it as no such thing. According to Banks, "we agreed to consent to a mechanism in which we would try to work things out with the special masters [panel] and not go to court unless we went to them first, which is what we had done with Ken Feinberg anyway so we didn't see it as a concession at all."[41] Part of the agreement was that "[a]t the end of the two year transitional period, the Panel will take account of all relevant factors and make whatever recommendations it believes appropriate as a result of its work, including any recommendations with respect to the resolution of the existing litigation involving family homelessness."[42] It was the city's hope that the SMP would eventually recommend an end to the litigation and court supervision. But from the point of view of Legal Aid, the key word in the agreement was that whatever the SMP had to say would be no more than "recommendations." But not all observers agreed with Banks that the panel's determinations would be entirely optional; to the *New York Law Journal*, "The panel has the look of an arbitration committee more than a group of mediators."[43] That is, to some people it seemed the SMP's conclusions were meant to be binding.

The members of the SMP were John D. Feerick, Gail Nayowith, and Daniel Kronenfeld. Feerick, who had been dean of the Fordham School of Law and head of an anticorruption commission appointed by Mario Cuomo, was, as Thomas Crane put it, "universally esteemed."[44] Feerick was also the lone lawyer on the panel; this was by design, as Bloomberg—the only mayor since homelessness litigation began under the Koch administration who was not a lawyer—felt it was important that the panel be a mix of lawyers and nonlawyers.[45] Gail Nayowith was, at the time, executive director of an advocacy group, the Citizens' Committee for Children of New York. Daniel Kronenfeld had been executive director of the Henry Street Settlement, one of the nation's first settlement houses, and had experience operating homeless shelters going back to 1972. The *Times* article reporting the creation of the SMP was titled "Members of New Panel Praised by Both Sides," but the city and Legal Aid had rather different conceptions of what to expect. According to Steven Banks, "from the plaintiffs' perspective you've got John Feerick, who's got an impeccable reputation for fairness, and two advocates who care about children." The city's analysis of the likely dynamic was, according to Thomas Crane, that "Gail was considered to be more pro-city and . . . Danny was considered to be more of an advocate. And Feerick, I think because he's so highly regarded, bridged whatever differences there were between the other two."[46]

The SMP issued several reports. *Family Homelessness Prevention Report*, issued in 2003, cited the literature showing that housing subsidies generally end family homelessness and recommended that DHS embrace prevention as an agency mission. A second document, *Report on the Emergency Assistance Unit and Shelter Eligibility Determination*, issued in 2004, entered into some of the bureaucratic details of how DHS would have to revise its intake procedures in order to implement the new mission of prevention.

The report on the Emergency Assistance Unit (EAU), which was the facility through which all families entered the shelter system, began by announcing that a professional consensus had developed among knowledgeable observers:

> Near universal agreement exists—among DHS, LAS [Legal Aid Services] and others—that the EAU as presently configured cannot process the flow of large

> numbers of families applying for shelter. This Report reflects that reality and the SMP's effort to understand the role and functioning of the EAU, the intersection of twenty years of competing and frequently piecemeal policy, program, and legal mandates, and the Panel's views for supporting DHS as it creates a better response to the problem of family homelessness in New York City.[47]

Here the SMP is delegitimizing the baseline shelter policy that developed after twenty years of incremental change. This was a crucial development, for incrementalism implicitly assumes that baseline policy is essentially acceptable. When the national welfare reform process of the nineties developed a similar rejection of baseline policy—expressed in the public idea, "end welfare as we know it"—the possibility of breaking decisively with sixty years of welfare policy was opened. A similar break with twenty years of homelessness policy in New York also began to develop.

And it was change of this magnitude that the SMP hoped to catalyze, as it made clear in the report on the EAU:

> It is clear that continuing to address efforts to improve the EAU on a case-by-case basis or respond to individual policy or operational issues, sequentially as they emerge, is bound to fail. This conclusion suggests that only a comprehensive approach will yield long-term improvement. The Panel's recommendations signal a departure from current policy and practice. They contemplate a complete restructuring of and significant improvements in application, eligibility determination and support functions.[48]

The family homelessness Special Master Panel report of June 2004 made it clear that the panel, and the department, envisioned a major change in the organizational culture of the department. The panel described the thrust of its recommendations as follows:

> The Family Homelessness Special Master Panel calls for a fundamental restructuring of the Emergency Assistance Unit . . . and a functional transformation of shelter application and eligibility process to shift from a shelter-only system of care to one with a homeless prevention focus where shelter is only one of many housing-related services and supports offered to homeless families with children.[49]

Gibbs briefly suggested the kind of changes that would have to happen with the department's front-line operators to complete the shift in organizational culture that she contemplated:

> The system before asked essentially one contentious question: Are you eligible for shelter on not. . . . Now, instead of hiring investigators, we are hiring staffers with social service backgrounds. We assume families that come to us have a problem and ask, "how can we help?" Sometimes the answer will be shelter, and sometimes it won't be.[50]

Perhaps the most striking indication of change was the improved conditions at the entry point to the family shelter system, the EAU. Throughout the 1990s and beyond, the EAU was by all reports "an infamous symbol of homeless policy gone awry."[51] Bloomberg himself acknowledged that the EAU was once "a symbol of shame for our great city."[52] According to a typical newspaper account,

> It is difficult to overstate the conditions inside the EAU, say those who have spent time in its dank chambers.
>
> "It is probably one of the most disturbing places on Earth," said Gail Nayowith, one of three court-appointed special masters who recommended the facility be leveled.
>
> It's a place where food is often spoiled, soiled diapers flow from trash cans and babies scream constantly.[53]

Rebecca Chew, who managed the old EAU and later the facility that replaced it, described the old EAU as follows:

> It was a 20-story brick building. . . . It was pretty overcrowded I would say [with] clients waiting inordinate amounts of time for service. We would have to walk over people who were sleeping on floors, benches. We had wing areas that we called classrooms, I don't know why, but they were just lots of benches and people would plug in their TVs and watch TV and play video games. Certain offices would have piles of donated clothing just sitting in a pile outside so people could sort through it. There was a cafeteria on the lower level that served hot meals throughout the day and clients would line up for meals. It was just a really kind of a dreary, terrible place, with lots of kids. It would be so chaotic that people would literally spill out into the neighborhood to get a breath of fresh air. It was very much like a sensory overload, in the sense that they were calling people's names to go to the appropriate windows so you heard a lot of noise, and on top of that people were stressing out and just acting out. It wasn't a great place.[54]

One reason for such terrible conditions was that families who applied for shelter often had to wait many hours, even overnight, in the EAU before they got an eligibility hearing. Families would camp out on benches or the floor to wait. Once their case was heard, families would be sent out to wherever there were vacancies in the system for ten days while their eligibility was being determined. Families would be bused out to temporary assignments all over the city and then bused back to the EAU to continue waiting. This process would go on for days. Those families that were found ineligible would frequently immediately return to the EAU to reapply—they had nowhere else to go, they maintained—and the traumatic experience would begin all over again. And on top of everything, food served at the old EAU was "notoriously awful."[55]

By about January 2003, conditions at the intake point of the system had much improved. The old EAU building was no longer used and was scheduled to be demolished and replaced with a new building built especially for the purpose. Most families were seen at the Prevention Assistance and Temporary Housing (PATH) intake center at 151 East 151st Street in the Bronx, which opened in November 2004 and where the average wait before a family had a hearing had dropped from twenty hours to about six.[56] Families no longer slept in the office. On a visit I made to PATH at that time there were no signs of the disorder and discomfort characteristic of the old EAU.

Very importantly, the city had addressed the problem of the repeated reapplications that used to back up the system. This was made possible by a state administrative directive promulgated on April 6, 2005, 05-ADM-07, which allowed DHS to deny shelter to anyone who reapplied within ninety days after their application was rejected, unless there had been a change in their circumstances. This new directive helped end the bottleneck. A court opinion in August allowed the city to implement the new ADM.[57] However, the city made certain exceptions to this policy to allow for the possibility that some families, within the ninety-day period, would nonetheless be in immediate need of shelter and city policy concerning these exceptions would become a major issue that the court would be forced to consider.

The implementation of 05-ADM-07was a significant relaxation of the right to shelter, one that allowed DHS to redefine the task performed at the intake point from one of sheltering and determination of eligibility to one of diversion and prevention. First-time applicants at PATH were given ten days of shelter as their eligibility was being determined. Clients who were found ineligible for shelter—usually because the city deemed that they had other housing alternatives—were referred to what was called the Resource Room. Unlike other PATH employees, the Resource Room staff were all degree-holding social workers. Their task was to meet with families who had been found ineligible and help them look for housing. Typically this involved mediating with the residents of whatever housing the family used to have. Resource Room workers did not provide any funds, but they could refer clients to Home Base offices, which could offer money and which will be discussed shortly. In short, Resource Room workers had to put together some kind of plan for where their families could go and then use their counseling skills to sell that plan to the parties involved.

Meetings with families were very personal and intensive exercises in crisis intervention, quite different from the impersonal sessions with the old EAU staff, in which front-line operators (who were not social workers) simply gathered information from the families for the purposes of eligibility determination and fraud investigation. According to the director of the Resource Room, "Our basic tool and modus operandi is the skills in terms of therapy and counseling and establishing rapport with people and making that connection. . . . Emotionally and mentally they have to buy in to what you are saying. So it's a very difficult thing."[58] However, a significant limitation of the Resource Room social workers was that they could not recommend reconsideration of negative determinations.

The city also tried to implement the SMP's call to focus on prevention. In 2004, the centerpiece of the effort to prevent homelessness was the Home Base program, then a half-dozen offices that served the six neighborhoods that had been identified by DHS as sending the most families to the shelters: Jamaica, Queens (CD 12); East Harlem (CD11); Bushwick (CD04); Bedford Stuyvesant (CD03); Crotona (CD06); and the South Bronx (CD01). The city contracted with a community-based organization in each neighborhood to identify and help families that were in danger of becoming homeless. These contracts were performance-based and specified a minimum number of target families each office must contact per month. Outreach workers knocked on doors, distributed leaflets, communicated with other community-based organizations, and sponsored and attended neighborhood events trying to identify families that were at risk of being homeless. Families who were doubled up were especially sought after. Home Base workers had access to funds to pay rent, utility bills, or anything else that might allow a family to stay housed. Of course, this was completely different from the situation of the eligibility-determination workers at the old EAU, who never distributed money.

Like Resource Room workers, Home Base operators also mediated with housed relatives who might be willing to take in, or let stay, an at-risk family. Sometimes the intervention arranged by a Home Base office can be almost trivial. For example, one Home Base director told me of the case of a family whose frisky young children were getting on the nerves of their grandmother, who was the lease holder. The Home Base office paid to hook the household up to cable television so the children could be babysat by Cartoon Network.

Home Base operators also helped clients with their search for affordable housing. One Home Base worker for Catholic Charities used the strategy of ingratiating herself with local landlords by calling them on their birthdays.[59] More generally the intervention took the form of paying bills, buying furniture, mediating disputes, and referring clients to other organizations or agencies. Eventually the Home Base program would be subjected to a rigorous, scientific evaluation, which will be discussed later, but by 2005 all the city had was a promising program of unknown effectiveness.

On October 19, 2004, in its efforts to reform the shelter system, the city made what would turn out to be a fateful and controversial decision. DHS abandoned its long-term policy of giving shelter residents priority for entering public housing and for receiving shelter subsidies in the form of Section 8 vouchers. The city gave several reasons for the change. The city had already assigned all of the Section 8 vouchers it had available. Such vouchers were available only when a current recipient left the program for whatever reason. But at the heart of the city's decision was the perversity argument. One DHS official explained the move as follows: "For a long time . . . we've known that Section 8 is seen as the pot of gold that you can get by declaring yourself homeless. We've heard it all the time that people are coming in order to get an apartment."[60] Commissioner Gibbs herself evoked the perversity argument, saying, "We don't want people to think that the best way to get housing is to bundle their children up and take them to the EAU."[61]

This was five years after Michael Cragg and Brendan O'Flaherty had refuted the perversity argument as it applied to the Dinkins administration's homelessness policy and thus raised serious questions about whether it applied in the context of New York City homelessness policy in general.[62] On firmer ground the city also made a fairness argument, arguing that it wanted to avoid "the cheating of working poor families who needed the benefit as well, but who stayed in difficult housing situations nonetheless."[63]

Instead, families applying to DHS would get rental-assistance grants—called Housing Stability Plus (HSP)—for up to five years. In the first year the grant would be for about $925 a month for a family of three, but the size of the grant would shrink each year by 20 percent. Families would only be eligible for the program after they had been in the shelters for at least three months, a provision that was intended to discourage applications to the system for the sole reason of getting quick rental assistance, which was, again, an evocation of the perversity argument. HSP represented the first time New York City had imposed any kind of time limits on rental aid. One enthusiastic writer claimed that this development marked "a banner day in the history of New York City housing—and in the history of American public assistance for the poor."[64] Gibbs argued that this decreasing subsidy would help homeless families "leave the shelters and achieve true self-sufficiency."[65]

This argument overlooked studies that suggested permanent housing subsidies were the most effective way to keep shelter families from relapsing into homelessness. HSP would eventually be presented to the court as yet more evidence that the city was reforming its shelter system during the hiatus on litigation. Thomas C. Crane, chief of the General Litigation Division of the city's Law Department, made this claim in an affirmation filed with the court in opposition to an order to show cause that had been filed by corporation counsel in February 2006 seeking dismissal of four consolidated actions, including *Yvonne McCain v. Bloomberg*. Robert Hess, who became DHS Commissioner in April 2006, would also point, in court, to the end of Section 8 priority and the development of HSP as great accomplishments: According to a *New York law Journal* report of a December 14, 2007 court decision: "He [Hess] also touts the City's program to move people out of shelter into permanent housing, contending that the City responded to the cut in federal Section 8 Vouchers with Housing Stability Plus (HSP). . . ." Besides its declining subsidy another feature of HSP that would become controversial was that it required families to remain on welfare to qualify, which sometimes would mean that a family would have to decline a job to stay eligible for welfare and HSP.

The administration thought the early results of what Commissioner Linda Gibbs called the "delinking" of Section 8 receipt and Housing Authority admission from shelter access were promising. In July of 2005 Gibbs said,

> [W]e delinked Section 8 . . . and the Housing Authority units from the shelter system. . . . This October is when we delinked. . . . Preceding the delinking, applications were high . . . the peak month had been August of 2004. When we delinked, we went below the prior year's demand. . . . And what that told us was, we had confirmed what everybody had expected, which is that there were a number of [applicants] who came toward the shelter because they were trying to do their best to access Section 8 and the Housing Authority Units. And when that wasn't available anymore, it did cause a decrease in demand.[66]

But by the end of the Bloomberg administration, the decision to end the practice of giving priority to homeless families for Section 8 vouchers and public housing would be seen as part of the reason why the shelter population was to grow to unprecedented levels.

By the beginning of 2005, the two-year hiatus on litigation that Legal Aid and the city had agreed to along with the creation of the Special Master Panel was at an end and the panel was to make recommendations concerning the resolution of *McCain* and related litigation. The city's interpretation of the question at issue was, Had the city made enough progress in the preceding two years to justify the resolution of the litigation and definitively end court supervision of the shelter system? The city, Legal Aid, and the members of the SMP had been involved in intense, almost 'round-the-clock negotiations. All parties felt they were within a finger's width of a resolution, but at the last moment negotiations broke down. One reason was that Legal Aid had a very different idea of what was required to end litigation than the city did. The city felt it deserved an end to litigation based on what it saw as two years of progress. Legal Aid, on the other hand, wanted a permanent order establishing a right to shelter for families and an agreement that the shelter provided had to meet basic standards of decency. Moreover, Banks contended that thousands of pages of depositions documented deplorable conditions and frequent improper denials of shelter and thus rebutted the city's claims of progress. But much to the distress of Steven Banks and Legal Aid, the SMP agreed with the city that great progress had been made and that litigation should simply come to an end. In a letter to the court dated January 18, 2005, the SMP wrote,

> We do not believe it appropriate at this time, in light of all the changed circumstances, for this court to remain in perpetual supervision of the system for homeless families. . . .
>
> In our view, the branches of government should be freed to perform to the fullest extent their responsibilities in our tripartite system of government. The judiciary, of course, will always be there for resort by citizens when government elsewhere fails, which is particularly critical when dealing with vulnerable children and families. We believe that after twenty-two years of system-wide litigation involving homeless families with children, the City of New York has earned the opportunity to go forward into a new era.[67]

To the plaintiffs, the panel's call for an end to court intervention was a disaster. Banks's reaction to the panel's statement was that

> [w]e were totally blindsided by it because there was no provision for issuing such a decision . . . no provision for issuing anything like that in the agreement we had entered into. I think it [the SMP] was a group of individuals, well meaning, that simply misread their mandate and in doing so caused tremendous problems for our clients and tremendous problems for Judge Freedman in particular. Because it created a launching pad for the city to continually attack her unmercifully and unfairly because she was, quote, "retaining litigation that

> these three individuals had said should end." When everybody knew, everybody knew that the litigation could only end with a settlement or a trial. And so I think these three special masters did a tremendous disservice to both our clients and Judge Freedman. And to the city as well because it created . . . a sense of "the case should be over, why isn't it being over?"[68]

The city, on the other hand, was mightily pleased with the panel's recommendation, which would serve as the basis of a show-cause order the city filed in February 2006 that would "urge the Court to adopt the views of the panel and dismiss the *McCain*, *Lamboy*, *Slade* and *Cosentino* cases because they are moot."[69] The city entered into detail about the improvements it had made in the shelter system since the establishment of the SMP and what it understood as a two-year hiatus in litigation:

> None of these changes came about as a result of threatened motion practice or Court orders. On the contrary, they were conceived and implemented in a litigation-free atmosphere which enabled DHS to design and develop comprehensive and far-reaching programmatic changes without the distortions which often result when litigation pressures and priorities, rather than rational planning, drive management's decision-making.[70]

While the debate continued over bringing the decades-old homeless litigation to an end, on November 3, 2005, the city and state reached yet another breakthrough agreement on developing permanent supported housing for the homeless, this one known as the New York/New York III Supportive Housing Agreement. Similar previous agreements had been the New York/New York Agreements to House Homeless Mentally Ill Individuals I and II. The difference in titles was significant, for one of the key innovations of the third agreement was that it expanded the population of clients to be housed beyond the mentally ill to include such homeless or at-risk-of-homelessness groups as youths aging out of foster care, people suffering from HIV/AIDS and other medical conditions, and people with a history of substance abuse—not only former substance abusers in recovery but active substance abusers who had not yet achieved sobriety. As this expansion suggests, the New York/New York III Agreement reflected, in its decision to include even populations who once would have been declared unready for housing, the ongoing influence of Housing First. The sheer size of the endeavor was also a milestone. New York/New York I had been a breakthrough when it added over three thousand units of affordable housing to the city's stock; the smaller New York/New York II Agreement added a still significant fifteen hundred units. New

York/New York III dwarfed them both by eventually creating nine thousand units. New York/New York III also represented a quantum jump in its level of complexity. There were five signatories to the first agreement: the governor and mayor and three agency heads. The second agreement carried seven signatures: those of both chief executives and five agency heads. New York/New York III was signed by Governor Pataki and Mayor Bloomberg and no fewer than ten agency heads. Besides the signatory agencies, New York State's Housing Finance Agency and New York City's Housing Development Corporation provided capital financing and were thus intimate participants. Total capital costs of developing the nine thousand units was to be $10 billion over ten years, which would be split evenly by the city and the state; once all units were up, operating expenses were estimated at $156 million per year, to be paid by the various state and city agencies.

Deputy Commissioner George Nashak was one of the representatives of DHS at the negotiations for the third agreement. Asked if discussions involved as many as twelve people around a table, he responded,

> More like 24 because no agency would go with just one person so each agency had multiple representatives. And so there were huge group meetings that took place over the course of a year and we hammered out these details. It's a very complicated deal with all kinds of complicated targets built into it. And, you know you had to create eligibility criteria, you had to create targeting criteria. You had to get the budget people on board to understand not only how much money we were going to invest in this but how that money was going to be spent and leveraged. And so it was a very complicated process. . . . It was tremendously hard work for a year, but it ended up being one of the best things that's ever been done with homelessness in the history of the city.[71]

A key sticking point was expanding eligibility beyond the mentally ill. According to Nashak,

> Everyone knew and accepted the fact that you really had an obligation to create housing for homeless mentally ill people. No one disputed that. The heavy lift in the deal was convincing people to put people with substance abuse issues into housing. People didn't accept that substance abuse was an illness. They believed it was a behavior choice. And the idea of putting someone with an addiction problem into housing and giving them housing, it felt to a lot of people, not to me but to a lot of people, as if we were rewarding people for bad behavior. And in fact, what ended up happening is we built this housing for people with addictions and it's been tremendously successful.[72]

What accounts for the overcoming of these two major obstacles to agreement: obtaining great interagency cooperation and opposition to serving "undeserving" populations? Further, what explains the dramatic change of heart of Pataki, whose initial apparent lack of interest led to the disappointing New York/New York II Agreement, but who finally signed off on the much larger, breakthrough third agreement? The persistence of the advocacy community and its ability to maintain an effective lobbying operation over a long period of time are part of the answer. According to the Albany lobbyist for Coalition for the Homeless, Shelly Nortz, the push for New York/New York III

> [w]as mostly . . . a grass-roots, rabble-rousing campaign. . . . You do not win the big stuff up here without causing there to be discomfort on the part of the executives and the elected officials and the appointed officials. . . . There has to be media coverage. . . . We had people marching and rallying and candlelight vigils and holiday heartstrings kind of stuff going on. . . . There's a lot of public pressure that goes into getting a big thing done.[73]

Nortz also credits Pataki with shrewdly deploying a governing strategy well known to Albany insiders. The stinginess of New York/New York II gave way to the relative generosity of the third agreement because Pataki

> [d]id what every new governor does. He scooped lots of money into a pile that he was saving by cutting the budget. And in subsequent years as he ran for reelection he was able to spend that money on signature initiatives. That is a traditional game book for a governor. So when you run for the second time and you run for the third time you've got resources to respond to the needs that are coming your way but it's your signature, it's not somebody else's old program.

But also part of the answer was the process of policy learning. Two decades of the homelessness crisis convinced all parties of the stakes involved. Previous New York/New York agreements created a template to follow. Earlier success taught how to make the agreements work and emboldened participants to try for more. Research into Housing First efforts and Culhane's research into the cost effectiveness of supportive housing proved that populations traditionally considered unpromising could be successfully served at a savings to the public. Culhane's research, sponsored by the Corporation for Supportive Housing (CSH), was particularly influential. According to Connie Temple of CSH, commenting on the strength of the Culhane study,

> We were able then to advocate for New York/New York III. Everyone started quoting this. The government people would quote it. We infiltrated it into the thinking of the government so that when it came time to do New York/New York III they all said this makes sense because it saves money. We presented it everywhere. They knew it. . . . People tell me that New York/New York III would have never happened without the New York/New York I cost study that CSH commissioned.[74]

DHS took various steps toward incorporating another research-supported policy initiative, Housing First, into its operations, when, on April 11, 2006, Robert V. Hess became DHS commissioner, replacing Linda Gibbs, who was promoted to deputy mayor for health and human services. Before coming to New York City, Hess had been deputy managing director for Special Needs Housing in Philadelphia, where he developed that city's ten-year plan to end homelessness and its first Housing First programs for the chronically homeless. According to George Nashak, his deputy commissioner for adult services, Hess was "passionate about street homelessness," and early in his New York tenure moved to introduce the Housing First approach to outreach that, it was said, had reduced street homelessness in Philadelphia by 60 percent.[75]

At the time of Hess's arrival in New York City, outreach to street homeless people was highly fragmented and unconnected to housing access. According to Sam Tsemberis, the developer of the Housing First philosophy who was brought in by Hess to speak to street outreach providers, Hess eventually "took back all of those old outreach contracts, where they were handing out sandwiches and referral cards and he made outreach connected to housing so that outreach performance criteria were connected to, not how many people do you serve on the street, but how many people did you help get off the street."[76] George Nashak described this process as follows:

> We decided that we were going to re-engineer street outreach services in the city. And so in the past I would argue that street outreach services, yes, the ultimate goal was bringing people indoors, try to get them to come into shelter, but in fact what we ended up with was a patchwork of services that very often helped people remain on the street. The feeding programs and clothing programs made it more comfortable to be on the street. . . . We blew up the entire system; we ended all of the street outreach contracts and we reprocured all of that money towards four contracts. Each of those contracts had a specific geographical area they were responsible for: the Bronx . . . Manhattan. . . . Brooklyn and Queens, and then Staten Island. And one of the innovations was, first of all, that we had one provider, not a patchwork of providers responsible for that

> geographic area. So each of those providers had a geographic catchment area that they were responsible for. And we gave them specific contractual goals with monetary incentives to reduce the number of people living on the street in those boroughs. And this was a very, very successful program. And the place where it was most successful was in the Bronx, where we reduced the homelessness by two-thirds within a number of years.[77]

This blowing-up process took place in the summer of 2006 at separate meetings for front-line outreach workers and their supervisors, as Hess remembered:

> I spent . . . many, many nights on the streets of this city. Talking to people experiencing homelessness, talking to outreach workers, and so forth. And in a nutshell what we found is that we had a number of departments that have outreach contracts. There was no common data sharing, no real strategy other than talking people on the street into coming in to a shelter system that they had already kind of rejected by not going in.
>
> And so that seemed like . . . a failed strategy and so what I decided to do is hold a meeting, an invite breakfast at the . . . New York Law Association Building . . . and invited all outreach workers. The only ticket for admittance that morning was you had to be a line worker, no supervisors, no directors, executive directors, none of that, you had to be a line outreach worker. . . . Turns out that 150 to 160 outreach workers showed up.
>
> We said to them, by our last count there are forty-three hundred people living on the streets. We want to get that number down dramatically, we want to do that in the next two years, tell us how to do it. Tell us what works and what doesn't work, what we need to do to bring down the number of people living in the street very significantly in the city.
>
> And first they told us all the things that weren't working. We don't talk to each other, we don't share data. . . . And they said we don't really have any resources to offer people on the streets, that they will accept, other than shelter. We need another model of housing [to offer].
>
> So, we listened for about three hours, copied everything [we] could on flip charts, and sent them all to lunch. [We] organized their thoughts [into] what we thought the priority areas were while they were at lunch. . . . After lunch, [we] gave them the infamous four stickers and said go vote for the stuff that is most important to you.
>
> In the afternoon we also invited in their supervisors, their directors, their executive directors. And what we said to them [was a] . . . recap [of what happened in] the morning: this is what we heard. . . . We want to move [the]

> majority of people off the street into housing. . . . [C]urrent strategies aren't working, these are the reason it's not working, these are the things that [your] folks [say] we need to do.
>
> As I talked through things [with] them . . . [it] was clear to me that people didn't have an appreciation or understanding of the Housing First strategy. And so I asked Dr. Sam Tsemberis at Pathways [to Housing] to come in and . . . lay out the research on the Housing First priority strategy. . . .
>
> And after he did that . . . I said, "Folks, I heard what we need to do is radically different than what we're doing now, what we're doing now will not get us fewer people on the street. People on the street deserve to be able to move indoors. So here's what we're going to do. I'm going to terminate all your contracts. . . . It's going to take a year but we're going to have a procurement process that has one winner. One organization [will] win and be solely accountable for each borough of this city . . . to house people that are on the streets and you can have as many subcontractors as you want, they could be multidiscipline if you want, but you've got to figure out what the plan should be and we'll fund that plan and then monitor and hold you accountable all the way."
>
> We did that. But it took a year to procure it and initially of course there was a lot . . . of political pushback, but we got it done because the mayor stood behind us.[78]

By October 2007, the procurement process was complete and the many outreach providers had been reduced to only a few: in Manhattan, Goddard Riverside Community Center; in Brooklyn and Queens, Common Ground Community; in the Bronx, Citizens Advice Bureau (later renamed BronxWorks); and in Staten Island, Project Hospitality.

BronxWorks provides perhaps the most striking example of the impact of the Housing First strategy on the city's street population.

A key element of Housing First practice is to have some way of offering street people access to permanent housing—not emergency shelter—as quickly as possible and therefore without requiring the potential client to become "housing ready" through lengthy treatment. The administrative challenges of doing so are formidable. People living on the street often lack identification or a source of income, both indispensable prerequisites to placement in permanent housing. Since, by hypothesis, potential clients had rejected emergency shelter, moving them there temporarily while such matters are attended to is usually not an option. Moreover, when a street dweller, perhaps after a long process of coaxing, decides to accept an offer of housing, the move must be made almost immediately to forestall a change of mind.

But how could a street outreach worker make an on-the-spot commitment to placement in sometimes scarce permanent housing? What was needed was a new type of housing, something other than a shelter, where bureaucratic details could be resolved and that offered a credible commitment to a speedy permanent placement. The Safe Haven system was the answer.

The Safe Haven system was developed under Hess as a way of integrating Housing First philosophy into street outreach programs. Street people had made clear their distaste for what they saw as the regimented regimes of the traditional shelters, with their curfews and prohibitions on drug and alcohol use. Safe Havens represented a low-stress alternative for street people who had rejected the shelters.

In keeping with its Housing First philosophy, BronxWorks's pitch to street homeless people was not that they should first deal with whatever disability they had (and according to the organization's staff, all, not just most, of the street-dwelling homeless had some kind of disability) but that they should come in and get an apartment. However, clients did not go immediately from the street to a permanent apartment. Some preliminary steps had to be taken before they got permanent housing. These preliminary steps were not focused on addressing the client's disability but rather on resolving some bureaucratic issues that had to be dealt with in order for a homeless person to be eligible for permanent housing. These included getting a source of income and getting necessary identification. While these steps were being undertaken, clients stayed in Safe Haven housing, of which BronxWorks had about fifty units on-site. (Eventually about five hundred Safe Haven beds were opened throughout the city.) Each room held one person and was private except that the rooms had no ceiling, which feature, according to staff, was designed to prevent clients from feeling that the Safe Haven rooms were intended to be permanent. Another sort of short-term, holding-pattern residence was the stabilization beds, which was a type of SRO facility provided off-site from BronxWorks's main building. Once clients got their identification, income, and other bureaucratic concerns in order, they moved to permanent supportive housing.

The emphasis on moving clients to permanent housing was a big change for BronxWorks. The organization's assistant executive director, Scott Auwater, described the nature of the change:

> We used to go up to a guy that had a serious crack-cocaine problem that was chronically homeless on the street. Our pitch to him was, "Look, you've got to clean up. We have got to get you drug free. Once you're drug free [and] in a program, then we can move you into housing."

And that didn't go over very well with our guys. . . . They'd tell you, "Yeah, I'm going to think about that. Why don't you come back next week?" And we'd come back next week for a year and get nowhere. And that's what's changed. Our pitch to them now is . . . "Let's get you into an apartment. Let's get your housing application done." . . . And then, we move him into our stabilization beds. . . . [A] stabilization bed is . . . a no-frills place. . . . There's no staff on-site. There's no security on-site. It is, however, heated, with bathrooms. There's a place they can heat up a meal. . . . It's the least restrictive environment for a street homeless [person]. . . .

I guess . . . [the] difference between the Housing First model and [what we did] previously is that . . . all we [now] care about is getting housed. . . . We just think you need to be housed. And we work on mental illness and substance abuse issues when appropriate in the appropriate way. [But] that's not a requirement. . . . So the pitch is pretty simple, it's not judgmental. "You need a house. We'll get you a house."[79]

The new Housing First strategy was extraordinarily successful at reducing the number of street homeless in the Bronx and throughout the city. In 2005 the city conducted the first methodologically sophisticated, all-borough count of street dwellers, which was called HOPE, for Homeless Outreach Population Estimate. The base estimate for the Bronx was 480 homeless people on the streets, to which an additional 107 were added as part of a methodological check for overlooked street dwellers, which made for a total of 587 street dwellers in that borough. When the 2011 count found only 115 street homeless people in the Bronx, the 80 percent decline in street homelessness in the borough received wide attention and was trumpeted as proof of the effectiveness of the Housing First approach.[80] In the city as a whole, street homelessness declined by 40 percent between 2005 and 2011, seemingly further confirmation of the success of Housing First, which had been adopted by outreach providers in all boroughs. However, by 2014, the count had inched back up to 193 persons in the Bronx and 3,357 in the city as a whole, which represented still impressive declines since 2005 of 67 percent and 24 percent, respectively.[81]

Successfully implementing the Housing First strategy required developing a very decentralized way of distributing Safe Haven accommodations. George Nashak explained how this major bureaucratic restructuring was accomplished:

Very often resources are deployed by government in a fairly centralized way with lots of eligibility criteria and lots of top-down kind of stuff. What we did is when we implemented the Safe Haven model . . . we said who amongst us

> is in the best position to decide when someone is going to move into housing. There's this sort of anecdotal belief, and as a street outreach worker myself . . . I believe this to be absolutely true, that with people who are living on the street you end up with . . . you end up with these little windows of opportunity to move someone indoors. You know, you work with somebody for six months or nine months [who says] no, no, no, no, no, no, no, and then some window opens and they say, today, all right. If you can do something in the next few hours, I'll take you up on it. . . . This is a well-established phenomenon. We said, OK, how do we deal with that? If I had a system where you needed five bureaucrats at DHS to make the decision to move [a street dweller] into a safe haven tonight, when my window opened for those three hours, I'm going to lose the opportunity. So what we did was we deployed Safe Havens in such a way that we put, metaphorically at least, the keys to the safe havens in the pockets of the outreach workers. . . . So the outreach workers made the decision who moved into the safe haven that night. . . . It challenged the Michael Lipsky *Street-Level Bureaucracy* story, where the street-level people were making the policy, changing the policy that was developed in the halls of government. And here we're actually asking them to do so. . . . No bureaucrat at DHS, including myself, and I was running the system, there was no bureaucrat at DHS who made a decision about a Safe Haven. It was all in the hands of the outreach workers.

Meanwhile, on November 14, 2007, Justice Freedman greatly aggravated the city when, instead of acting on the city's request to dismiss the *McCain*, *Lamboy*, *Slade*, and *Cosentino* cases, she appointed a new Special Master Panel. The circumstances of this decision highlight some basic realities of how difficult it is to make decisions in a social service context, and of how difficult it can be for courts to interpret social science analysis. As was mentioned above, state administrative directive 05-ADM-07 allowed the city to deny shelter to reapplicants for ninety days after a family was denied shelter unless the family could demonstrate that there was a change in their circumstances. There was, however, a way that a family in that ninety-day period could get shelter. Such a family could attempt to demonstrate that it had an "immediate need," and if the family applied for shelter at PATH after 5:00 p.m., it was entitled to "late arrival placement" for one night. By October 2007, the city believed that some families were taking advantage of this provision and decided that late-arrival families seeking immediate-need shelter and who were still within the ninety-day period would no longer be granted one night of shelter. The plaintiffs believed that there were systemic errors in the eligibility process for immediate-need families, and for applicant families in general, and moved to enjoin the city to remedy those errors. The plaintiffs submitted thirty-nine case histories of families who had been denied shelter, sometimes several times, only to be eventually found eligible; the city responded to those case histories. A summary of one such point-counterpoint provides a sense of the challenges of eligibility determination:

> In the case of I.L., plaintiffs allege that she was rejected on four separate occasions for "immediate needs" shelter on the ground that the family, consisting of a mother and children, could live with I.L.'s "abusive father." However, DHS contends that it was not until her fourth application and after a State Administrative hearing that she disclosed her "sensitive history of abuse." Ms. I.L., who is apparently illiterate, claims to have told PATH workers, and been referred to ACS, that her father physically and verbally abused her children, but DHS contends that Ms. I.L. abandoned her first application, changed her story several times, did not cooperate by refusing to tell where her fifteen year old son, who had been with her the day before, was, and refused to tell the PATH workers where her father was. It was also not until her fourth application that Ms. I.L. described the abusive behavior and not until the State Administrative hearing that DHS agreed to refer Ms I.L. to NOVA. (NOVA is a program that helps victims of domestic violence.) When NOVA precluded her father's home, she was found eligible. The Court notes that Ms. I.L. was referred to ACS early on, but relevant information was not obtained at that point.[82]

This and similar complex cases raised the questions, How accurate was the eligibility-determination process at PATH; how many families endured multiple rejections only to finally be accepted without any change in their circumstances; and was the eligibility-determining process getting more or less accurate over the time period in question, 2005–2006? Both sides engaged experts to analyze the available data. The plaintiffs relied on one David B. Monk, a business consultant with an M.S. degree in statistical science. The city worked with John Mollenkopf, distinguished professor in the Political Science and Sociology Departments of the Graduate School of the City University of New York.

The result was a complex set of claims and critiques that the court seemed unable to evaluate on its own. The court claimed that "interestingly, the experts, Monk and Mollenkopf, reach similar conclusions. . . . Both found that the percentage of reversed determinations increased, not insignificantly, from 2005 to 2006,"[83] even though they differed on fundamental methodological points. Nor was it correct that both experts found a significant increase in the reversed determinations from 2005 to 2006. For his part, Mollenkopf found that "[i]f one looks only at what happened to those families deemed ineligible because they were found to have other housing available, meaning a determination by DHS that the family had a housing option, the comparable rates of change were 4.3% in 2005 and 4.7% in 2006, *i.e.*, a minor difference."[84]

After all the expert analysis and the picking-over of the thirty-nine case histories, Justice Freedman could not see a bottom line. As to the effectiveness of PATH's eligibility determination process, Freedman held that "[t]here must be objective facts that would support a proper determination of the dispute. While hearings might resolve the dispute, they would be polarizing, they would probably repeat the allegations in the affidavits, and they would be costly to all parties." Thus, rather than get to those objective facts, Freedman appointed three distinguished lawyers as a new set of "short-term temporary Special Masters," who were to "engage in a limited investigation as to what actually happened that caused or causes the allegedly erroneous denials on first or subsequent applications."[85] Why a limited investigation by three eminent jurists who were nonetheless nonexperts in social science analysis would provide any more insight into this matter than the already extensive investigation had produced was not clear. But in any case, the *McCain* case and related litigation now had a third set of special masters.

The city was aghast that Justice Freedman had created what it characterized as "yet another" special master panel.[86] The judge's credibility with the city was not advanced by the fact that one member of the new panel, Alexander Forger, in the course of a long and distinguished legal career, had served for seventeen years as a director of the plaintiff group, that is, of the Legal Aid Society.[87] On November 20, 2007, the city filed a motion that castigated Judge Freedman for not acting on its motion to end court oversight of the shelter system.

Meanwhile, Legal Aid had been responding to what it saw as the highly destructive 2005 recommendation of the Feerick-Nayowith-Kronenfeld SMP and developing evidence for the court that it should retain its oversight of the shelter system. According to Steven Banks, after the 2005 recommendation,

> [We] took three long years of depositions, thousands of pages, and our papers were going to be due in the middle of September of 2008. And those papers would rebut the city's claims [of progress]. . . . We had extensive evidence that we had taken from the depositions of deplorable conditions, of improper denials of shelter, and it would make the case that we should on paper get a permanent order requiring the provision of shelter and a permanent order saying if shelter is habitable and if the court felt there was a dispute we would be entitled to a trial and we would be marshaling evidence and putting forth evidence.[88]

The stage was thus set for an extraordinary courtroom confrontation in September of 2008. The few weeks before then represented, Banks thought, "the last clear chance before this entire case [was] going to become an explosive issue."[89]

Then, in July, Justice Freedman was promoted by Governor Paterson to fill a vacancy in the Appellate Division, First Judicial Department, in Manhattan. Events then began to develop rapidly. On September 17 a breakthrough was achieved. As Michael Cardozo, the city's corporation counsel, put the matter, "on the very day plaintiffs' responsive papers were due, the parties reached a settlement that brought to an end the twenty-five years of court oversight of the city's family shelter services system."[90] Steven Banks concurred on the suddenness with which resolution was reached. Agreement, he said, was possible "only today" once the city acknowledged its "legal obligation" to provide shelter and accepted a "legal framework to protect families in the future no matter who the mayor is."[91]

Cynics immediately concluded that Banks had hastily resolved the litigation when he saw that he would no longer be dealing with the sympathetic Justice Freedman. In good tabloid fashion the *Daily News* shouted, "Bang the gong! The longest, costliest, most damaging exercise in self-indulgent judicial overreaching is coming to an end after almost a quarter-century on the court docket. . . . Gov. Paterson promoted Freedman to a higher court. And, all of a sudden, with the case headed to a new judge, Legal Aid's indomitable Steven Banks agreed to a settlement."[92]

Banks denied this charge and believed that it was the city that was most discomforted by Justice Freedman's departure:

> Actually I think . . . the pressure was on the city from that change. Because the city had spent several years, particularly intensified from the moment of the special master announcement, vilifying her [Justice Freedman] mercilessly and unfairly. . . . So the city consciously was battering away at the judge . . . for three years. And getting her ready for the moment when now she was going to be asked to vacate all these orders after brutally beating her up publicly for a number of years. And then she's gone. . . . And so from a city perspective, they no longer had the . . . judge who they had been attacking [and] was going to be asked to vacate a series of court orders. . . . And from our perspective, the facts are the facts, the law is the law. The appellate law was very clear. Whoever heard this was going to have to confront the fact that if men and women had a right to shelter, children should too, and if men and women were entitled to shelter that met basic standards, children were too. And so we felt very strongly about this that we would prevail no matter who the judge was. Ultimately something

> changed because the city had said they would never settle this case with a permanent order. And they did. And they did.[93]

Banks is correct to note that in the 2008 resolution the city acknowledged, as it never had before, "a right to shelter for families who had no other place to go . . . and that the conditions of shelter would have to meet basic standards of habitability."[94] For the final agreement provided that

> [e]ligible homeless families with children, defined as families with children who lack alternate housing, and families with children seeking shelter who, pending the City's eligibility determination for shelter pursuant to applicable local and/or State law, codes, regulations, and agency guidances ("applicable law"), are entitled to emergency shelter and the City shall not deny shelter to such families. . . . The City shall provide shelter facilities for families with children that are safe, sanitary and decent as defined by applicable law.[95]

Banks observes that the settlement with the city was reached just before Bloomberg announced he would seek a third term and speculates that the mayor may have been motivated to settle in order to keep embarrassing evidence of the continuing shortcomings in city homelessness policy out of the courts and media. It may also be that Bloomberg wanted to be able, in his upcoming campaign, to claim credit for resolving a major problem that had bedeviled the previous three mayors.

In any case, though Legal Aid retained the right to commence new litigation if the city failed to live up to the final agreement, it has not done so. So the Bloomberg administration achieved its long-time desire to get out from under the supposedly stultifying court oversight. What was the record of the newly liberated DHS after the final court settlement?

The much-touted Home Base program, a key part of the city's efforts to reform DHS by reemphasizing prevention, continued to develop. In 2007 the program expanded citywide to all five boroughs and fifty-nine community districts. But was the program working? In 2008, the Independent Budget Office, in a review of the city's prevention efforts, noted that "[w]hile the city is undertaking many strategies to prevent homelessness, including the Home Base program . . . little is known about their overall effectiveness."[96] In 2009 the *Mayor's Management Report* trumpeted that the program was a "highly successful model" based on the fact that by 2007, 91.7 percent of families who worked with Home Base did not enter the shelter system within eighteen months of enrollment.[97] As the administration probably understood, this claim was question begging because without a control group it was not known what percentage of similar families that did *not* receive services would have avoided the shelter system. A scientific evaluation of Home Base was therefore necessary.

Beginning in 2008, in keeping with the administration's data-driven management style, DHS engaged Abt Associates and the City University of New York and the subcontractor University of the Sciences to conduct a scientific evaluation of the program's effectiveness. This involved recruiting Home Base applicants who would form both a test group and a control group. From June through September of 2010 the researchers recruited from program applicants 295 families with at least one child; 150 families became the treatment group and 145 were assigned to the control group. Through December 2012 the families' use of the homelessness system, other housing programs, and a range of services, including TANF, SNAP, child welfare programs, and HRA emergency financial assistance, was tracked. The total cost of the evaluation was $577,000.[98]

In September 2010, the evaluation ran into a snag. On September 30, the *New York Daily News* ran an article on the evaluation of Home Base entitled, "City's Cruel Test for Poor Families: 200 Denied Aid Are Being Treated like 'Rats in a Lab Experiment.'"[99] The focus of the article was concern for the families randomly assigned to the control group, who, unlike the treatment group, received no services from Home Base, but who were given a list of other city agencies they could receive help from. Many city officials were appalled. Scott Stringer, the Manhattan borough president, shot off an announcement in which he thundered,

> The New York families who approached the Home Base Program, in desperate need of assistance, were placed in this bone-headed experiment for 18–24 months. And what's worse is that it has been funded with federal stimulus dollars, money that should be used to help people, not humiliate them. Homeless families are not statistics. Nor should they be targets for bureaucratic tinkering. This is the kind of barbaric approach to dealing with poverty that fell out of favor years ago. It is disheartening to see it alive and well in New York City today.[100]

City Council members were also shocked. Councilwoman Melissa Mark-Viverito remarked, "Just when you think you've heard it all. It's inhumane. How cold-hearted and callous." Councilwoman Gale Brewer said, "It's bizarre. It's like they're being cast to the wind."[101] Even as sophisticated an analyst as

Patrick Markee of the Coalition for the Homeless commented, "These are real parents and children, not rats in a lab experiment."[102]

On December 9, 2010, City Council hearings on the experiment did not go well for the investigators. The senior researcher for Abt, Howard Rolston, provoked an audible murmur from the packed hearing when, in explaining the idea of a control group, he noted that "[y]ou can opt out of the research, but you can't opt into the services."[103] Despite the furor, the evaluation went through to completion, with Bloomberg defending this example of his data-driven decision-making process with a characteristically terse statement: "In the end, we are only going to spend money on things that work, so we have to find out what works."[104]

Final results of the evaluation were available in June 2013. The study found that the treatment group spent on average 22.6 fewer nights in the shelters than control group families (9.6 nights versus 32.2 nights). The treatment group was 6.5 percentage points less likely to spend at least one night in the shelters (8.0 percent versus 14.5 percent). And families in the treatment group were 8.9 percentage points less likely to apply for shelter than control group families (9.3 percent versus 18.2 percent).[105] All of these results were statistically significant at the p=.10 level. (See table 5.2.) Home Base also turned out to pay for itself, with each family served by the program costing $140 less than the shelter services that would have been provided in the absence of the program.[106]

TABLE 5.2: Shelter Outcomes of Home Base Program

Treatment Outcome	Control Group Average	Treatment Group Average	Effect of Program	90% Confidence Interval for Effect of Program	p value
Nights in Shelter	9.6	32.2	-22.6	[-41.7, -3.4]	p=.03**
Spent at least one night in shelter	8.0%	14.5%	-6.5 percentage points	[-12.8, -.002] percentage points	p=.04**
Ever applied for shelter	9.3%	18.2%	-8.9 percentage points	[-15.9, -2.0] percentage points	p=.02**

Note: The regression-adjusted control group is equal to the unadjusted treatment group average minus the regression-based estimate.

**Impact estimate is significantly different from zero at the .10 level using a one-tailed test.

Source: Abt Associates, *Final Report: Evaluation of the Homebase Community Prevention Program*, June 6, 2013, table 1, p. 13.

Thus the much-touted effort to refocus DHS on prevention ended up bearing fruit. But, as we shall see, in the face of the policy of ending subsidies and preferences for shelter clients, prevention did not forestall the worsening of the homelessness crisis.

Another major development after the 2008 settlement came on May 3, 2011, when the new PATH building, begun in October 2007, began serving clients. Located at 151 East 151th Street, Bronx, the PATH center stands on the footprint of the old EAU building, which was demolished to make way for the new structure. While the old EAU building was described as "squat and terminally dreary,"[107] the new building has been described as "a gleaming modern building . . . with artwork on the walls and an airport-like 'departure lounge.'"[108] The edifice looks like a high-tech wedge and features a terra cotta façade with zinc and metal trim. The building was completed for $65.5 million.[109] The center is managed by Associate Commissioner Rebecca Chew. Asked to describe the management challenges of running PATH, Chew quoted a former deputy commissioner for family services, Roger Newman, as saying that "running PATH is like trying to put socks on an octopus." She explained,

> PATH is intake. It is that initial triaging and figuring out what is this family's degree of crisis that we're looking to stabilize. So it's that initial intake process. [Then] you've got all the collaboration with the sister agencies. You've got HRA and our liaising with them and ensuring that clients are given the right amount of services and that . . . [HRA] understands our processes as much as we understand their processes to help manage client expectation. You've got that whole piece of collaboration with all the agencies. You've got the whole investigation piece, the interview piece, all the family workers who are doing all the in-depth interviews. And then you've got our separate hub of investigators to oversee in the different boroughs . . . [who] are co-located in certain shelters. . . . Then you have the transportation piece, when families are ready to go to [the] shelters, and also interfacing with HERO [Housing Emergency Referral Operations], the vacancy control folks, and getting that information together and managing . . . that client and where they're going to go. And that's rapid fire, nonstop. . . . Yes, lots of tentacles. It's sort of like an ER.[110]

The city had invested considerable resources to make this necessarily active environment manageable. One source of constant confusion and noise at the old EAU was the "pass system." The object of this system was to prevent clients from missing school or work while waiting through the eligibility-determination system, which could take up to twenty hours. Passes therefore had to be issued to anyone who needed to leave the building to get food, or go to school or work. This would stretch out the application process and generate confusion as away clients would not be there to hear their turn called. PATH now uses an automated Q-matic customer flow management system, similar to those used at airports. Digital message boards now indicate whose turn it is so that names do not have to be called out.

When they enter the building, clients go to a window to register. They are given a welcome packet containing toiletries and other items and the worker, called a community associate, gathers basic information. All data gathered are entered into the Client Assessment and Rehousing Enterprise System (CARES), which is the department's on-line case management system. Families that have suffered domestic violence are immediately referred to a NOVA (No Violence Again) worker who contacts the HRA domestic violence shelter system to see if a space is available. Families with a member who has medical problems are sent to an on-site medical staff that is available seven days a week.

All other families go on to the diversion operation, which occupies the entire second floor. Diversion workers explore with families options other than shelter. Alternatives can include anti-eviction legal services, resolving issues with the family's public assistance case, or getting access to public assistance subsidies that the family might not be aware of, and resolving issues with a primary tenant.

Families who are not diverted are sent to a family worker who conducts a program interview. The family's housing history for the last two years is developed. According to Chew,

> We interview every adult separately. So we are getting the names of the people with whom they resided . . . the primary tenants, the number of rooms in that location, which rooms were used for sleeping, where everyone slept, their relationship to the primary tenant, their reason for leaving, whether it was their own apartment. There . . . [is] another series of questions about . . . how much was rent, the landlord's number . . . if they owed rent, how much rent . . . phone numbers, contact information, we get their emergency contact person's information. . . . We also have a worker-connected portal that links to other health and human services agencies recruiting . . . and the HRA documenting depository. [The] technology is hugely impressive. If you think about the light years from the old EAU to today's world, it's pretty phenomenal.

Family workers deal with the family on their first day at the facility. Typically that visit takes about six hours. The department aims at determining eligibility within ten days. During that time families are given a conditional shelter placement and the case is passed on to a team leader who coordinates a field investigation to determine eligibility. Chew described that process:

> Based on the information given by the family, we also have a team of field investigators . . . who go out in pairs and . . . visit homes, knock on the doors. They have handheld computer devices that sync up to CARES. So when we are submitting our request for a field investigation because there is, say, [an allegation of] overcrowding or unsafe conditions, our field investigators . . . get all the requests. And then we geo-code it based on the location and that's how we distribute the work to the investigators, and also based on priority. We've self-imposed on ourselves a ten-day time frame to complete and render a final eligibility determination. So we prioritize work based on what's coming closest to the tenth day.
>
> So the investigators will go out and ask the tenant a series of questions. And they're not arriving [without notice]. We also ask the client when the best date and time are to visit [and] for any language issues so we can set up a language line service system. . . . So during the field investigation we're asking, similar to what we ask the client, how long did the client live there, why did they leave, what's the relation to the client's family, where did everyone sleep? We ask to tour the premises to see if there are any health or safety hazards and note all of our findings [which are] . . . then synced back into CARES.[111]

Final eligibility determination is based on state regulations, court orders, and final judgment in the *McCain* litigation. If the family is found eligible, the team leader submits a shelter assignment request to HERO, which is located in the department's central office in Manhattan, and which determines exactly what shelter opening the family will receive. No one stays at PATH or sleeps in its halls. PATH provides transportation to the site.

Approximately 34 percent of applicant families are found eligible and receive shelter. Twenty-four percent are found ineligible. The rest are either diverted to a shelter alternative or fail to complete the eligibility process. As was discussed earlier, clients who are found ineligible are referred to the Resource Room. Ineligible families can request a legal conference, during which on-site department lawyers will review their case, or a fair hearing, where the review is done by lawyers who do not work for the city. Families found ineligible can reapply for shelter as often as they like, but within ninety days of their first application will not get shelter unless they can demonstrate that their circumstances have changed.

The opening of the new PATH building and the documented success of the Home Base program were important successes for the Bloomberg administration. Unfortunately, not all of the administration's initiatives worked out. A major disappointment was that the mayor's 2004 pledge to reduce the city's shelter population of 36,000 by two-thirds by 2009 was not achieved. In February 2009 the total shelter census was still 36,298.[112] The year 2004 was also the point when, with great fanfare, the city abandoned the practice of giving shelter families a priority for Section 8 vouchers and public housing (i.e., units in the New York City Housing Authority, or NYCHA). Instead, shelter families were eligible for Housing Stability Plus (HSP), which began by providing a monthly rent subsidy of about $925 a month for a family of three for five years, but with the subsidy declining by 20 percent each year. Families had to be enrolled in Public Assistance and to have been in the shelter system for at least ninety days to be eligible for HSP. Part of the justification for the switch from Section 8 vouchers and NYCHA placements to HSP was that the lure of receiving these subsidies was creating a perverse incentive for families to move into the shelter system and become eligible for them. HSP, with its time limit of five years and its declining subsidy schedule, was supposed to be much less of an incentive.

HSP was seen as being a reform analogous to the 1996 reform of federal welfare, which placed a five-year lifetime limit on welfare receipt and therefore supposedly discouraged dependency. As the Manhattan Institute's housing analyst Howard Husock put the matter, "[T]his so-called Housing Stability Plus program would carry a five-year time limit, with the subsidy declining 20% every year from the outset until it hits zero. This is the first proposal for a major new housing program in New York that includes a time limit, similar to the one that has been attached to cash public assistance since welfare reform passed in 1996."[113] So the perverse incentive was supposed to be mitigated, which, in theory, ought to reduce demand for shelter. Thus, according to Husock, "we can now expect the surge of those entering the city's shelter system to slow, as the message goes out that the Section 8 pot of gold is now empty."[114]

Things didn't work out as planned. One problem was the poor quality of some of the apartments into which families were placed under HSP. In 2007 Coalition for the Homeless documented the deficiencies of many of the units that received HSP clients, as follows:

> Two of every five HSP families—1,136 families—were placed by the City into buildings that have at least two or three hazardous violations per apartment (depending on building size), as documented by City housing inspectors. . . . One of every five HSP families was placed into an apartment with five or more

hazardous violations per apartment. . . . Half of HSP families in Brooklyn and 40 percent of all families receiving HSP in the Bronx were placed in buildings with more than two or three hazardous violations per apartment (depending on building size).

Violations documented in HSP buildings include lead paint hazards, broken windows, collapsed ceilings and floors, non-working appliances and fixtures, as well as a lack of heat, hot water, and electricity.[115]

Another problem was the requirement that HSP families remain on public assistance. The idea was that HSP would add to the rental supplement that welfare families received as part of their welfare grant. But staying on welfare meant keeping one's income low enough to remain eligible, which was a work disincentive. Then-councilman Bill de Blasio called attention to one family that got caught up in this dilemma:

Councilman Bill de Blasio . . . cited the handling of the case of Lisa W. Hendley, 26, as an example. . . . Ms. Hendley and her daughter, now 5, moved into a one-bedroom apartment in the Bronx in February 2005 after living in a shelter for victims of domestic violence. Ms. Hendley, a high school graduate, found an $8-an-hour job packaging groceries for Fresh Direct, the online grocery delivery service, in June 2005. But she said she quit the job after a Department of Homeless Services caseworker told her that she could not continue to work and receive the rental assistance.[116]

The *Times*, in March 2007, reported another such case, that of

Jennifer Robertson, 29, who was homeless for more than a year starting in 2003. She was a graduate of George Washington University and making $15 an hour as a FedEx courier, but that wasn't enough to cover her student loans, support her two children and pay her rent of more than $500 a month.

The staff at the shelter where she stayed, she said, told her that the only help they could offer was Housing Stability Plus, but that she earned too much to qualify. So in March 2005, Ms. Robertson quit her job, took the $925-a-month allowance and found a one-bedroom apartment in Far Rockaway, Queens. . . . In December 2005, the city notified Ms. Robertson—who had started work again, this time as a cargo handler at Kennedy Airport—that she was earning too much to keep the housing subsidy, and it was cut off. She disputed the action in a hearing and won, but, she said, the city still did not pay her rent for 11 of the next 13 months, and she has received numerous eviction notices.

> "It is crazy how they don't want you to work," she said. "All I want is a little help with the rent. I'll take care of everything else. But no, it can't be like that."[117]

The welfare requirement also meant that any disruption in welfare receipt would end eligibility for HSP, and remaining a client in good standing was not always an easy feat, considering the bureaucracy that a family had to negotiate. This problem turned out to be much larger than DHS had anticipated. Robert Hess noted that while the city had anticipated that disruptions in welfare might affect as many as 20 percent of client families, in fact 65 percent had been affected.[118]

By 2007 the city realized it had a problem. Little progress had been made on the mayor's pledge to reduce homelessness by two-thirds by 2009. The shelter census in March 2007 was 35,208 people, just a hair lower than it had been when the pledge had been made in June 2004.[119] Apparently the end of the priorities for Section 8 vouchers and NYCHA placements, and their replacement with HSP, was not driving down the census. Rather than restoring the priorities, the administration decided that the problem was HSP and that a new form of subsidy was needed. Commissioner Hess held a meeting with shelter providers in March 2007 in which he acknowledged problems with HSP and announced his plan for a new program. The *Times* reported,

> Several people who attended Mr. Hess's meeting with nonprofit housing agencies last week said the commissioner proposed eliminating the 20 percent annual decrease in the Housing Stability Plus vouchers and the requirement that families must be on welfare.
>
> However, because the city wants to discourage long-term dependence on the subsidy, it will limit the vouchers to two years, a move opposed by advocates for the homeless.[120]

Thus was born the Advantage program, officially announced in April 2007. Key features of Advantage were that it was a one-year subsidy with a second year extension available to certain clients; it did not require receipt of public assistance; like HSP it was available to families only after they had been in the shelter system for at least ninety days; participants were required to be employed; to deal with concerns about housing quality, apartments rented by participants would be subject to Section 8–level inspections; and it involved a savings subsidy program in which the city matched savings made by the client.[121]

Like HSP before it, Advantage was conceived of by the Bloomberg administration as an example of an important reform it had been able to achieve once DHS overcame the "culture of caution" that years of being subject to court supervision had encouraged. Thus, according to Commissioner Hess,

> HSP . . . didn't help families move out to shelter quickly enough for a variety of reasons. And so we ended that program and started the Work Advantage Program and I think that . . . sent a message to our staff that it was OK . . . [to] be creative and to think differently and to say that if something wasn't working, then do something else.[122]

June 2009 marked the end of the five-year period during which the Bloomberg administration had striven to reduce the shelter population by two-thirds. Unfortunately, the number of shelter residents in June 2009—36,329 people—was virtually unchanged from what it had been in June 2004—36,399 people.[123] In a 2008 progress report on Bloomberg's plan, *Uniting for Solutions beyond Shelter*, the administration had taken note that the shelter census of June 2008 was about 9 percent lower than it had been in June 2004, but no note was taken when a year later the census was back up to where it had been.[124]

Rather than rethink its policy of not granting Section 8 vouchers or NYCHA placements to shelter families, the administration stuck with the Advantage program, to which it made some adjustments in July 2010. Now, families would be eligible for the program after only sixty days in the shelters rather than ninety; the work requirement was strengthened, with first-year clients now being required to work at least twenty hours a week and participate in an additional fifteen hours of work-related activities or housing searches and second-year clients being required to work at least thirty-five hours a week.[125] Previously, Advantage families typically paid about fifty dollars a month in rent. In the revised program families had to pay 30 percent of their income during the first year of the program, and in the second year they would pay 50 percent of the total rent.[126]

Advantage continued to be criticized on several fronts. In July 2010, an audit by the city comptroller found that the program was poorly administered, with responsible DHS workers often being misinformed about the terms of the program. The audit also showed that many Advantage tenants, to secure an apartment, had to enter into a side deal with the landlord and make extra rent payments beyond what was indicated in the lease.[127] In February 2011 the Coalition for the Homeless reported that 25 percent of Advantage families who did not receive another rent subsidy when the program's term ran out ended up back in the shelter system. (The coalition's percentage used the total number of families who began the program as a baseline. The city pointed out that if the baseline were the number of families who completed the two-year program, the return rate was 10 percent.[128] Patrick Markee, the coalition's senior policy analyst, remarked, "The fact that they're only counting people who completed the program is like a high school that says, '100 percent of our students graduate from high school, but we're only talking about students who make it up to senior year.'")[129] The coalition argued that Advantage was an inherently flawed program and that the administration should reinstate the policy of directing available Section 8 vouchers and NYCHA units to homeless families.[130]

Advantage ran into a crisis, not because of these criticisms but as a result of a falling out between the city and the state over funding of the program. Governor Andrew Cuomo's proposed 2011–2012 budget eliminated state funding for Advantage. Exactly what the budget numbers said was a matter of dispute. The city claimed that the total annual cost of Advantage was $140 million; the state said the cost was $103 million. The city said its share of the cost was $48 million, with the rest coming from the federal government and the state. Federal help would be lost with the end of state funding, which, according to the city, would result in a total loss to the city of $92 million; the state calculated that the total loss to the city would be $68 million.[131] In any case, the state did end its funding and along with it went federal funding. The question then was what to do next.

The advocates argued that the loss of funding represented an opportune time to end what they saw as the flawed Advantage program and return to the policy of supplying homeless families with Section 8 vouchers and NYCHA units. Thus the Coalition for the Homeless argued that "Governor Cuomo's 2011–2012 budget proposes eliminating State funding for the Advantage program, offering City and State officials the chance to abandon the flawed program and replace it with a better, more cost-effective alternative: Targeting proven Federal housing assistance to homeless families."[132]

The city disagreed. Seth Diamond, commissioner of DHS after April 2010, argued as follows:

> Nowhere is this need for new debate more clear than in the discussion of how to help homeless families move out of shelter. Here the city has attempted to make up for a lack of state and federal support by putting in place innovative programs that invest in the success of homeless families who work and leave the shelter system, the most recent of these being the Advantage rental supplement. At every turn, our attempt to discuss and support these programs was met with one refrain—no program is acceptable unless it awards Section 8 vouchers or NYHCA housing to those in shelter. It doesn't matter that the city's program

is the most generous municipal subsidy in the country, far exceeding what is available elsewhere. It doesn't matter that the city adjusted the subsidy to better meet the needs of families and developed one that was far more costly for city taxpayers than prior subsidies, but better supported those in shelter who wanted to work and grow their income. It doesn't matter that nearly nine out of ten families who exited shelter on Advantage succeeded in remaining stably housed or that even by the most conservative measure, seven out of ten families succeeded in doing so. The response of some was not a measured inquiry about how to fashion a better subsidy that recognizes present-day realities, but a reflexive call to end the local subsidy immediately and award Section 8.[133]

In March 2011, DHS sent a letter to the housing brokers who connected shelter families with landlords, notifying them that it would no longer conduct lease signings under the Advantage program. Thus no new families would be added to the program. The department also announced its determination to end Advantage entirely by April 1, and letters were sent to some fifteen thousand families and individuals indicating that their rent would no longer be subsidized by the program. Throughout March and April all forms of news media were filled with stories about the coming demise of Advantage.[134]

The reason why the city ended Advantage was that the state ended its funding of the program. When the program was gone, some administration officials offered justifications for its demise. At the beginning of June, the *Times* ran a front-page article that suggested that the perversity argument was still on the minds of Bloomberg administration policymakers. The story, entitled "City Sees End to Rental Aid for Homeless," ran, in part, as follows:

With New York City's shelter population near all-time highs, the Bloomberg administration is on the verge of ending its signature housing program for homeless families, saying the program's generosity might have contributed to the problem.

The program, called Advantage, started in 2007 and offers subsidies for up to two years to help people in shelters afford their own apartments, provided they work or take part in job training. But several months ago, the administration warned that if the state followed through with its plan to stop its financial support, the city could not afford to maintain the program and would cut off aid even to those already participating.

After those warnings, the number of applicants to enter shelters dropped by 17 percent, evidence, the city said, that the program might have enticed some people to leave their homes for the promise of the subsidy.

> "You never know what motivates people," Mayor Michael R. Bloomberg said during a recent radio show. "One theory is that some people have been coming into the homeless system, the shelter system, in order to qualify for a program that helps you move out of the homeless system." . . .
>
> When questioned about the figures, the department acknowledged that the decline could be partly a result of seasonal variations. But normal fluctuations could not explain all of the drop, officials said. "Those are the people who were coming in maybe because of the subsidy," said Seth Diamond, the homeless services commissioner.[135]

Perhaps Bloomberg administration actors believed that the perverse incentives of subsidies were so strong that they continued to operate even when the Section 8 and NYCHA priorities had been replaced with the time-limited, work-enforcing Advantage program. In any case, a situation in which there were finally absolutely no subsidies to aid families in leaving the shelter system developed on the Bloomberg administration's watch.

By the end of March 2011, the Legal Aid Society won a temporary restraining order from Supreme Court Justice Judith J. Gische that barred the city from ending rent subsidy payments under the Advantage program until the expiration of the tenants' leases or until further court orders.

The city appealed, and on February 21, 2012, a state appellate court ruled that the city was not required to continue paying the rent of Advantage tenants. Legal Aid had argued that the city had to continue paying rent because the city in effect had a contract with Advantage landlords. But the court found that the contract was between, not the city and the landlords but the tenants and the landlords. Thus Advantage came to an end, and there were now no housing subsidies to aid families in exiting the shelter system.

The reported drop in applications to the shelter system turned out to be a blip, with the number of individuals sheltered going up almost steadily throughout the remainder of Bloomberg's term. In November of 2013, the number of individuals in the shelter system was at a record high, 53,270 persons.[136]

The Bloomberg administration's homelessness policy presents a frustrating case history. With great fanfare the new mayor tried to usher in a new policy paradigm, one that emphasized preventing and ending homelessness rather than accepting and managing it. Also innovative was the strongest emphasis on supportive housing of any administration yet and the embrace of Housing First. Together these new initiatives might be termed the post-paternalistic moment of homelessness policy. This approach is founded on the most sophisticated and validated policy research on homelessness so far. Yet homelessness rose to new heights under Bloomberg. Part of the answer to this paradox may be that while he embraced certain features of post-paternalism, Bloomberg clung to the paternalistic fear of perverse incentives and ended the preferential access of homeless families to Section 8 vouchers and public housing. The ending of the Advantage subsidy program turned out to be a disaster, for which it is hard to apportion responsibility between the city and the state. An interview I conducted in 2011 with Richard Motta, president and CEO of Volunteers of America, which operated family shelters in the city, suggests both how much the Bloomberg administration tried to change the paradigm of homelessness policy from paternalism to post-paternalism and the problem with ending subsidies. According to Motta, homelessness policy changed under Bloomberg in that

> [t]wenty years ago when a family came into shelter the first question you . . . would ask is why you're here, what's the underlying reason for your homelessness? And . . . the motivation was to try and solve that underlying reason. It was substance abuse. It was lack of income. It was lack of education. And then twenty years ago, you would try and put that family into a community program that solved the underlying problem that was causing homelessness.
>
> Today . . . the first question we ask them is, let's get an exit strategy for you. Where are you going? So it's a Housing First approach. . . . The whole dynamic has changed over the last five years. The Department of Homeless Services is really going to a Housing First model. The discussion is mainly how can we get you housed, not why are you homeless?[137]

The Bloomberg administration had successfully communicated to the shelter providers that policy was moving away from a paternalistic, underlying-cause model and embracing the post-paternalistic Housing First model. But if the main question, from the first day a family enters shelter, is to be "how can we get you housed?" what sense does it make to end the subsidies that offered the best prospect of in fact getting that housing? The answer that this author and others offered during the Dinkins administration and later was that subsidies of various sorts would unleash perverse incentives, but that argument had been rebutted by Cragg and O'Flaherty's analysis of the Dinkins deluge, and was further undermined when the shelter census rose to historic highs after subsidies were ended under Bloomberg.

Bloomberg's failure to follow through as much as he might have on the post-paternalistic model contributed to the political crisis of the conservative governing coalition on which his administration, like Koch's and Giuliani's, rested. The growth of homelessness, poverty, and inequality during the reign of that coalition left it open to the progressive charge that it had allowed two parallel but unequal cities to develop on its watch. De Blasio was to make that claim convincingly and win election as the first progressive mayor since the one-term Dinkins administration. Will de Blasio be able to realize the promise of post-paternalistic policies? Or will the homelessness crisis turn out to be, in New York City at least, more intractable than anyone would like?

6

Homelessness Policy under de Blasio

In some obvious ways, the election of Bill de Blasio, New York City's first progressive mayor since the ill-fated David Dinkins, represented a sharp break with the conservative governing coalition that had elected his predecessor, Michael Bloomberg. Bloomberg's policy of attracting wealth to the city and his lack of concern for economic inequality contrasts sharply with the tale of two cities that was at the heart of de Blasio's political vision and of the progressive mayor's passionate conviction that inequality is the great issue of our time. These contrasting overall visions are reflected in homelessness policies that also show obvious differences. De Blasio is explicitly and strongly committed to the idea of a right, not just to shelter but to housing. Bloomberg, despite showing more interest in homelessness policy than might have been expected from a billionaire Republican-Independent and even though in settling the litigation related to family homelessness he finally left the right to shelter in place, never embraced the idea of a right to housing. Also, Bloomberg, while he acknowledged homelessness as a serious problem, never saw it as a product of the city's overall economy, which would need to be modified if the problem were to be solved. De Blasio sees homelessness as part of the overall crisis of inequality that he was elected to address and, more particularly, as caused by a gap between the demand for and supply of affordable housing that policy must fill.

So there is no denying that the change from Mayor Bloomberg to Mayor de Blasio is a big change, what I have been calling in this book a nonincremental change, but it is a rather different type of nonincremental change than I have focused on so far. Much of this account has presented nonincremental change as something precipitated by policy entrepreneurs who crystallize galvanizing public ideas and market them in a highly fragmented political environment. Bob Hayes and Steven Banks and the idea of a right to shelter, Andrew Cuomo and Rudolph Giuliani and the paternalistic paradigm, and Sam Tsemberis and Housing First are the most salient examples of local policy entrepreneurs who identified a social problem, distilled from the available research an easily graspable public idea, and remade homelessness policy by promoting that idea through whatever avenues might be most responsive, including courts, regulatory agencies, bureaucracies, the media, and policy networks. For this type of change I have borrowed the term "ideational/entrepreneurial change," and an important theme of this book is that such change has happened frequently in the case history examined here.

De Blasio's election represents a different, more traditional style of nonincremental change. In this model, a candidate for the chief executive identifies a perceived crisis, runs on a platform that promises a response, achieves a strong victory, brings the rest of the political system along with him, and is thus able to make changes that were previously politically impossible. At the national level this phenomenon has been termed "presidential/majoritarian change," and its most obvious examples are Roosevelt and the New Deal, Johnson and the Great Society programs and, perhaps, Obama and health care reform. At the level of New York City, similar episodes of what might be called "mayoral/majoritarian change" can be identified, including the mayoralties of LaGuardia and Lindsay. Both these path-breaking mayors responded to an emergency—the Depression and what was called the "Urban Crisis"—made explicit calls for dramatic change central to their campaigns, won election convincingly, and used a unified government to usher in an era of striking reform. De Blasio's rise seems so far to also exemplify this mode: He responded to a perceived crisis—the inequality crisis—ran on a platform calling for dramatic change, won overwhelmingly, and is setting out to implement his mandate. Whether he will be as successful as LaGuardia in terms of achieving lasting change or will set the stage for a financial crisis, as Lindsay did, remains to be seen.

One very striking charge wrought by de Blasio's victory is one of personnel: Steven Banks, the legal advocate who had litigated with the city from the Koch through the Bloomberg administrations to advance the right to shelter for homeless families, has become commissioner of HRA. Some observers argued that Banks's background as an advocate and litigator would not serve him well in his new role as a public administrator. In an article entitled "No Managers Need Apply," Heather Mac Donald, writing in the conservative publication *City Journal*, argued that "[w]ith his choice of Banks, de Blasio has signaled that he's not interested in even the illusion that he seeks nonpartisan technocratic managers for his administration."[1] But Banks turns out to have more managerial experience than is sometimes recognized. In 2004 Banks's organizational base, the Legal Aid Society, ran into a financial crisis and needed to be rescued. According to Banks,

> I received a battlefield promotion. The organization was about half a second away from going bankrupt. I became the head of the organization under that circumstance. We were literally on the verge of going bankrupt. We had a $21

million deficit. . . . Together with the Board of Directors and the managers and the unions, the Association of Legal Aid Attorneys, Auto Workers, and 1199, we worked together to save the organization. I ran it for ten years. It's an organization with nineteen hundred employees, including eleven hundred lawyers, a budget of $225 million. So I had the experience of running a large organization, the largest legal services program in the United States, with a large budget, complex financial needs, and complex personnel needs. So I had experience in running a large organization and now I'm running an even larger organization. . . . I had actually extensive experience running an agency that needed reforms. Legal Aid needed reforms and HRA is in the middle of a reform process that we're implementing and making substantial reforms. So the kinds of management approaches, albeit on a larger scale, are similar.[2]

Nonetheless, Banks's transition from an outside, oppositional advocate to an inside manager and team player is striking and could only have come about through the era-marking change from Bloomberg to de Blasio.

But in certain senses de Blasio's homelessness policy does not represent a root-and-branch repudiation of Bloomberg's approach so much as a reaffirmation, consistent application, and extension of some of the former mayor's most promising initiatives and a correction of his most egregious mistakes. The main Bloomberg initiative that de Blasio has embraced and is extending is prevention. The big Bloomberg mistake that de Blasio is correcting is the ending of housing subsidies to help shelter clients relocate rapidly to some form of permanent housing. The de Blasio administration would like to remain faithful to Bloomberg's push for more supportive housing and emphasis on Housing First, but for political reasons to be discussed, has had trouble doing so. The commitment to ending homelessness has been abandoned for the short term, although the research and analysis behind the focus on chronic homelessness is still accepted and policies consistent with it are being deployed. Overall, de Blasio has not rejected the post-paternalistic paradigm broached, but insufficiently followed up on, by Bloomberg, but rather modified it in light of changing political realities and the new administration's progressive ideology.

The most obvious point of policy continuity between the Bloomberg and de Blasio administrations is the continued emphasis on preventing rather than just reacting to homelessness. As we saw, Bloomberg made a great fuss of elevating the goal of preventing homelessness to equal status with the goal of sheltering the homeless in the organizational culture of DHS, and even incorporated prevention into the agency's mission statement. Prevention was to be achieved in various ways but especially by the new Home Base initiative, into which Bloomberg put considerable effort and achieved a certain amount of vindication when methodologically sophisticated analysis showed that the program was in fact reducing the number of families entering the shelters below what it would have been absent the effort. De Blasio embraced and greatly expanded Home Base, nearly doubling funding for the program in FY 2015 from $22 to $42 million and increasing the program's offices from fourteen to twenty-three.[3]

However, the de Blasio administration's commitment to prevention goes far beyond just expanding Home Base. Much of the new prevention effort is based at HRA on the theory that that agency is responsible for poor people before they lose their housing while DHS is responsible for them once housing is lost. Within HRA a Homelessness Prevention Administration headed by a deputy commissioner has been created. Legal services to prevent evictions and tenant harassment have been centralized at HRA. Writing of rent arrears checks, previously done at many locations all over the city, has been centralized at HRA to make for faster delivery. Redirecting HRA welfare policy away from strict enforcement of regulations and swift imposition of sanctions is also expected to play a role in homelessness prevention. "We found," says Banks, "that 23 percent of the applicants for DHS shelter during a particular period in 2013 had an HRA case closing or sanction within 12 months of applying," which is one reason why his agency is backing away from efforts of previous administrations to shrink the welfare rolls through administrative actions.[4]

The Bloomberg administration mistake that de Blasio is most visibly correcting is the ending of housing subsidies, such as Advantage and preferential access of shelter families to NYCHA apartments and Section 8 vouchers. Perhaps the new administration's biggest initiative in homelessness policy is the Living in Communities (LINC) programs, which are a batch of rental subsidy programs designed to help various sorts of shelter clients move out of the system. LINC represents, in a certain sense, a reinstatement of Advantage. De Blasio's deputy mayor for health and human services, Lilliam Barrios-Paoli, went so far as to partially defend Advantage against its critics:

> Well, Bloomberg did Advantage, which was a rental assistance. The census plummeted down and when Advantage stopped the census went right up. And I think it's clear that that was the one thing that works, which recognizes that people just don't have enough money to pay the rent. Now, how long you do it for, what social services you build in, all of that is a little bit different [in LINC]. But I don't think it's a complete departure. It's acknowledging what works and the fact that when they stopped the whole thing just exploded again. . . . I feel

> that in criticizing Advantage, we sort of threw the water out and the baby with it.[5]

But LINC does more than simply reinstate Advantage; de Blasio's initiative extends and refines the program Bloomberg abandoned in three ways. First, while the Advantage rent subsidies lasted only two years—reportedly because the Bloomberg administration felt such a short period would "discourage long-term dependence"[6]—LINC payments go on for five years, perhaps because under de Blasio there was less concern about possible perverse incentives. Second, LINC, unlike Advantage, requires recipients to participate in various social services designed to encourage housing stability. Third, LINC subsidies are available to a much wider variety of shelter clients than the working families to whom Advantage was limited.

LINC is in fact a set of programs, each tailored to the needs of a different type of shelter client. LINC I is for working shelter families, that is, families with a member working at least thirty-five hours a week for at least ninety days. LINC II is for families that have experienced multiple shelter stays. Survivors of domestic violence are targeted by LINC III. LINC IV is for the elderly or medically frail and for adult families (that is, families without children). Working singles or adult families are covered by LINC V. LINC VI relocates families with relatives or friends by paying a portion of the host's rent.

The various LINC programs, and the de Blasio administration's general embrace of rental subsidies, are more consistent with the insights of the early Bloomberg years than was Bloomberg's own abandonment of subsidies. Under the influence of the research of Sam Tsemberis and his colleagues on Housing First, Bloomberg had succeeded in communicating to shelter managers that the paternalistic concern with diagnosing and treating the underlying cause of clients' homelessness was to be dropped in favor of planning to rehouse them as soon as possible. But clearly rental subsidies are likely to be an important part of any realistic rehousing plan. In this sense LINC represents an extension of the post-paternalistic emphasis on Housing First.

The de Blasio administration would like to extend Bloomberg's commitment to supportive housing, the most striking manifestation of which was the signing of the New York/New York III Agreement, by continuing to place street dwellers and shelter clients in supportive housing units and by bringing to fruition a fourth New York/New York Agreement. But as the supply of new supportive housing units produced under New York/New York III has declined, negotiations for a fourth agreement have been stalled due to budgetary politics in Albany. Patrick Markee, deputy executive director for advocacy of the Coalition for the Homeless, who follows the politics of homelessness and city/state relations perhaps as closely as anyone, commented on the city's dilemma concerning supportive housing:

> When de Blasio comes in you've already seen the fact that very few new permanent supportive housing units are still left in the . . . New York/New York III pipeline. There's only about one hundred units that are still left to be created under that agreement. Almost all of the existing stock of New York/New York housing is full and has very low vacancy rates. . . . So the de Blasio administration has been stuck with the reality of the shortage of the supply of that stock of [supportive] housing while the needs have been growing. That's one of the reasons that the one part of the shelter population that is growing, and I believe will continue to grow until we see a significant fourth New York/New York Agreement, is the single adults in shelters. That's one of the reasons you also see the street population beginning to rise. Historically in New York there's only one policy tool that has really made a dent in the number of single adults in shelters and that has been additions to the supply of permanent supportive housing. You saw that happen in the late eighties, early nineties, you saw that happen in the 2005 period. I don't think there's another way you really get at that population in a significant way.
>
> So I think the reason you haven't seen the de Blasio folks talking about it [supportive housing] as much has been this frustration. You have seen this dance . . . between the de Blasio and Cuomo administrations, around permanent supportive housing. . . . Many of us who had started this campaign to get a fourth New York/New York Agreement were hopeful, as was the city, that the Cuomo administration was going to come out in a positive place on the idea of a permanent supportive housing agreement. Fran Reiter, who was the point person for the [Cuomo] administration, spoke very favorably last summer at the Supportive Housing Network's annual conference about the governor wanting to do a fourth agreement. . . . When the governor proposed his version of a New York/New York IV Agreement in January, we were all just stunned at how paltry it was: five thousand units over seven years. They called it five years but when we talked with state budget officials it became clear that it was really a seven-year development timeline. Only thirty-nine hundred of those units would be in New York City. Even that thirty-nine hundred was counting on eighteen hundred units being created by the city. . . .
>
> So de Blasio to his credit went up [to Albany] and proposed . . . a twelve-thousand-units-over-ten-years agreement, still smaller than what we would like to see but obviously larger than what the governor was proposing and significantly larger than what the New York/New York III Agreement had

> proposed. . . . The Cuomo administration was just deeply unhelpful. . . . From a policy perspective they totally embrace the idea of permanent supportive housing, the de Blasio folks. They want more of it. You saw that de Blasio's capital budget significantly expanded funding for permanent supportive housing and other specialty housing . . . [I]t's about $2 billion over ten years just of special needs housing in his budget. It would fund, as I understand it, on its own the city's portion would fund over twelve thousand.[7]

The decision to deemphasize the push for a New York/New York IV Agreement means that not too much can be said about Housing First either, for with no new supportive housing units in the pipeline, the promise implicit in Housing First to move street dwellers immediately into such housing has to be extended cautiously. It may also be that recent financial troubles into which the New York office of Sam Tsemberis's organization, Pathways to Housing, has fallen, which resulted in the termination of contracts with the state Office of Mental Health and the transfer of the organization's clients to other housing providers, has made it inconvenient for the city to publicly reiterate its commitment to Housing First.[8] However, the de Blasio administration quietly continues to expand use of that approach by, for instance, recently having DHS take over contracts to provide outreach services in the subways from the Metropolitan Transit Authority for the sake of better coordination and to ensure that the Housing First strategy that has been successful above ground will be applied in the subways.

Another signature move of the de Blasio administration has been to reinstate the priority access of shelter families to available public housing (New York City Housing Authority, or NYCHA) units and Section 8 rental vouchers that had been ended with considerable controversy by Bloomberg in 2004. Linda Gibbs had stated that the object of ending this priority was to eliminate the perceived perverse incentive to enter the shelter system in order to qualify for the units or vouchers. This decision failed to appreciate that research by Cragg and O'Flaherty and others showed that in fact access to these types of housing assistance produced only a weak incentive for nonhomeless families to enter the system and therefore did not drive up the shelter census. The de Blasio administration grasped this point. As Barrios-Paoli put the matter,

> There is that belief that if you, if people get good things, whether it's NYCHA or Section 8 or rental assistance, by becoming homeless or being in shelter, more people will do that to access housing. There may be a kernel of truth in that but it has to be a pretty desperate situation for people to do that. And you and I are not going to resort to that, right? These are people who are asking out of des-

peration or people who are very precariously housed, who are doubled up, who are very crowded, people who eventually would be homeless, maybe not tomorrow but will be. And maybe they accelerate their route to homelessness because of this. But I don't really believe that. It's like believing that people voluntarily go onto welfare, even if they had other options. I don't think that's the case. I worked on these issues for close to forty years. . . . Poor people are logical like you and me, they're intelligent like you and me. And they make choices that are good for them. But if they have a better option they don't opt for these things.[9]

While de Blasio's executives were confident that reintroducing the preferences for shelter families would not ignite perverse incentives, a number of moves were made to respond to other criticisms that were launched against the Dinkins administration when it relied on extensive placements into NYCHA to reduce the shelter census back in the early nineties. For one thing, the preferences were reintroduced on a quite limited basis. While Coalition for the Homeless called for the new administration to relocate 2,500 shelter families a year into NYCHA under de Blasio, only 750 families are scheduled to get vacant units. Why so few? One concern was with retaining the right "mix" of working, elderly, and very poor tenants in NYCHA. Barrios-Paoli explained,

During the Koch years, even Giuliani, Dinkins, even the beginning of Bloomberg, most NYCHA vacancies went to homeless families. And I think that was in recognition of the fact that this is public housing, it's our housing. Who's more deserving than people who are really poor and cannot afford more than 30 percent of their income for this? And that's one philosophy. I think over the years HUD and NYCHA felt that it was better to have a mix in public housing. That it worked better when you had people who were working, people who were on Public Assistance. You had a mix so there was better role modeling. It would be a better life for everybody. That's the other philosophy. . . . They still believe that. . . . I don't think it's such a big danger. But they have a point. And I think to put everybody with the same problem in the same building is not a good thing.[10]

Also, eligibility for NYCHA placement is stricter than it was under Dinkins. To receive a unit a family must have a working member or some source of income such as SSI or other public benefits. Families must also be already on the NYCHA waiting list to partly address the concern that shelter families got to jump the line into public housing. Another issue broached during the Dinkins years resolved itself. In the early nineties, established NYCHA tenants expressed considerable resentment of the newcomers from the shelters and even staged demonstrations to keep them out. But by the time de Blasio came to office, attitudes had changed. According to Barrio-Paoli,

> Now, because of the policy of allowing most of the vacancies to go to homeless families since the Koch administration, a lot of families that are in NYCHA have been homeless at some point. And they got their life together and their life went on and so forth. . . . We've never had a problem with families that have moved in. In fact there was a rally not too long ago where there were NYCHA tenants saying that it's okay to bring homeless families in. . . . I think at the end of the day, in poor families, homelessness is not such an unknown phenomenon. Your cousin has been homeless, your neighbor has been homeless, maybe you have been homeless at some point. The recognition is that homeless people are just like us, one pay check away.[11]

In one interesting respect, however, the de Blasio administration did break with at least the rhetoric of the post-paternalistic paradigm. Part of the appeal of that approach was its commitment to ending, not merely managing, homelessness. Culhane's refocusing of homelessness policy on the more manageable problem of chronic homelessness brought the goal of ending homelessness within reach. Mangano and others promoted to cities and states the idea of developing ten-year plans based on Culhane's analysis to reach that goal. And under the influence of these policy entrepreneurs Bloomberg developed, not a ten- but a five-year plan to at least very substantially reduce homelessness and even incorporated the aim to "overcome" homelessness into the DHS mission statement. One might have thought that a progressive mayor would be at least as enthusiastic about eliminating a salient manifestation of inequality as a billionaire mayor had been. But under de Blasio the rhetoric of overcoming homelessness was quietly taken out of the DHS mission statement, which now reads, "With our partners, our goal is to prevent homelessness when possible; to provide temporary, emergency shelter when needed; and to help individuals and families transition rapidly into permanent housing. We do this through providing coordinated, compassionate, high-quality services and supports."[12]

Asked whether the new mission statement represented a backing away from the Bloomberg goal of ending homelessness, de Blasio's commissioner of DHS, Gilbert Taylor, wouldn't quite put the matter that way. "I'm a realist," Taylor replied. "I believe that if you want to make God laugh, tell him your plans."[13] Deputy Mayor Barrios-Paoli expanded on the matter. She felt that ending homelessness might be a realistic goal in jurisdictions like Utah where the housing market is slack and the homeless population is mostly made up of single individuals. In New York City, with its great gap between demand for and supply of affordable housing, and with a homeless population made up mostly of families, who are harder to place than singles, Barrios-Paoli felt the old statement of intention to overcome homelessness was an "overpromise":

> It is impossible to eradicate homelessness [in New York City] unless you produce apartments that are deeply affordable for people. And so until the time we do that we have to acknowledge the fact that there will be people living in shelters. [Will the number be] much less than fifty-seven thousand? I sincerely hope so. I really, really hope so. But what is that irreducible number? I don't know. But we know zero is not something that's going to happen in the next three or four years simply because the supply of housing isn't there.

The deputy mayor was optimistic that after that period of time a fourth New York/New York Agreement would be negotiated and de Blasio's would start to kick in and then some real progress—perhaps not overcoming homelessness, but at least making a substantial dent in it— would start to happen. In that sense de Blasio's homelessness policy remains faithful to the post-paternalistic aim of not merely managing homelessness but trying to end it. Further, the LINC programs, by incorporating a broader range of clients than had been covered by Advantage, is consistent with the concern with chronic homelessness. LINC IV and V cover that population, according to Banks, and represent the continuing impact of Dennis Culhane's identification of the chronically homeless:

> If you look at the segmentation of the LINC program, that gives you a sense that it's not a one-size-fits-all approach. And so focusing on seniors in the single adult system, or focusing on adults who have disabilities and are receiving federal benefits, this is all aimed at getting people out of the system who can be linked back to housing in the community. I think some of the flaws of the Bloomberg approach were it was broad brush: chronic homelessness. Chronic homelessness is a constellation of individuals that have individual needs. And so the LINC program and the other things that HRA and DHS are doing are focused on what are the individual needs. . . . What we're doing is consistent with what Dennis [Culhane] has said.[14]

Asked about continuity and change in homelessness policy over the years, Banks, from his perspective as HRA commissioner after a thirty-year career in advocacy, responded as follows:

Well, let me tell you a story. I remember cross-examining an executive deputy commissioner during the Dinkins administration, Jeff Carples, who was ultimately held in contempt along with other city officials for violating certain court orders. I remember cross-examining him about what it would take to be able to comply with right-to-shelter requirements. The judge interrupted and said I would really like to know what your answer is about what it would take to comply. And Carples answered, it's a combination of prevention, having adequate shelter for people who become homeless, and you need a place to move people to out of the shelter system. Those have been the basic truths for years. The first Bloomberg term, that was the focus. The second and third Bloomberg term he totally turned his back on that focus and that's how we got into this mess that the current administration has inherited and is embracing the basics: prevention, adequate shelter, some place to move people to.[15]

Conclusion

What, then, does the story we have just unfolded imply for urban politics? Or more specifically, what are the implications for urban politics New York style? To answer this question, let us go back to the beginning of modern political analysis of New York City, which is that classic of postwar American pluralism, *Governing New York City*, by Wallace Sayre and Herbert Kaufman. They famously wrote that "[n]o part of the city's large and varied population is alienated from participation in the system."[1]

The pluralist school of political science would come under fire from a wide range of power-elite, structuralist, and, later, regime theorists. The criticisms of pluralism were wide ranging. One was that there were, in fact, important interests that were alienated from the political process. As Bellush concludes in her updating of the Sayre and Kaufman account, "The outcome of the urban political process is not necessarily a little something for all the players."[2] Clearly, the argument goes, the pluralist system wasn't working for some.

What does the story of New York City's homeless over the last thirty years imply for this critique of the pluralist picture? Of course, conclusions drawn from the experience of one numerically small group cannot radically change the large picture. However, the homeless, despite being relatively few in number, are an especially significant part of that picture. As Dr. Johnson has noted, and as John Rawls has elaborated upon, the conditions of the worst off members of a community are a particularly important consideration in judging the justice of that community. And, as we have seen, the homeless, many of them, are perhaps the worst of the worst off in New York City. If the city has not addressed their needs, that is a damning reflection on the pluralists' optimistic evaluation. On the other hand, if the homeless have gotten a fair shake, perhaps there is hope for any disadvantaged group.

New York's record on the homeless is mixed. An evaluation of it depends on whether we focus on how far the city has come or on what the situation is now in the early years of the de Blasio administration. Very striking progress has been made since homelessness was first pushed onto the city's political agenda in the late seventies. On the other hand, the city's shelter population—about fifty-five thousand people in the summer of 2015—is nearly as large as it has ever been since that beginning. A fair evaluation of the city's record has to take both of these realities into consideration.

It would be hard to find an interest group less likely to be successful in the urban political arena than the homeless. David Snow, Sarah Soule, and Daniel Cress point out the obvious when they write that

> [a]t first glance the homeless . . . are unlikely candidates for protest mobilization. The homeless not only suffer severe resource deficits materially and socially, but they are more impoverished in both realms than most other marginalized individuals and groups. . . . They also rarely have ready access to the kinds of material facilities and resources that most social movement activists and organizers take for granted such as a meeting place, a telephone, and a few office supplies.

Other obstacles to the political efficacy of the homeless are also noted, including high rates of disability and the transitory nature of homelessness.[3]

And yet, despite this unpromising position, New York City's homeless have been quite successful in certain ways. We have recounted the development of the Department of Homeless Services with an annual budget, recently, of about $1 billion; the demise of such hellholes as the big room of the Men's Shelter at 8 East Third Street, the Emergency Assistance Unit, the flophouses and welfare hotels; their replacement with state-of-the-art facilities, including the PATH building and Project Renewal's recovery program; the rise of much-improved temporary accommodations such as those operated by a network of nonprofit providers; and the development of high-quality permanent shelter for the disabled, as was provided for in the various New York/New York agreements. Despite some qualifications that we will get to shortly, the experience of the homeless of New York implies a degree of openness that is consistent with the pluralists' account of the city's political system and that tells against the arguments of the pluralists' critics.

Obviously, one might disagree with this assessment for a number of reasons. Donna Wilson Kirchheimer denies that homelessness policy is a pluralist success story and concludes that the city's efforts have all fallen "well within the historically acceptable protective functions of the partial U.S. welfare state."[4] But the question here is not whether New York's response to the homeless has transcended the parameters of the partial American welfare state. It hasn't, not by a long shot. The question at the moment is whether the homeless "got something" in the way that pluralists conceive of everybody getting something out of the city's political system. If the homeless got something, that represents, perhaps not a "pluralist's dream" but a degree of openness that is consistent with the pluralists' picture of urban America. The pluralists never argued that the degree of openness they found allowed for breaking beyond the boundaries of the American welfare state.

How large, then, are the resources devoted to homelessness in New York City? The Department of Homeless Services is allocated $1.04 billion in the city's 2014 expense budget of $69.8 billion, only about 1.5 percent of the total.[5] By other measures the resources devoted to the homeless in New York City are more impressive. As was noted earlier, in 1978, or the year before the *Callahan* litigation began, the city government spent $6.8 million on the homeless,[6] for an increase of more than 4,000 percent in constant dollars.[7] It would be illuminating to compare New York City's efforts with those of other cities. However, most cities do not have an analogue to New York's DHS, which makes comparisons difficult. An exception is Los Angeles, with its Los Angeles Homeless Services Authority, which spent $72 million in FY 2014–2015.[8] The findings of Daniel Cress and David Snow on "The Outcomes of Homeless Mobilization" for fifteen organizations of the homeless in eight U.S. cities are also telling. The greatest success was that of the Oakland Union of the Homeless, which achieved what the authors describe as the "stunning" victory of getting built a twenty-six-unit, $4.7 million housing project.[9] But as we have seen, this outcome is small potatoes compared to New York City's efforts. The resources New York City spends on the homeless, then, are small relative to the city's entire budget, but large compared to the city's past efforts and the efforts of other cities. In short, the city's homeless, at least by some relevant measures, did indeed end up getting quite a bit. That result, at first blush, seems consistent with the pluralists' account of city politics as a system open to a wide range of participants.

Yes, the homeless got something, but what they got, for the most part, was not what they were most desperate for, permanent housing; what they usually got was emergency shelter and some associated services. From this perspective, Kirchheimer's criticism of the limits of the city's homelessness policy has more force, although it needs to be reformulated. Certainly the city's efforts have not transcended the "protective functions of the partial U.S. welfare state";[10] the real problem is that those efforts have not lived up to the accomplishments of the American welfare state at its best. New York's shelter system, as impressive as it is in many respects, pales in comparison with LaGuardia's achievements in slum clearance, providing affordable housing, and establishing the New York City Housing Authority (NYCHA).[11] In recent decades, housing reform of such ambition has not been politically possible. New York City has had to develop its homelessness policy under the constraints of conservative dominance, neoliberal globalization, and, often, financial austerity. The result has been a shelter system, not in the grand tradition of the New Deal but one that reflects the flexibility and limitations of what has been called the "post-Fordist welfare state."[12]

The homeless have indeed gotten something out of the city's political system, and yet it cannot be said that they have been active participants in that system. In important ways they have indeed accepted passively the policies that the system has dealt out. The homeless did not make use of the organizing resources or strategies that have been effective for the other urban interest groups described by the pluralists. Kirchheimer correctly reports that

> the beneficiary population was a weak political force. The homeless were the poorest people in New York City and had no financial resources for political mobilization. The poor did not have an organizational base from which to press for their own needs. They tended to be inactive in electoral politics, and their support was not heavily courted by elected officials. The homeless also did not exert their force of numbers through organized protests or street demonstrations, which have been important to New York City's day care and senior citizen movements. About a third of homeless single persons were handicapped by major mental disabilities, and many suffered from substance abuse. Most heads of homeless families were young single women who had less than a twelfth grade education and less than a year of work experience, and they were preoccupied with caring for small children in unstable residences from which they had to move almost every other year.[13]

New York City's homeless won the substantial resources they did not through their own political action but through the political action of others on their behalf. It is telling that it was the activist lawyer Robert Hayes who sought out and represented the plaintiffs to the *Callahan* litigation, and not the homeless who organized themselves and sought out representation. The Coalition for the Homeless has been an effective advocacy organization, but although in its earliest days homeless people were a significant part of the milieu out of which it developed, for the most part the organization has been, as its name says, a coalition *for* the homeless, rather than *of* the homeless. At no point did the coalition's leadership or staff consist mainly of homeless people or formerly homeless people, although there was, as we have seen, some participation of the homeless in the formative days of the coalition.

The exact nature of the experts who were at the center of homelessness politics in New York City has been usefully termed by Kirchheimer as a policy community, which she described as follows:

> Within this milieu, a new policy community sprang up to specialize on the issue of homelessness. It was an identifiable community of shared values, which consciously challenged the existing institutional structure. It consisted of people who were committed social advocates, not neutral technicians, and they were not based in the city bureaucracy. The internal structure of this policy community was loose and open, and contacts were ad hoc and informal. Many members knew each other, exchanged information, shared strategies, and at times coordinated particular actions.[14]

This picture of the homeless of the city as politically inactive needs to be qualified in one respect. The homeless did not organize, but they did occupy public spaces and may be said to have disrupted the routines of passersby who saw them. Research has shown that simply by being visible, the homeless gain sympathy and support.[15] Joel Blau, in his book *The Visible Poor: Homelessness in America*, writes that "perhaps the single most significant attribute of homelessness is its visibility. Visible poverty disrupts the ordinary rhythms of public life. It undermines the rules governing the use of public space."[16] There is no research on how often New Yorkers see homeless people or on how that sight impacts them. However, a 2007 study by the Public Agenda Foundation found that 63 percent of New Yorkers reported that there were some or a lot of homeless people in their neighborhood and that 47 percent reported directly helping a homeless person within the past year.[17] My own interest in homelessness was provoked in the early 1980s by the sight of homeless people in the subways that I used to go to work. Mayor Koch would eventually say that simply "seeing people in the street itself" forced the homelessness issue on his attention.[18] Homeless people have undoubtedly been visible over the last thirty years in New York City, and that visibility was most likely part of the reason why the city devoted more resources to the homeless. Insofar as visibility disrupted ordinary routines and resulted in more sympathy and resources, it may be thought of as a political phenomenon.

The finding that the homeless did not organize but did disrupt is similar to the thesis of Frances Piven and Richard Cloward's book, *Poor People's Movements*, which claims that "[w]hatever influence lower-class groups occasionally exert in American politics does not result from organization, but from mass protest and the disruptive consequences of protest."[19] On closer examination, however, the case of the homeless in New York City does not confirm the Piven and Cloward thesis. First of all, mass protest did not play much of a role in developing the city's homelessness policy. The Thompson Square Park riot got attention at the time, but it happened well after the *Callahan* and *McCain* litigation had begun and did not have a major impact on policy. And as we saw, the continuing disruption in the park during the early Dinkins administration led to the park's closure and then reopening after an extensive renovation rendered it less hospitable to the homeless. There is not much evidence to suggest that the city's homeless people considered themselves to be part of a larger movement or that they shared a set of protest beliefs. The type of disruption they mainly engaged in—inappropriately occupying public spaces—did not require any type of collective consciousness. More coordinated forms of disruption were rare. In January 1989, Parents on the Move (POM), a self-help organization of homeless parents living in the Brooklyn Arms welfare hotel, seized the offices of the city's Crisis Intervention Services at the hotel and refused to be relocated to anywhere except permanent housing. A survey of twenty members of the group found that thirteen of them considered the organization a success in the sense of "making people feel good about themselves and their homeless situation," but POM folded soon after the demonstration.[20] The Philadelphia Union of the Homeless tried to develop a New York City branch, which "promised civil disobedience," but according to one sympathetic observer, the group soon "dissipated" when its main organizers moved on to other cities.[21] Homeward Bound Community Services (HBCS) organized a sleep-in at City Hall Park that lasted for hundreds of days, but according to a review of the history of the protest, "the encampment fell apart after a while, a victim of disorder, neglect, and the instability of its residents."[22] Robert Hayes praised the efforts of HBCS but acknowledged that "[h]omeless people organizing themselves has been rare."[23]

The sheer visibility of the homeless was an important contribution to the politics of homelessness in New York City. Otherwise, however, homelessness politics in the city has mostly been made on behalf of the homeless, not by them. This reality has received very little comment. The one sustained consideration of this fact has been the passionate denunciation by Theresa Funiciello in her book *Tyranny of Kindness*. Funiciello, a formerly homeless mother, welfare activist, and advisor to the New York State commissioner of social services, Cesar Perales, fulminates against what she calls "the creation and marketing of homeless people," writing that "[u]nder the rubric of helping homeless people, little empires were built, expanded and strengthened, careers were boosted, and media stars created overnight." The problem is that "the poverty industry has become a veritable fifth estate. Acting as stand-ins for actual poor people, they mediate the politics of poverty with governmental officials."[24]

Whatever one makes of Funiciello's overwhelmingly negative caricatures of many policy actors, and her blistering invective, mediating the politics of poverty with governmental officials is a pretty fair description of the work of the city homelessness-policy community identified by Kirchheimer. What Funiciello does not succeed in doing is showing, rather than asserting, that this mediated or paternalistic mode of policymaking has been bad for the homeless. Her main argument is that the homeless would benefit immensely if all the resources devoted to their problems were simply delivered directly to them in the form of a check and/or permanent housing, rather than being routed through the public and nonprofit bureaucracies. The problems with such a guaranteed-income-and-housing scheme—which are rooted in perverse incentives, fairness, and behavioral issues—have been developed in detail elsewhere.[25] What is interesting here is that implicit in Funiciello's argument is the recognition that the resources devoted to the homeless in New York are quite considerable. It is also true that since Funiciello's writing in 1993, most of the poor shelter conditions described in her book have been dealt with. All this is to say that the politics of dependency, with the homeless as a group mostly passively organized by others on their behalf, have been beneficial to the city's homeless. Or again, the politics of homelessness in New York City are dependency politics, and it's a good thing too.

As this book has demonstrated, New York City homelessness policy, as it has developed since the beginning of the *Callahan* litigation, has passed through three moments: a moment of entitlement, a paternalistic moment, and then a post-paternalistic moment. These moments can be summarized as follows.

The Entitlement Moment

As it was developed by advocates working through the courts in the early 1980s, and by the city bureaucracy reacting to that pressure, city homelessness policy began by focusing on rights and offering shelter with no quid pro quo asked of the clients. Delivering on that entitlement was the central challenge to policy during the Koch and most of the Dinkins years. The courts and various advocacy groups such as Coalition for the Homeless are primarily concerned with this aspect of homelessness policy. These interests pushed policy in the direction of developing a shelter system that was large, court supervised, and primarily concerned with delivery of emergency accommodations.

The entitlement or right to shelter completely transformed the city's homelessness system. The system grew tremendously in the early eighties. While 7,584 individuals were sheltered in 1982, 21,154 were sheltered in 1985. Spending grew from $6.8 million in 1978, the year before the litigation to establish a right to shelter began, to $100 million in 1985. To cope with the rapidly expanding demand, the city rushed to open large, barracks-style shelters where hundreds of clients would sleep in cots laid out in open spaces. During these years the city also relied on commercial welfare hotels to shelter homeless families at the cost of $72 million in 1986. The shelter system during these years was satisfactory neither from a conservative nor from a liberal point of view. The right to shelter was absolute, and unbalanced by any requirements to work, participate in rehabilitation, or seek permanent housing.

Shelter quality was often very poor during the Koch and Dinkins years, when the focus was on establishing the right to shelter. That a right or entitlement to shelter should result, at least at first, in poor-quality shelter is not a paradox but a necessary outcome of the advocates' decision to apply the rights premise to the problem of homelessness. If homelessness had been conceived of as an "ordinary" social problem, like poverty or mental illness, it would have been addressed legislatively, just as other social problems are. A legislative solution—such as developing more affordable housing—would likely have been an incremental solution as various interests fought to have an influence on policy. An expanded affordable housing program would thus probably have been implemented over time, with new housing coming on line over a period of some years. This approach would have left more people homeless for longer but would have avoided the implementation problems associated with suddenly providing access to shelter on a day certain.

If homelessness was to be addressed through the right to shelter, the main forum in which policy would play out would be the courts. Courts, being relatively independent of multiple political interests to satisfy and less sensitive to implementation concerns, were free to impose a nonincremental solution to homelessness, one in which the basic right to shelter was established with the signing of the *Callahan* consent decree on August 26, 1981. The result was a sudden crush of demand for shelter, one that the city had to meet immediately in a catch-as-catch-can fashion. Large barracks-style shelters based in armories—with all the problems of privacy, security, and hygiene they implied—were a foreseeable part of that response; there was no time to go through the politically demanding process of opening up many smaller, neighborhood-based shelters as the advocates had wanted. Use of the infamous welfare hotels expanded, as they were the supply of emergency shelter for families most available to hand. And few services were offered to clients, as the main concern was simply providing the mandated emergency shelter. Approaching the problem of homelessness as a matter of right or entitlement meant that, in the short run, the city would create a system that guaranteed the right to free, low-quality shelter.

Dinkins tried to extend this entitlement by providing shelter clients with rapid transfers into permanent housing, still without making any demands of clients. Entries into the shelter system began to go up. As we saw, by 1991, key figures in the Dinkins administration came to believe that this entirely rights-based policy had created a perverse incentive for more potential clients to enter the system. Later research by Cragg and O'Flaherty indicated that this belief was incorrect and that more placements would have decreased, not increased, the shelter population. This observation raises the tantalizing possibility that had the Dinkins administration persisted in its original course it might have come as close to solving the homelessness problem as was possible at that time.

The Paternalistic Moment

But even if the Dinkins administration had known that it had not created a perverse incentive, political considerations suggest that it was likely that the generous distribution of permanent housing units would not have continued for long. During the early 1990s, strong opposition was building to purely rights-based, services-oriented welfare programs in general, which, at the national level, would result, by 1996, in the passage of the quite demanding Personal Responsibility and Work Opportunity Reconciliation Act. In New York City, a similar process and a similar disappointment with the city's service-oriented welfare program, BEGIN, would result in the very work-oriented welfare reforms under Giuliani.[26] In this political environment, it is inevitable that the city's purely rights-based homelessness policy would, sooner or later, have become the object of a similar, paternalistic reform.

That the change in direction came sooner, under Dinkins, rather than waiting for the arrival of Giuliani, is probably to be attributed to the arrival of an effective local policy entrepreneur, Andrew Cuomo. As chairman of the New York City Commission on the Homeless, usually known as the Cuomo Commission, Andrew Cuomo acknowledged the concerns of Nancy Wackstein, Cesar Perales, and other Dinkins administration officials who believed that the homelessness system had become over-generous. He borrowed the policy idea of "mutual responsibility," which had been developed in the national welfare reform debate, and ingeniously applied it in detail to city homelessness policy. He outmaneuvered traditionally liberal welfare policy actors, such as Barbra Sabol, the commissioner of the Human Resources Administration under Dinkins, and eventually sold his plan to the possibly somewhat reluctant Dinkins. The paradigm that the Cuomo Commission produced—one that insisted that homeless clients do something, such as work, search for housing, or participate in rehabilitative programs in return for shelter and services—was essentially paternalistic and would become the basis for policy under Giuliani.

Lawrence M. Mead defines paternalistic policies as "social policies aimed at the poor that attempt to reduce poverty and other social problems by directive and supervisory means."[27] Many of the homelessness policy developments since the Cuomo Commission have been consistent with the paternalistic paradigm. That paradigm rests on two assumptions. First, paternalism subscribes to the "underlying cause" theory of homelessness. It assumes that there is "something wrong" with the homeless that importantly contributes to their homelessness. This might be mental illness, substance abuse, or simply a "dysfunctional" or underclass lifestyle that, it is thought, makes housing hard to hold onto. Paternalism assumes that this underlying cause has to be addressed, otherwise the subject will remain homeless. Therefore, the second assumption of paternalism is that if clients are to receive housing, whether shelter or some form of permanent housing, they have to participate in a rehabilitative regime that will address the underlying cause of their homelessness. Such participation could involve enrollment in a substance abuse rehabilitation program, or mandatory compliance with psychiatric treatment, or, for homeless families, participation in various sorts of housing-search, work-preparation, or family-living programs.

Paternalism thus conditions the right to shelter on various "good behaviors" of the clients. Paternalism began to manifest itself as the limits of the early, entitlement-based, emergency-oriented system became apparent. An obvious problem was the poor quality of the shelter that was provided by the jerry-built system. The unconditional right to shelter also proved to be problematic. Behavioral problems, such as substance abuse, nonwork, and criminal activity, enacted by some of the homeless, seemed to require that the entitlement to shelter be conditioned on participation in work, treatment, and job-search programs. It was thought that strong conceptions of the rights of the mentally ill sometimes had to be limited in order to provide necessary protection and therapy. This line of thinking resulted in the efforts of Project HELP to involuntarily transport mentally ill street people to psychiatric services, which represented an early manifestation of the paternalistic impulse. Improving shelter conditions made more acute the possibility that a perverse incentive to become homeless in order to qualify for housing had been created that had to be counterbalanced in various ways. This set of challenges is of particular concern to mayors and administrators who, unlike the courts or advocates, are responsible for the actual operation of the shelter system, and for spending. These actors therefore pushed policy in a paternalistic direction, one in which rights are conditioned on good behavior and participation in programs such as drug-treatment, job-search, and housing-search activities.

The development, under Giuliani, of an eligibility process for homeless families was a first, necessary step in moving from a purely rights-based policy in a paternalistic direction. Bloomberg's efforts to develop an eligibility process in the shelters for singles continued this direction. Not-for-profitization also expanded greatly during the paternalistic moment, partly because of the demonstrably better management of nonprofit shelters as compared with public shelters but also because creating a two-tier system of public intake shelters and nonprofit program shelters made it possible to require client participation in rehabilitative programs without violating the right to shelter as it was developed through the courts. And of course the program shelters themselves, focusing as they did on rehabilitation and quid pro quo, were also a paternalistic policy development. Even the improvement in shelter conditions, while obviously pursued on humanitarian and legal grounds, has reinforced the paternalistic regime, since if one is to demand a quid pro quo, it helps to offer a benefit that is worth having.

The Post-Paternalistic Moment

The limits of paternalism started to manifest themselves by the final years of the Giuliani administration. It was then that DHS executives began to notice that substantial numbers of shelter clients refused to take up the paternalistic deal offered by the then newly developed program shelters: admission to a better-quality shelter in return for participation in a rehabilitative regime. That deal was also being offered to street dwellers, to whom outreach teams would offer access to permanent, supported housing, but only if they demonstrated themselves to be housing ready by abstaining from substance abuse, participating in psychiatric treatment, and in general behaving themselves. A frustratingly high number of street dwellers declined this deal, making inroads against public homelessness hard to achieve. The option of involuntarily transporting street dwellers who refused treatment and shelter to hospitals, as was attempted for a time by Project HELP under Koch, turned out to be impractical. So paternalism ended up not being able to reduce homelessness, which left city policymakers in the difficult position of having to manage the homelessness problem apparently indefinitely without being able to end it.

One response to these problems was Housing First. At the least, Housing First substantially modifies the paternalistic quid pro quo of housing in return for compliance with various sorts of rehabilitative programs by offering the housing before expecting compliance, or rather, by offering housing and not expecting, but perhaps hoping for, compliance. Now, if we interpret Housing First as simply a variation on paternalism—that is, if we see it as a tactic for in fact increasing compliance with treatment by *offering* the treatment *after*, rather than *requiring* treatment *before* housing is provided—then Housing First seems not to deliver on the paternalistic quid pro quo. Housing First clients use, for example, substance abuse services *less* than treatment-first clients do, even though there is no difference in actual substance abuse among these two groups.[28] Housing First clients also use psychiatric treatment services less than treatment-first clients do, though the differences are for the most part not statistically significant.[29] Housing First, then, does not work if it is conceived of as a perhaps counterintuitive tactic for increasing compliance and thus making real the paternalist quid pro quo.

Housing First is more radical than that. Housing First doesn't increase, and in some cases even lessens, compliance, but it *improves outcomes*, and thus obviates the need for compliance. Housing First clients, despite the fact that they use substance abuse services less, do not engage in substance abuse any more than treatment-first clients do.[30] And, whatever their use of psychiatric services, Housing First clients show fewer psychiatric symptoms than do treatment-first clients.[31] If mental illness and substance abuse are supposed to be underlying causes of homelessness, Housing First does a better job of addressing them than do treatment-first programs that paternalistically insist on the use of services that are supposed to address those underlying causes. In other words, Housing First radically undermines the paternalistic paradigm.

Housing First strikes at both the underlying cause and quid pro quo assumptions of paternalism. First, consider the underlying-cause assumption. It is important to understand that, unlike some of the formulations of the antipsychiatry movement of the sixties and seventies, such as those of Thomas Szasz and R. D. Laing, Housing First philosophy does not deny that its potential clients are mentally disabled. What is denied is not the reality of disability but that this real disability precludes subjects from being housed. In other words, Housing First admits that there is "something wrong" with its clients. Housing First's point is that providing permanent housing need not be delayed until this disability is dealt with. Housing First is not housing only; clients' disabilities are dealt with by the extensive support services provided with the permanent housing. But access to the permanent housing is not *contingent* on use of the services. Disability remains a real and serious problem, but it is no longer a "cause" of homelessness in the sense that provision of housing is futile if the disability is not dealt with first.

But if there is no underlying cause of homelessness, demanding a quid pro quo of clients—housing in return for compliance, with a rehabilitative regime to address the cause—makes no sense; thus Housing First undermines the mutual responsibility or quid pro quo assumption of paternalism. Another way of putting this is to say that Housing First rejects the "directive and supervisory" nature of paternalistic policy. Under paternalism, clinicians or front-line workers or operators have to provide clients with what Mead calls the "help and hassle" they need to overcome their disabilities, which are presumed to be the cause of their poverty or homelessness. When disabilities are no longer thought of as causes of homelessness, the role of the providers is reduced as their intervention is no longer considered essential to overcoming privation. This is not to say that clients' disabilities do not need to be treated, but that housing no longer need be contingent on treatment and that therefore clients can choose when and if to take up treatment. Tellingly, Housing First rhetoric designates program beneficiaries not as "clients" but as "customers," and speaks of its "shift from 'expert' service provider to the 'expert' consumer of the provided service."[32] Tsemberis has said that "the whole point of consumer-driven services is putting the people that the services are intended to serve in charge of the program. Turning the asylum over to the inmates."[33] For all of its clear-headedness about the reality of mental illness, Housing First clearly represents a fundamental break with paternalism. It was under the Bloomberg administration that Housing First policies began to be widely implemented, especially in new outreach techniques to the street homeless, including the use of Safe Havens, and in changing intake procedures for homeless families to deemphasize diagnosis of underlying causes and instead stress quick planning for rapid rehousing.

Another response to the limits of paternalism was Culhane's refocus of policymakers' attention on chronic homelessness. By demonstrating that a relatively small percentage of shelter clients accounted for a greatly disproportionate percentage of shelter use, Culhane identified a strategy by which a dramatic impact on homelessness might be made: concentrate on housing the chronically homeless and thus reduce shelter use strikingly. Thus the possibility of achieving something like an end to homelessness began to seem within striking distance. Making use of Culhane's analysis, Philip Mangano of the United States Interagency Council on Homelessness, proselytized to any state and locality that would listen the importance of developing ten-year plans aimed at ending homelessness. As we saw, one of the jurisdictions that headed Mangano's call was New York City, where Bloomberg ambitiously adopted not a ten- but a five-year plan to "make the condition of chronic homelessness effectively extinct in New York"[34] and reduce the city shelter population by two-thirds. Thus the never-ending stalemate of managing homelessness that the paternalistic paradigm seemed to hold forth would be "overcome," as the mission statement of DHS under Bloomberg came to read.

Also integral to the goal of ending or at least dramatically reducing homelessness would be the strategy of prevention. Prevention represents a step away from the paternalistic paradigm because it assumes that in most cases there is nothing so very "wrong with" potentially homeless families and singles that they can't be maintained in housing with a little bit of help. Here again it was under Bloomberg that prevention was prioritized and raised to coequal status beside the task of providing shelter in the DHS mission statement. The main programmatic manifestation of that reemphasis was the Home Base program, which Bloomberg initiated, very publicly subjected to scientific evaluation, and made a centerpiece of his homelessness policy.

Thus it was during the early years of the Bloomberg administration that a post-paternalistic approach to homelessness began to be embraced in New York. The main elements of this paradigm were articulated by that administration in the 2004 overall plan to reduce the shelter census by two-thirds within five years. Not only was this goal not met, but by the end of the Bloomberg years the shelter population was at an all-time high of about sixty thousand people. What had gone wrong? Had the post-paternalistic paradigm spectacularly failed?

Rather than fail, post-paternalism was broached and then abandoned under Bloomberg. As was discussed earlier, the post-paternalistic concern with immediately planning to rehouse homeless clients implies that sufficient resources must be deployed to make those plans work, which implies that rental subsidies ought to be available. But under Bloomberg, first the priority assignment of NYCHA units and Section 8 vouchers to shelter families was stopped, then the limited rental subsidy program, Advantage, which was implemented partly to compensate for the end of these preferences, came to an end. The end of the subsidies amounted to a break with or a failure to follow through on the logic of the post-paternalistic paradigm and also precipitated the dramatic rise in the shelter census.

How is it that subsidies came to an end under Bloomberg? The administration seems to have ended the preferential access to NYCHA units and Section 8 vouchers for shelter families because it believed that policy created a perverse incentive for families to enter the system. On the basis of a temporary decline in admissions to the family system, Linda Gibbs at the time believed that "we had confirmed what everybody had expected, which is that there were a number of [families that] came toward the shelter because they were trying to do their best to access Section 8 and the Housing Authority Units. And that—when that wasn't available anymore—did cause decrease in demand."[35] Why the Advantage program came to an end is less clear. The city and the state got into a disagreement over funding, and after weeks of intense lobbying by the city to maintain the program, the state withdrew its funding, the city declined to support the program on its own, and Advantage came to an end. Having that happen on their watch had very unfortunate consequences for the Bloomberg administration. Rapidly rehousing shelter clients became much more difficult, the shelter census rose to unprecedented levels, and the very promising beginning Bloomberg made in introducing a new direction in homelessness policy came to a disappointing end.

De Blasio revived and greatly expanded the post-paternalistic paradigm that came to an end in the later Bloomberg years. The new administration did not take up some of the rhetorical flourishes of its predecessor. De Blasio declined to promise to overcome homelessness or set a specific goal for shelter census reduction, but that is the case because it was acknowledged that it would take some years before new policies could be expected to make a dent in those problems. But the Bloomberg emphasis on prevention was reinforced with the expansion of Home Base and the consolidation of various prevention programs at HRA. Subsidies, in the form of the LINC programs, consistent with the interest in rapidly rehousing rather than rehabilitating clients, were introduced. Some iterations of LINC were aimed at the chronically homeless. Homelessness is highly relevant to de Blasio's political commitment to fighting inequality, so it seems likely the new paradigm will be implemented as consistently in his administration as political reality will allow.

Nonincremental Change in a Conservative Era

Another remarkable feature of homelessness politics in New York City is that the rise of a well-funded, high-quality system of care took place, mostly, during the tenure of what John Hull Mollenkopf describes as a "conservative dominant coalition."[36] In his book *A Phoenix in the Ashes: The Rise and Fall of the Koch Coalition in New York City Politics*, Mollenkopf describes how Koch was able to forge a "conservative, white, pro-growth coalition" at a time when biracial and neighborhood-oriented coalitions were in power in other cities.[37] Mollenkopf shows in detail how the political and economic environment of New York City caused this conservative coalition to be in power more often than alternative progressive coalitions. The course of politics during the years we have discussed bear out Mollenkopf's prediction, with Koch, Giuliani, and Bloomberg all putting together variations on the conservative coalition and with Dinkins being the sole representative, before the election of de Blasio, of an alternative progressive coalition. Although Mollenkopf notes the increase in spending for the homeless under Koch, his few remarks on homelessness present the issue as one of concern primarily to white liberals and other constituents of the Dinkins progressive coalition.[38] But if that is the case, why was expansion and improvement of the homelessness system pursued not only by Dinkins but also by Koch, Giuliani, and Bloomberg, all, within the New York City context, conservatives of various stripes?

Part of the answer is the creative use made of the court system by Robert Hayes, Steven Banks, and others within the city's homelessness-policy community. To a considerable extent, the courts forced the conservative mayors to attend to a problem they otherwise might have ignored. But the power of the courts is not the whole answer. Consider, for example, Koch's decision to sign the *Callahan* consent decree. Koch himself claims that he signed the decree on the advice of his corporation council, Allen Schwartz, whom he claims said, about the *Callahan* decree and other decrees, "it's better that we sign these decrees, because otherwise they'll impose even heavier sanctions."[39] But most of the other participants on the city's side reported that one key consideration was that they felt that signing the decree was simply the right thing to do. Robert Trobe and Bonnie Stone of HRA both felt that the city could not take the position that it would not mind if some homeless people froze to death on the streets as a result of there being no decree. And according to Len Koerner of the city's Law Department, "at some point during the litigation in *Callahan*, everybody agreed that it wouldn't be so terrible if men had a right to shelter. . . . [E]verybody agreed that it was a good thing to do and therefore we signed it."[40] No doubt the city's decision to sign the *Callahan* decree was driven as well by very practical considerations, including the possibility that had the city decided to litigate the case, it might have lost and been faced with more demanding requirements. But a sense that signing the decree was the right thing to do played a hard-to-quantify role. Thus an administration representing the city's conservative-dominant coalition with few strictly self-interested reasons to care about the homeless found itself moved by what Kelman calls "[p]ublic spirit . . . [the] inclination to make an honest effort to achieve good public policy."[41]

Another key decision of the Koch administration that was motivated in part by public spirit was his decision to invest $4 billion in his ten-year housing plan. About 150,000 units would eventually be developed. Only 10 percent of those units would go to homeless families, partly because a program that featured benefits for moderate-income families was politically more tenable. Nonetheless, building support for the plan was not easy. In his recent biography, *Ed Koch and the Rebuilding of New York City*, Jonathan Soffer writes, "In practice the mayor got flack for his program from both the Left and the Right. The Right wanted an unregulated private housing market. . . . [T]he Left. . . . deplored Koch's decision to build significant amounts of middle-income housing, demanding that the needs of the poor should come first."[42] Mollenkopf argues that Koch "felt compelled" to adopt his housing plan, despite his political base, which included "real estate developers, investors . . . their lawyers . . . the city's business elites and the leading voices for the establishment," because of "intense conflicts" that his otherwise pro–private developer and pro-gentrification policies precipitated.[43] But a sense that rebuilding low- to moderate-income New York was simply good public policy was also important.

Public spirit was perhaps also a factor in the Bloomberg administration's early efforts to emphasize and forge a new direction in homelessness policy. Exactly why that administration did not follow up on its insights is hard to determine. Too much concern with perverse incentives seems to have played a role. And perhaps Bloomberg's public-spirited desire to address homelessness was in the end overcome by the fact that the problem was simply not central to his main political concern of economic development.

Public spirit was perhaps less obvious during the Giuliani administration than under Koch or Bloomberg. Certainly Giuliani devoted considerable attention to homelessness policy—more, perhaps, than one might have expected of a conservative. Giuliani's main policy direction was implementing the recommendations of the Cuomo Commission. No doubt Giuliani believed that this represented good public policy. But it also represented good political instincts, for during his second, successful campaign for mayor, Giuliani achieved considerable political mileage from promising to be a more energetic supporter of the Cuomo Commission than Dinkins seemed to be. Other signature Giuliani policies, such as the campaigns against squeegee men and in favor of public order, were essentially what would be expected from a mayor with a white, middle- and upper-middle-class base.

Public spirit played a role in the Dinkins administration. The most striking feature of Dinkins's homelessness policy was its U-turn from a conventional liberal approach emphasizing rights and rapid access to permanent housing to a paternalistic style that focused on rehabilitation, eligibility, and quid pro quo. It is true that this paternalistic turn was more a matter of intention than implementation under Dinkins. We have discussed how Dinkins was slow to embrace the change of direction supported by the Cuomo Commission, perhaps for ideological reasons, so that when he eventually did, little time was left for implementation. But Dinkins did finally accept the commission's recommendations even though they flew in the face of the progressive policy direction outlined while he was Manhattan borough president and endorsed by the city's liberal coalition. A number of factors explain this shift. The apparently incorrect perception that a perverse incentive had been created by the rapid rehousing of homeless families had an impact. So did the emergence of Andrew Cuomo as a skilled policy entrepreneur. But the simple fact that the Cuomo Commission put together a convincing case that persuaded Dinkins that a change in direction was the right policy decision was also important.

The development of an improved shelter system during a time of domination, mostly, by a conservative ruling coalition becomes less incongruous if it is placed in the context of other policy developments during that time. We have already mentioned the rebuilding of the city's marginal housing stock. The decline in crime and the development of safer public spaces is well known. A less noticed accomplishment is the vast improvement in public transportation since the early 1980s.[44] We usually think of a conservative-dominant coalition as being narrowly concerned with balancing budgets and economic development. During the time period covered here, New York City's conservative coalition did more than that.

In that it has achieved things one might not expect of a city dominated for a considerable period by a conservative coalition, New York City resembles Atlanta as it is described by Clarence N. Stone in *Regime Politics: Governing Atlanta, 1946–1988*. Stone describes a governing coalition in which the downtown business elite plays a preponderant role. Yet the Atlanta governing coalition has a record of accomplishments that go beyond a narrow business focus. Stone writes,

> Governance requires the power to combine necessary elements for a publicly significant result—whether it is building a downtown expressway system, developing new housing for blacks in the outer area of the Westside, hiring black police officers in a Jim Crow city, redeveloping substandard areas next to the business district, peacefully desegregating the school system in an era of massive resistance, launching a mass-transit system, putting on a National Black Arts Festival, or rebuilding Underground Atlanta as a major entertainment district. Atlanta's postwar governing coalition has accomplished all of this and more.[45]

In Atlanta, the downtown business elite governs, not by domination, as is described in Floyd Hunter's classic account of the power structure of that city during the 1950s,[46] but because the resources it commands and the internal coordination it has achieved makes it an attractive partner to any interest group hoping to achieve significant change. The result is that Atlanta's business elite usually works in partnership with the city's black middle class, and anyone else who wants to get something done. Atlanta's governing coalition is "activist but not progressive."[47] It focuses, as the phrase goes, not on exercising *power over* the populace, but on deploying *power to* "carry on great enterprises."[48]

New York City's dominant governing coalition looks nothing like Atlanta's. In particular, the black middle class in the Big Apple plays nothing like the role that it does in Atlanta. The regimes resemble each other, however, in both being activist but not progressive, which is the phenomenon we are trying to understand. Stone's analysis of Atlanta is also relevant because in New York, with its decades-old tradition of civic enterprise, power is most usefully understood as power to, rather than power over. But the way in which power to is exercised in New York City is very different than in Atlanta, or perhaps than in any other American city.

Exercising the power to in New York City involves getting things done in a highly fragmented political environment. One sense in which that environment is fragmented is that there are simply very many formal governments. It is still true that, as Robert Wood famously wrote in his 1961 book *1400 Governments*, the New York City metropolitan area is "a governmental arrangement perhaps more complicated than any other that mankind has yet contrived or allowed to happen."[49] If we focus on just the formal city government, it too is fragmented in various ways. It is a strong-mayor form of government, meaning that the executive and legislature are independent of each other. Unlike most cities, New York encompasses five separate counties, which are also boroughs and which were each represented on the city's Board of Estimate before that entity was abolished in 1989. Moreover, as Theodore Lowi wrote in his classic account, *At the Pleasure of the Mayor*, New York City government is "highly articulated," in the sense that it consists of many different agencies trying to do many different things.[50] Each agency is lobbied by and responds to its own set of interest or "satellite" groups, with the result that "there are as many 'governments' as there are areas of public responsibility."[51] Those who would exercise power to carry on great enterprises in New York City face a blooming, buzzing confusion of a political environment.

Such fragmentation is supposed to frustrate change. As one textbook on urban politics put the matter, "In addition, political fragmentation makes it difficult to assemble sufficient political resources to address problems. It may be impossible to arrive at consensus among so many different jurisdictions, and this may lead to 'immobilism and non-decisionmaking.' . . . Urban political structures change slowly in an incremental, evolutionary fashion."[52]

But as we have seen, homelessness policy in New York City has over the last thirty-six years developed in a series of striking leaps with dramatic, short-term changes in funding, administration, and policy "philosophy." How was this possible?

Part of the answer is that New York City's fragmented governance system creates many opportunities for policy entrepreneurship, and policy entrepreneurship is capable of precipitating nonincremental change.

Policy entrepreneurship refers to political activity by middle men (and women) who simplify and distill expert knowledge and disseminate it in a broader political arena. Political actors—private individuals, elected officials, organizations—resort to entrepreneurship when they find it difficult to organize a potential interest group. Policy entrepreneurs stand a better chance of getting their ideas adopted in fragmented governance structures. By hypothesis, policy entrepreneurs represent an unorganized interest. Such interests will not necessarily prevail in a general political contest (for example, in a national election for a parliament), where voters must weigh many different policy ideas and make one vote that is only slightly influenced by any one of them. Policy entrepreneurs have a better chance when there are many political contests. For one thing, the more contests, the more chances of an unorganized interest prevailing. Further, where there are many political contests, some of them are likely to be nonelectoral. Court cases are a good example. In court, a policy entrepreneur need only convince one citizen—the judge—to adopt a policy idea.

But fragmented governance structures are favorable to policy entrepreneurs for another reason. Fragmented governance almost necessarily implies separation of powers. The separate election and independent standing of the executive and the legislature is the most fundamental of all government fragmentations. In the centralized system of parliamentary governments, policy entrepreneurs, if they cannot capture a majority of the all-powerful legislature, are completely out of luck. In a separation-of-powers system, policy entrepreneurs have a chance of getting their way if they can achieve the less daunting task of capturing the executive. Of course, capturing the executive is of little use if the executive has little power. In a strong-mayor system, in which a sole executive has direct authority over the bureaucracy (as opposed to weak-mayor systems, in which the mayor is but one member of a council to whom the bureaucracy is collectively responsible), policy entrepreneurs, when they capture the executive, have a better chance of seeing their ideas implemented.

Finally, policy entrepreneurs have better chances when the political environment is not only fragmented but competitive. Where there are lively contests between two parties, there are two happy outcomes political entrepreneurs may achieve. Both parties may struggle to "own" a particular policy idea. This is what happened in Washington in the 1980s with tax reform and in the 1990s with welfare reform. Republicans and Democrats competed with each other to see who could come up with the flattest tax, the most demanding welfare system. Nonincremental policy change is the likely result of such a "bidding up" competition. Another possibility is that one party may win possession of a policy idea and go on to capture some branch of government with it. In that case the winning party has a clear mandate to implement its idea. Again, nonincremental change is a likely result.

In most respects, fragmented New York City fits the bill of an entrepreneur-friendly environment. To begin with, in New York City, courts have jurisdiction over administrative decisions by the bureaucracy. Hayes's strategy of translating a political demand—"help the homeless"—into a litigable right—"the right to shelter"—is a textbook case of judicial political entrepreneurship. It was also a classic example of the "rights strategy"—converting a potentially unpopular political demand into a right—which is particularly effective in the context of American political culture and a strong judiciary.[53] This strategy helped Hayes to sell his cause to the public and the media, for an unprepossessing interest had been transformed into a hard-to-deny cause.

It is precisely because in New York policymaking power is fragmented between the courts and the other branches that advocates could achieve real power by winning in the courts. With the court effectively on their side, advocates had great say in remaking the shelter system, as the mayor had few choices besides defying the court or going along. Thus, for practical purposes, the nonincremental change of a right to shelter for singles, with all its fiscal and programmatic implications, had arrived.

As we have discussed, *McCain* and related cases and regulations are good examples of how a fragmented political environment, usually thought to generate many veto points, can sometimes create many opportunity points.[54] The fact that the state, as well as the city, had jurisdiction over the shelters was crucial here. As we saw, the question of what homeless families were entitled to bounced back and forth between various cases and various courts and the state Department of Social Services, receiving new additions or modifications each time. The result of many incremental steps turned out to be the nonincremental step of creating what was effectively a right to shelter for families.

When nonincremental change is achieved, future changes are more likely to be nonincremental as well. For past policy is an influence on future policy. Where past policy has been characterized by dramatic breaks, future dramatic breaks are legitimated. Moreover, when one interest wins a striking victory, other interests mobilize to fight back. By 1989 advocates for the homeless were seen, correctly or not, as having gotten almost everything they wanted. When the right to shelter appeared to have its own problems, the advocates for the homeless, correctly or not, were seen as having been discredited. Yet the idea that radical change was not per se bad had been established. It was inevitable that a counter idea would start to crystallize in such an environment.

That New York City homelessness policy was based on the idea of a right to shelter was a potential barrier to the crystallization of a counter idea. Significantly, the counter idea that did crystallize—mutual obligation—specifically did not reject the right to shelter but only stressed that with a right should come a responsibility. In this way the popular rights premise was not challenged directly. Two features of New York City politics account for the sudden success of this counter idea. First was the newly competitive political environment. As a Republican competed strongly for the mayoralty for the first time in decades he, Giuliani, was naturally eager to find some idea to use against the Democrat. Of course, Dinkins too had an incentive to embrace new ideas, but to do so in the case of homelessness policy would have required of him a 180-degree turn. That was by no means impossible, but Dinkins was ideologically and psychologically not disposed to it, and Giuliani had the easier task of picking up a new idea and running with it.

Further, New York City's strong-mayor government made the counter idea of mutual obligation relatively easy to implement. In a weak-mayor system, Giuliani would have had to resell his idea to the other members of the council, and then turn it over to a general administrative officer or city manager to implement. As an institutionally strong mayor, Giuliani could choose and hold accountable his own policy team. Thus a second bout of nonincremental change, the paternalistic moment, came about.

We are still left with the problem of distinguishing incremental and nonincremental change. The changes wrought by *Callahan v. Carey* in the New York City shelter system, even in budgetary terms, surely count as a nonincremental change. But the changes in the shelter system stemming from *The Way Home*, while extensive and important, did not generate such a striking quantifiable change. Was this second bout of change, then, really nonincremental? We might respond by noting that magnitude is not necessarily the main measure of nonincremental change. The feature of nonincremental change that especially interests us is that it breaks with the incrementalist model by producing changes that that model would predict are not possible during times of ordinary politics. Put another way, nonincremental change is the product of the "politics of values and ideas," with its key features of expertise, policy entrepreneurs, institutional fragmentation, competitive political environments, and, especially, public ideas. Defined in these terms, the paternalistic reform of the shelter system under Giuliani was nonincremental, for it did involve public ideas, policy entrepreneurs, and so on, as discussed here.

Thus the first two moments in New York City homelessness policy—the entitlement moment and then the paternalistic moment—can be considered nonincremental changes that were precipitated by policy entrepreneurs marketing attractive public ideas in a competitive, highly fragmented political environment. What about the third policy moment we have identified, the post-paternalistic moment characterized significantly by the rise of the Housing First "philosophy" and movement?

Housing First might be considered an instance of "policy feedback," in which a new policy is forged in reaction to perceived failures or successes of past policy.[55] As we saw, one of the earliest manifestations of the paternalistic reaction to the entitlement moment that characterized most of the Koch and Dinkins administrations was Koch's attempt to involuntarily transport mentally ill street dwellers to Bellevue Hospital under the Project HELP outreach program. Whatever one thinks about the mental competency of Project HELP's most famous client, Joyce Brown, and of the ethics of mandatory psychiatric treatment, the policy of involuntary transportation proved to be a failure, as mental health law, a strong advocacy community, and limited hospital facilities made it impossible to permanently remove mentally ill homeless people from the streets against their will. Tsemberis was hired as director of Project HELP shortly after the Joyce Brown affair cost the earlier director her job, and he saw the futility of the revolving door between the streets and psychiatric wards that the project created. And later, after the development of the paternalistically oriented program shelters during the Giuliani administration, more policy actors would become aware of the limitations of the paternalistic model as many clients of the shelters for singles declined to accept the quid pro quo of better services for enrollment in the therapeutic services of a program shelter and remained in the city-operated general intake shelter. Housing First was conceived and implemented as a feedback response to the failures of paternalism to reduce the number of street people to acceptable levels and to enroll enough clients in therapeutic services.

There appeared at this moment of policy failure a charismatic policy entrepreneur, Sam Tsemberis. He faced a formidable challenge in marketing his proposed policy change. With the report of the Cuomo Commission and its adoption and implementation by the Giuliani administration, the paternalistic reaction to the initial entitlement moment had crystallized. Housing First represented a radical rejection of the "underlying cause" and "quid pro quo" assumptions of paternalism. Moreover, Housing First had roots in a number of ideologies that were unpopular among many mental health service providers. Tsemberis has described himself as a follower of R. D. Laing, the radical psychiatrist whose work seemed to question the whole idea of mental illness. Although Tsemberis never denied the reality of mental illness, his insistence that the homeless were "experts in their own lives," and his emphasis on making services customer-centered rather than clinician-centered meant that Housing First was likely to meet with at least initial opposition from the mental health service providers who were *ex hypothesi* to be put out of charge of their programs. Tsemberis, along with his coauthors, has also noted that "[m]ainstream housing and treatment providers were also extremely skeptical about the efficacy and consequences of the PHF (Pathways Housing First) model of service delivery. Some voiced concern for consumers, saying that placing homeless persons with mental illness in permanent housing was reckless and potentially damaging."[56] How then did this radical departure from settled policy make any headway?

Again, part of the answer is that New York City's unusual political environment is conducive to policy entrepreneurship. Deborah Padgett, former president of the board of Pathways to Housing and a Housing First researcher, has argued that "[p]athways . . . could have only happened in New York. . . . because we have such a chaotic, fragmented system that this little upstart could take root."[57] At the time Pathways to Housing was founded, New York City's homelessness service system had been privatized, or more accurately not-for-profitized. Housing and services were provided not by a single entity like the city, but by a wide range of private organizations. In this environment it was possible for a single, small provider with a distinctive philosophy to spring up. Convincing a single city- or state-wide provider to abandon its settled practices and embrace a radical policy departure would have been much more difficult.

Another aspect of New York's fragmented policy environment was also crucial: Authority over homelessness policy was shared among the city, state, and federal governments. At crucial moments Tsemberis received help from the state and federal governments at a time when the city, having bought into the paternalistic paradigm, was less sympathetic. The first support for Pathways to Housing came not from the city but from New York State, whose progressive commissioner of the Office of Mental Health, Richard Surles, was more open to the radical message of Housing First than the Giuliani administration would have been. Later, the federal government also played a hand in the institutionalization of Housing First when Phil Mangano, executive director of the U.S. Interagency Council on Homelessness, became a convert to the cause. Mangano, who had given up on the strategy of trying to coordinate the behemoths of the federal bureaucracy, instead conceived of himself as an advocate and was in search of an idea he could market to cities and states. During Mangano's tenure on the council (2002–2009), the scholarly literature supporting Housing First had come to a critical mass, providing him with material to disseminate. As we saw, it was Mangano who was instrumental in selling Housing First, and the idea of a plan to end homelessness, to the Bloomberg administration.

This brings us to another feature of the new politics of public policy that played a key role in New York City's, and the world's, adoption of Housing First: professional consensus. Housing First went from being a radical initiative to international standard operating procedure in large part because the academic literature overwhelmingly supported Tsemberis's claim that his approach provided better outcomes in housing retention, cost savings, and other key goals than did traditional approaches. Indeed, it was with an idea of developing such a consensus that Tsemberis from the beginning subjected his approach to rigorous evaluation; he knew that such convincing evidence would be necessary to overcome initial skepticism. Tsemberis also showed good judgment in taking the results of arcane scientific analysis and boiling them down into one easily communicated public idea: "Housing First."

Overall, Housing First is a striking example of how an idea, based in professional consensus, effectively communicated by policy entrepreneurs, and developing a toe-hold in a fragmented policy environment, can effectuate nonincremental change in what has traditionally been thought to be a situation unfriendly to dramatic innovation.

We are not in a position to make sweeping claims about the nature of urban political change. But perhaps urban political science can look at the history of homelessness policy in New York City and consider the possibility that fragmentation leads, not to stasis or gridlock but to change.

APPENDIX

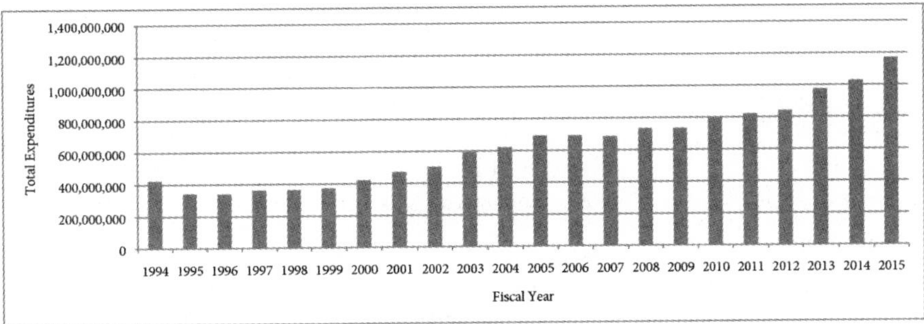

Department of Homeless Services expenditures (1994–2015). *Source:* Comprehensive Annual Fiscal Reports of the Controller; figure for 2015 comes from the New York City Office of Management and Budget, Current Modified Budget, Adopted Budget FY 2016.

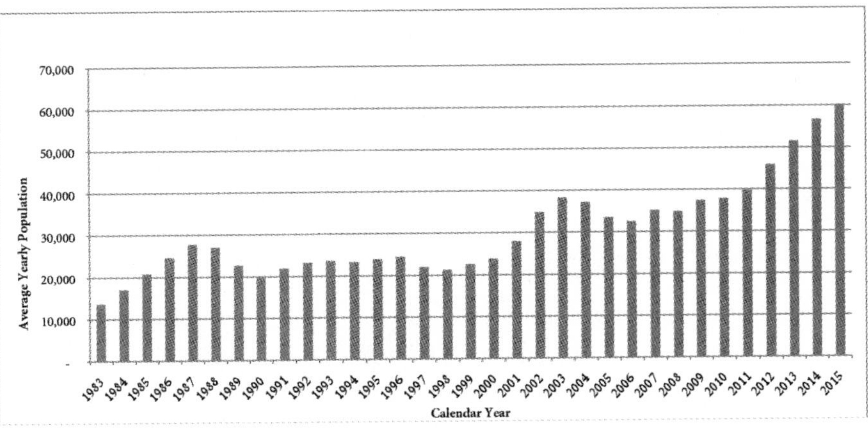

New York City homeless municipal shelter population, 1983–present: total population. All New York City homeless municipal shelter population figures from NYC Department of Homeless Services and Human Resources Administration and NYCStat shelter census reports. *Note:* For data through September 2011, figures for homeless families, children, and adult family members reflect end-of-month census data. All numbers for families after September 2011 and for homeless single adults (men and women) for all months reflect average daily census data.

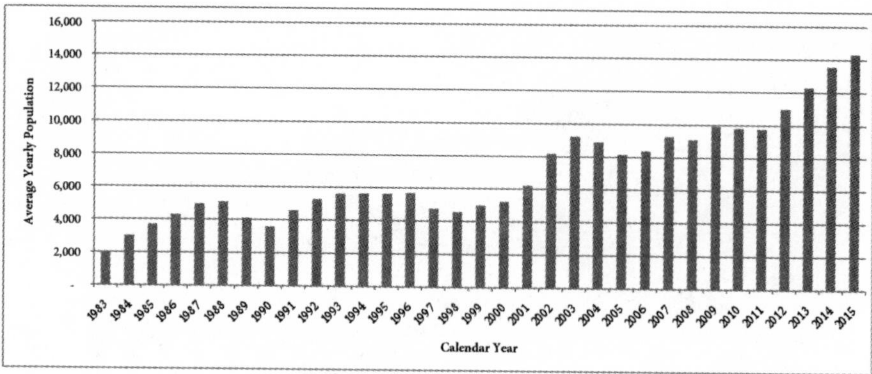

New York City homeless municipal shelter population, 1983–present: total families.

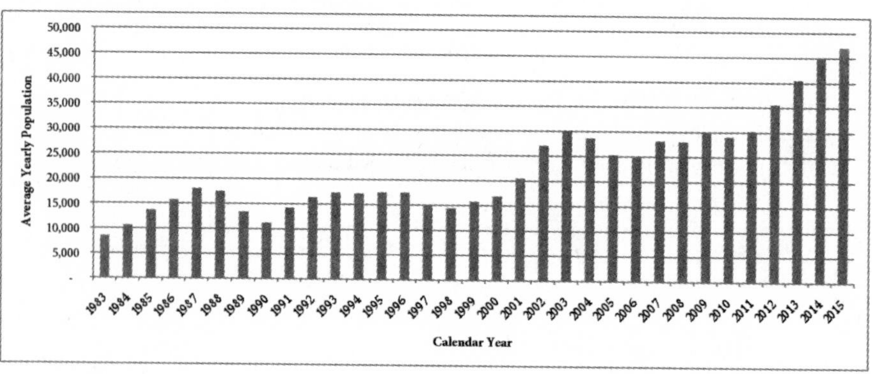

New York City homeless municipal shelter population, 1983–present: total persons in families.

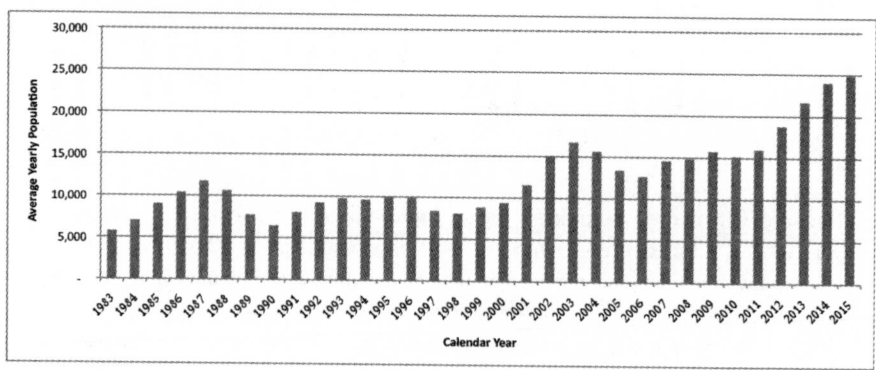

New York City homeless municipal shelter population, 1983–present: children.

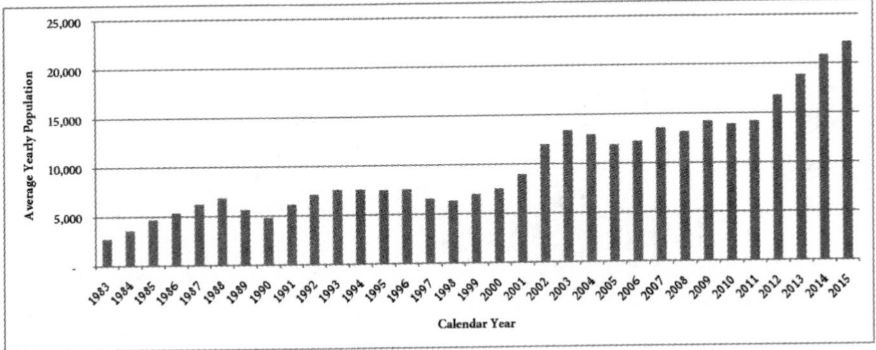

New York City homeless municipal shelter population, 1983–present: adults in families.

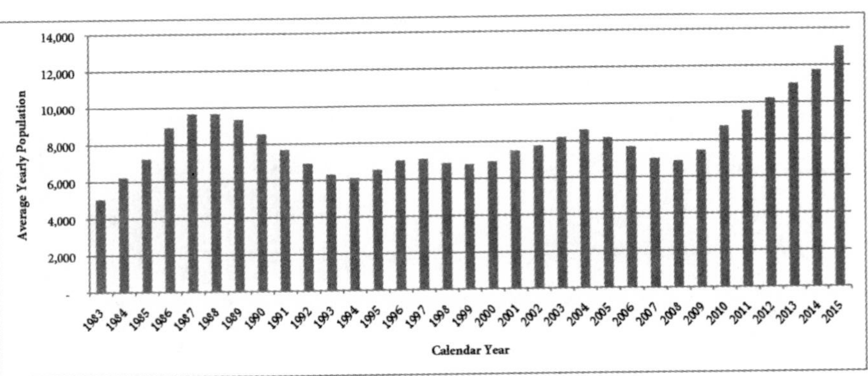

New York City homeless municipal shelter population, 1983–present: single adults.

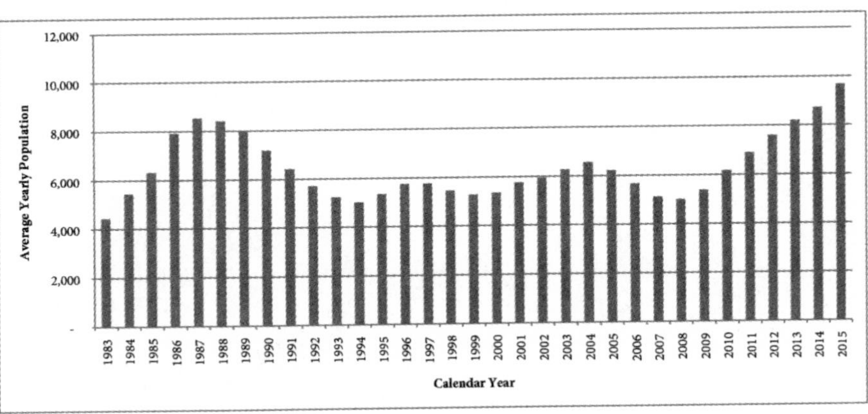

New York City homeless municipal shelter population, 1983–present: single men.

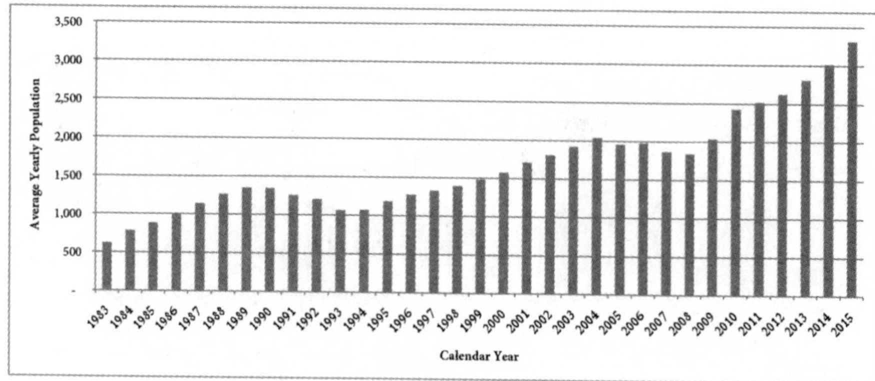

New York City homeless municipal shelter population, 1983–present: single women.

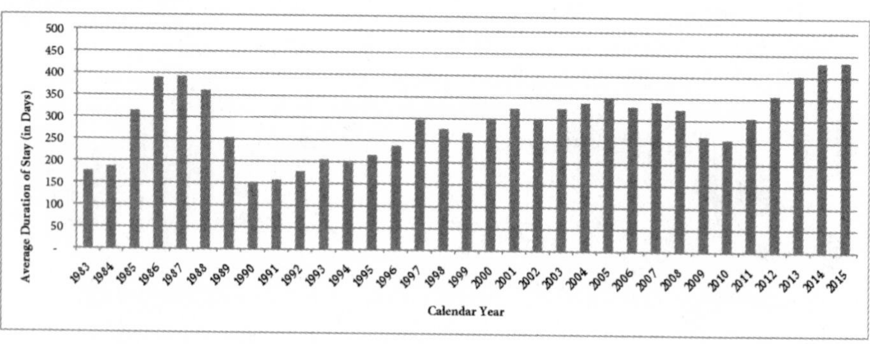

New York City homeless municipal shelter population, 1983–present: average shelter stays for families (in days).

NOTES

PREFACE TO THE PAPERBACK EDITION

1 Eric Alterman, *Inequality in One City: Bill de Blasio and the New York Experiment, Year One* (New York: Nation, 2015), 18.

2 Nikita Stewart, "Fight Looms as de Blasio Plans to Seek 90 New Homeless Shelters," *New York Times*, February 28, 2017, www.nytimes.com.

3 Dina Temple-Raston, "Bloomberg Vows to Make Chronic Homelessness 'Extinct,'" *New York Sun*, June 24, 2004.

4 City of New York, "Uniting for Solutions beyond Shelter: The Action Plan for New York City," undated, pp. 4, 34, http://www.nyc.gov.

5 New York City Independent Budget Office, "Further Increases to Homeless Rental Assistance, but Additional Funds for Shelter Still Necessary," May 2015, p. 2, http://www.ibo.nyc.ny.us.

6 "New York City Department of Investigation: Probe of Department of Homeless Services'Shelters for Families with Children Finds Serious Deficiencies," March 12, 2015, www.nyc.gov.

7 E-mail from HRA spokesperson to Thomas J. Main, April 13, 2017.

8 Giselle Routhier, "Family Homelessness in NYC: City and State Must Meet Unprecedented Scale of Crisis with Proven Solutions," Coalition for the Homeless, January 2017, p. 9, www.coalitionforthehomeless.org.

9 City of New York, "Turning the Tide on Homelessness in New York City," undated, pp. ii–iii, http://www.nyc.gov.

INTRODUCTION

1 B. G. Link et al., "Lifetime and Five-Year Prevalence of Homelessness in the United States," *American Journal of Public Health* 84, no. 12 (1994): pp. 1907–12.

2 U.S. Department of Housing and Urban Development, Office of Community Planning and Development, *The 2013 Annual Homeless Assessment Report to Congress*, part 2, *Estimates of Homelessness in the United States*, p. 23. https://www.hudexchange.info/onecpd/assets/File/2013-AHAR-Part-2.pdf, p. 23.

3 U.S. Interagency Council on Homelessness, Fiscal Year 2013 Federal Government Homelessness Budget Fact Sheet, p. 2. http://usich.gov/resources/uploads/asset_library/FY13_Budget_Fact_Sheet_final.pdf

4 National Alliance to End Homelessness, Homelessness Research Institute, Data Point: Homeless Assistance Funding: Federal versus State and Local Assistance,

July 2011. http://www.endhomelessness.org/library/entry/data-point-homeless-assistance-program-funding-federal-versus-state-and-loc

5 U.S. Department of Housing and Urban Development, *The 2010 Annual Homeless Assessment Report to Congress*, p. 18.

6 Gallup Poll, March 2013. Retrieved April 16, 2013, from the iPOLL Databank, The Roper Center for Public Opinion Research, University of Connecticut. http://www.ropercenter.uconn.edu/data_access/ipoll/ipoll.html. See more at http://www.spotlightonpoverty.org/polling.aspx?id=a7a5c9dc-e2e6-4204-8958-1a003e09abca#sthash.LlSlkfGY.dpuf.

7 C. Lindbloom, "The Science of Muddling Through," *Public Administration Review* 19, no. 2 (1959): pp. 79–88; C. Lindbloom, "Still Muddling, Not Yet Through," *Public Administration Review* 39 (1979): pp. 517–26.

8 See, for example, Harold Meyerson, "Did the Founding Fathers Screw Up?" *American Prospect*, September 26, 2011, which argues that "Gridlock in Washington is no accident. It's built into the Constitution."

9 Examples of works expressing such concerns include James MacGregor Burns, *The Deadlock of Democracy* (Englewood Cliffs, NJ: Prentice Hall, 1963); Lloyd N. Cutler, "To Form a Government," *Foreign Affairs* 59 (Fall 1980): pp. 126–43; James L Sundquist, *Constitutional Reform and Effective Government* (Washington, DC: Brookings Institution Press, 1986); Daniel Lazare, *The Frozen Republic: How the Constitution Is Paralyzing Democracy* (New York: Harcourt Brace, 1996); Sanford Levinson, *Our Undemocratic Constitution: Where the Constitution Goes Wrong (and How We the People Can Correct It* (New York: Oxford University Press, 2006); Larry J. Sabato, *A More Perfect Constitution: 23 Proposals to Revitalize Our Constitution and Make America a Fairer Country* (New York: Walker, 2007).

10 Timothy J. Conlan, David R. Beam, and Margaret T. Wrightson, "Policy Models and Political Change: Insights from the Passage of Tax Reform," in Marc K. Landy and Martin A. Levin, eds., *The New Politics of Public Policy* (Baltimore, MD: Johns Hopkins University Press, 1995), p. 121.

11 National Alliance to End Homelessness, Homelessness Research Institute, Data Point: Homeless Assistance Funding: Federal versus State and Local Assistance, July 2011. http://www.endhomelessness.org/library/entry/data-point-homeless-assistance-program-funding-federal-versus-state-and-loc

12 For the count of the city's sheltered homeless see Coalition for the Homeless, "New York City Municipal Shelter Population, 1983–Present," undated, http://www.coalitionforthehomeless.org/wp-content/uploads/2014/04/NYCHomelessShelterPopulation-Worksheet1983-Present4-Sheet1.pdf; for the count of the city's homeless people who live in public spaces, see New York City Department of Homeless Services, "Homeless Outreach Population Estimate (HOPE) Shows Five Percent Decrease in Unsheltered Population since 2014," May 17, 2015. http://www.nyc.gov/html/dhs/downloads/pdf/03-15-HOPE-Count-Findings-Release.pdf

13 For an account of the welfare hotels that helped establish their infamous status, see generally Jonathan Kozol, *Rachel and Her Children: Homeless Families in America* (New York: Crown, 1988).

14 Jennifer Toth, *The Mole People: Life in the Tunnels beneath New York City* (Chicago: Chicago Review Press, 1993); Teun Voeten, *Tunnel People*, updated edition (Oakland, CA: PM Press, 2010). Toth's account of "a city beneath the streets" seems exaggerated. Better documented is Voeten's estimate of some thirty to fifty people living in the relatively accessible Amtrak railroad tunnel on Manhattan's Upper West Side.

15 Diana R. Gordon, "A Hotel Is Not a Home," chapter 7 in *City Limits: Barriers to Change in Urban Government* (New York: Charterhouse, 1973), pp. 255–93.

16 Ronald K. Vogel and John J. Harrigan, *Political Change in the Metropolis*, 8th ed. (New York: Pearson Longman, 2007), p. 27.

17 Wallace S. Sayre and Herbert Kaufman, *Governing New York City* (New York: Russell Sage Foundation, 1960), p. 716; Theodore J. Lowi, *At the Pleasure of the Mayor* (New York: Free Press of Glencoe, 1964), p. 199.

18 Martin Shefter, in *Political Crisis/Fiscal Crisis* (New York: Columbia University Press, 1992), emphasized the "boundaries within which the game of urban politics is played and the imperatives confronting the players of that game" (p. xxviii). Similarly, Ira Katznelson in *City Trenches* (Chicago: University of Chicago Press, 1981), emphasizes the "boundaries and rules" of urban politics (p. 6). In *City Limits* (Chicago: University of Chicago Press, 1981), Paul E. Peterson argues that "city politics is limited politics," p. 4.

19 Blanche Blank, "Bureaucracy: Power in Details," in Jewel Bellush and Dick Netzer, eds., *Urban Politics New York Style* (Armonk, NY: M.E. Sharpe, 1990), chapter 5.

20 Charles Brecher and Raymond D. Horton with Robert A. Cropf and Dean Michael Mead, *Power Failure: New York City Politics and Policy since 1960* (Oxford: Oxford University Press, 1993), p. 14.

21 Michael Lipsky, *Street-Level Bureaucracy: Dilemmas of the Individual in Public Services* (New York: Russell Sage Foundation, 1980), p. 192.

22 Marc K. Landy and Martin A. Levin, eds., *The New Politics of Public Policy* (Baltimore, MD: Johns Hopkins University Press, 1995), p. x.

23 See Thomas J. Main, "Quantum Change in the Fragmented Metropolis: Political Environment and Homeless Policy in New York City," in *Review of Policy Research* 23, no. 4 (2006): pp. 903–13; and Thomas J. Main, "Nonincremental Change in an Urban Environment: The Case of New York City's Human Resources Administration," in *Administration & Society* 37, no. 4 (2005): pp. 483–503.

24 Michael Cragg and Brendan O'Flaherty, "Do Homeless Shelter Conditions Determine Shelter Population? The Case of the Dinkins Deluge," *Journal of Urban Economics* 46 (1999): pp. 377–415.

25 Mayor Bloomberg has been quoted as saying that "[o]ne theory is that some people have been coming into the homeless system, the shelter system, in order to qualify for a program that helps you move out of the homeless system." Mosi

Secret, "City Sees End to Rental Aid for the Homeless," *New York Times*, June 1, 2001, p. A1.

26 See Albert O. Hirschman, *The Rhetoric of Reaction: Perversity, Futility, Jeopardy* (Cambridge, MA: Harvard University Press, 1991).

27 Sarah L. Kellerman, "Is Deinstitutionalization Working for the Mentally Ill?" (New York: Department of Mental Health, Mental Retardation, and Alcoholism Services, 1982), p. 9.

28 See Thomas J. Main, "Shelters for Homeless Men in New York City: Towards Paternalism through Privatization," in Lawrence Mead, ed., *The New Paternalism* (Washington, DC: Brookings Institution Press, 1997), pp. 161–81.

29 In the early eighties there was a single EAU, which was at 241 Church Street in Manhattan. In the mid-1980s there were four EAUs, one in each borough except Staten Island. Through the nineties and the early twenty-first century, there was again a single EAU, this time at East 151st Street in the Bronx. It was the EAU at that location that developed the infamous reputation.

30 Gail Nayowith, one of three court-appointed special masters who recommended the EAU be eliminated; quoted in David Saltonstall with Mark Fass, "Despised Homeless Intake Office to Be Gutted," *Daily News*, June 27, 2004, p. 24.

31 New York City Department of Homeless Services, Power Point presentation, Hope 2014: The Street Survey, slide 2.

32 Thomas J. Main, "The Heuristics of Homelessness: Balancing Structural and Individual Causes," *Journal of Social Distress and the Homeless* 7, no. 1 (1998): pp. 41–54; Thomas J. Main, "Analyzing Evidence for the Structural Theory of Homelessness," *Journal of Urban Affairs* 18, no. 4 (1996): pp. 449–57.

33 National Multifamily Housing Council, *Tabulations of 2013 American Community Survey, 1-Year Estimates*. Updated Sept. 2014. Table, "Large Cities: Population, Housing, and Renters." Accessed at http://www.nmhc.org/Content.aspx?id=4708, February 12, 2015.

34 Mireya Navarro, "In New York, Having a Job, or 2, Doesn't Mean Having a Home," *New York Times*, September 17, 2013. Navarro reports that "[m]ore than one out of four families in shelters, 28 percent, include at least one employed adult, city figures show, and 16 percent of single adults in shelters hold jobs," but does not otherwise indicate the source of these numbers. Researcher Elizabeth Brown of the Independent Budget Office has tried to confirm these numbers with the city but has so far been unable to do so. Coalition for the Homeless obtained data from the Department of Homeless Services through a freedom of information request that showed 3,214 homeless families and 1,486 single adults reporting some income from employment in 2013. Blog post, Patrick Markee, "NY Times: Working New Yorkers without Homes," posted September 18, 2013, at http://www.coalitionforthehomeless.org/ny-times-working-new-yorkers-without-homes/.

35 Milton Friedman and George J. Stigler, "Roofs or Ceilings? The Current Housing Problem" (Irvington-on-Hudson, NY: Foundation for Economic Education, 1946).

36 Rachana Sheth and Robert Neuwirth, "New York's Housing Underground: A Refuge and Resource" (Brooklyn and Jackson Heights, NY: Pratt Center for Community Development and Chhaya Community Development Corporation, March 2008).

37 Unpublished master's thesis, Mari Kanai, "The Solution to the Crisis of Low-Cost Housing in New York City: Creating an 'Accessory Dwelling Unit' Category," Baruch College, 2013.

CHAPTER 1. THE BEGINNINGS OF HOMELESSNESS POLICY UNDER KOCH

1 Howard M. Bahr and Theodore Caplow, *Old Men Drunk and Sober* (New York: NYU Press, 1973). Research for this study of Bowery men began in 1963, p. v.

2 John Darnton, "Alone and Homeless, 'Shutouts' of Society Sleep in Doorways," *New York Times*, October 26, 1971, p. 82.

3 Pranay Gupte, "The Derelict Population Is Declining, but the Whole City Is Its 'Flophouse,'" *New York Times*, October 23, 1973, p. 49.

4 John L. Hess, "Vagrants and Panhandlers Appearing in New Haunts," *New York Times*, August 6, 1976, p. B15.

5 Kim Hopper, *Reckoning with Homelessness* (Ithaca, NY: Cornell University Press, 2003), pp. 100–102.

6 David C. Anderson, "A Good Neighbor Shelter: No Longer a Horror on East Third Street," *New York Times*, December 11, 1991, p. A26.

7 Personal interview with Bonnie Stone, October 26, 2011.

8 For a detailed description of the Men's Shelter and the big room as they were during the late seventies and early eighties, see Hopper, *Reckoning with Homelessness*, pp. 85–86, 93–100.

9 Kim Hopper and L. Stuart Cox, "Litigation in Advocacy for the Homeless: The Case of New York City" (New York: Coalition for the Homeless, May 1982), p. 8.

10 Gerald Benjamin with Melissa Cusa, "Social Policy," in Gerald Benjamin and Henrik N. Dullea, eds., *Decision 1997: Constitutional Change in New York* (Albany, NY: Rockefeller Institute Press, 1997), p. 310.

11 Jeffrey Omar Usman, "Good Enough for Government Work: The Interpretation of Positive Constitutional Rights in State Constitutions," *Albany Law Review* 73 (2010): p. 1503.

12 *Tucker v. Toya*, 43 NY 2d 1, 400 N.Y.S. 2d 728 (1977).

13 43 NY 2d 437 and 448–49.

14 Ibid.

15 Christine Robitscher Ladd, "Note: A Right to Shelter for the Homeless in New York State," *New York University Law Review* (May 1986): p. 272.

16 Doron Gopstein (with George Gutwirth), "Litigation Affecting the Homeless," paper presented August 9, 1988, American Bar Association, Governmental Liability Committee, Toronto, Canada, p. 4.

17 "Judge to Hear Suit on Derelict Shelter," *New York Times*, October 27, 1979, p. 23.

18 Hopper, *Reckoning with Homelessness*, p. 92.

19 Glenn Fowler, "Koch Pays Visit to New Shelter on Wards Island," *New York Times*, January 4, 1980, p. 82.

20 *Mayor's Management Report*, May 9, 1980, Section on Human Resources Administration, Family and Adult Services.

21 *Callahan v. Carey*, Index No. 42581/1979, 12/5/1979 Sup. Ct. Order.

22 Jonathan Soffer, *Ed Koch and the Rebuilding of New York City* (New York: Columbia University Press, 2010), p. 281.

23 Gopstein with Gutwirth, "Litigation Affecting the Homeless."

24 *Callahan v. Carey*, Index No. 42581/1979, 12/24/1979 Sup. Ct. Order.

25 Personal interview with Robert Hayes, January 19, 2012.

26 Robin Herman, "Some of City's Homeless Gather in Convention's Shadow," *New York Times*, August 14, 1980, p. B10.

27 Personal interview with Robert Hayes, January 19, 2012; personal interview with Kim Hopper, December 20, 2011.

28 Personal Interview with Kim Hopper, December 20, 2011.

29 Ellen Baxter and Kim Hopper, *Private Lives/Public Spaces: Homeless Adults on the Streets of New York City* (New York: Community Service Society, February 1981).

30 Kim Hopper et al., *One Year Later: The Homeless Poor in New York City, 1982* (New York: Community Service Society, June 1982).

31 Laurie Johnston, "A Journey into the City's Netherworld," *New York Times*, March 11, 1981, p. B3. Another sponsor of CSS's early work on the homeless was the Van Ameringen Foundation.

32 Baxter and Hopper, *Private Lives/Public Spaces*, p. vi.

33 Human Resources Administration of the City of New York, "Monthly Shelter Report" (November 17, 1982), table A1.

34 Baxter and Hopper, *Private Lives/Public Spaces*, p. 103.

35 Personal interview with Kim Hopper, December 20, 2011.

36 David Bird, "Help Is Urged for 36,000 Homeless in City's Streets," *New York Times*, March 8, 1981, sec. 1, part 1, p. 1.

37 Personal interview with Ellen Baxter, August 11, 2011.

38 Hopper et al., *One Year Later*, p. 44.

39 Baxter and Hopper, *Private Lives/Public Spaces*, p. iii.

40 Cynthia J. Bogard, "How Many Homeless? Experts, Advocates, and the Struggle over Numbers," in *Seasons Such as These: How Homelessness Took Shape in America* (New York: de Gruyter, 2003), chapter 5, pp. 97–123.

41 Thomas J. Main, "The Homeless of New York," *Public Interest*, no. 73 (Summer 1983): p. 12.

42 *Callahan v. Carey*, Index No. 42582/79 Sup. Ct. NY County, final judgment by consent.

43 Personal interview with Edward Koch, February 29, 2010.

44 Deirdre Carmody, "The City Seen on Solutions for Homeless," *New York Times*, October 10, 1984, p. A1.

45 Personal interview with Robert Trobe, July 7, 2010.
46 Personal interview with Bonnie Stone, October 27, 2011.
47 Personal interview with Ellen Baxter, August 11, 2011.
48 Personal Interview with Robert Hayes, January 19, 2012.
49 Hopper and Cox, "Litigation in Advocacy for the Homeless," p. 16.
50 Human Resources Administration of the City of New York, "Providing Services for the Homeless: The New York City Program" (December 1982), pp. 9–13.
51 David Bird, "Study on Homeless Sees Some Gains on Shelters," *New York Times*, July 28, 1982, p. B22.
52 Robin Herman, "New York Struggling to find Permanent Homes for Homeless," May 24, 1982, *New York Times*, p. B1.
53 Personal interview with Bonnie Stone, October 27, 2011.
54 Ibid.
55 Sarah Kellermann, "Is Deinstitutionalization Working for the Mentally Ill?" (New York: Department of Mental Health, Mental Retardation, and Alcoholism Services, 1982), p. 9.
56 See Thomas J. Main, "The Homeless of New York," *Public Interest*, no. 72 (Summer 1983): pp. 3–28. This article was condensed into an op ed piece published as "New York's Lure to the Homeless" in 1984 in the *Wall Street Journal*, thus extending its impact.
57 See Michael Cragg and Brendan O'Flaherty, "Do Homeless Shelter Conditions Determine Shelter Population? The Case of the Dinkins Deluge," *Journal of Urban Economics* 46 (1999): 377–415. This article is discussed in more detail in chapter 4.
58 New York City, Department of Homeless Services, "Average Daily Census (Adult System)," undated.
59 I am indebted to Jack Krauskopf for these insights on how the city charter influenced homelessness policy in the early eighties.
60 *Mayor's Management Report*, September 17, 1982, p. 410.
61 *Callahan v. Carey*, Index No. 42582/79 Sup. Ct. NY County, Memorandum of Law in Support of Motion for Modification of Consent Judgment, by Doron Gopstein, Chief Assistant Corporation Council, October 8, 1992, p. 6.
62 Ibid., p. 8.
63 Ibid., p. 8.
64 Ibid., p. 17.
65 Lindsey Gruson, "City Asks Judge to Alter Agreement on Homeless," *New York Times*, October 16, 1982, sec. 1, p. 29.
66 *Callahan v. Carey*, Index No. 42582/79 Sup. Ct. NY County, colloquy, October 27, 1982, p. 22.
67 Gruson, "City Asks Judge to Alter Agreement on Homeless."
68 *Callahan v. Carey*, Index No. 42582/79 Sup. Ct. NY County, colloquy, October 27, 1982, pp. 37, 31.
69 *Callahan v. Carey*, Index No. 42582/79 Sup. Ct. NY County, deposition of Robert M. Hayes, October 14, 1982, p. 3. par. 7.

70 "Showers, Shelters," *New York Times*, October 20, 1982, p. A26, Editorial Desk.
71 *Callahan v. Carey*, Index No. 42582/79 Sup. Ct. NY County, decision of Judge Richard Wallach, November 4, 1982, p. 3.
72 *Callahan v. Carey*, Index No. 42582/79 Sup. Ct. NY County, Memorandum of Law in Support of Motion for Modification of Consent Judgment, by Doron Gopstein, Chief Assistant Corporation Council, October 8, 1992, p. 16.
73 *Callahan v. Carey*, Index No. 42582/79 Sup. Ct. NY County, decision of Judge Richard Wallach, November 4, 1982, p. 6.
74 E. R. Shipp, "City Loses a Bid to Alter Accord on the Homeless," *New York Times*, November 5, 1982, p. B1.
75 Hopper and Cox, "Litigation in Advocacy for the Homeless," p. 17.
76 Edward I. Koch, "Homeless: One Place to Turn," *New York Times*, February 26, 1983.

CHAPTER 2. THE DEVELOPMENT OF HOMELESSNESS POLICY UNDER KOCH

1 Interim Order, June 20, 1983, *McCain* (Index Number 41023/83).
2 18 NYCRR 352.3 (g)-(h) (1983).
3 Susan V. Demers, "The Failures of Litigation as a Tool for the Development of Social Welfare Policy," *Fordham Urban Law Journal* 22, no. 4 (1994): article 7, pp. 1022–23.
4 Personal interview with Steven Banks, November 25, 2013.
5 83 ADM-47 issued September 29, 1983.
6 Personal interview with Steven Banks, December 9, 2013.
7 83 ADM-47, IV, A, 2, a.
8 *McCain v. Koch*, 484 N.Y.S.2d 985, 987 (Sup. Ct. 1984).
9 Ibid.
10 Josh Barbanel, "City Barred from Sheltering Homeless Families in Offices," *New York Times*, August 28, 1985, p. A1.
11 Ibid.
12 Matter of *Lamboy v. Gross*, 126 AD 2d 265—NY: Appellate Div., 1st Dept. 1987 126 A.D.2d 265 (1987) March 26, 1987.
13 Barbanel, "City Barred from Sheltering Homeless Families in Offices."
14 Matter of *Lamboy v. Gross*, 126 AD 2d 265—NY: Appellate Div., 1st Dept. 1987 126 A.D.2d 265 (1987) March 26, 1987.
15 Barbanel, "City Barred from Sheltering Homeless Families in Offices."
16 *Lamboy v. Gross*, 129 Misc.2d 564 (1985), Supreme Court, Special Term, New York County, August 26, 1985.
17 Order, Freedman, J., Oct. 2, 1985, at 5, *Lamboy* (Index No. 41108/85).
18 New York State Department of Social Services, letter dated June 19, 1985.
19 Susan V. Demers, "The Failures of Litigation as a Tool for the Development of Social Welfare Policy," p. 1028.
20 *Lamboy v. Gross*, Supreme Court of New York, Appellate Division, First Department, 126 A.D. 2d 265; 513 NYS 2d 393; 1987 NY App. Div. Lexis 41227, March 26, 1987.

21 Ibid.
22 Personal interview with Steven Banks, December 19, 2013.
23 Human Resources Administration, New York City, "An Observational Study of Toilet and Shower Utilization at Three Men's Shelters," Stephen Levine and James M. Svrcek, February 4, 1985, p. 6.
24 *Callahan v. Carey*, Index No. 42582/79 Sup. Ct. NY County, decision of Judge Stanley Sklar, October 1, 1987, pp. 6–7.
25 *Callahan v. Carey*, Index No. 42582/79 Sup. Ct. NY County, Plaintiffs' memorandum in opposition to city defendant's motion for modification of the consent decree and in support of plaintiffs' cross-motion, December 19, 1986, p. 26.
26 Ibid., p. 15.
27 Ibid., pp. 14–27. On p. 13 of his decision of October 1, 1987, Judge Sklar notes that one of the study's observations had been conducted while a World Series game was on television.
28 *Callahan v. Carey*, Index No. 42582/79 Sup. Ct. NY County, decision of Judge Stanley Sklar, October 1, 1987, pp. 14, 18.
29 Robert B. Cooper, "Queuing Theory," in Anthony Ralston, Edwin D. Reilly, and David Hemmendinger, eds., *Encyclopedia of Computer Science*, 4th ed. (Groves Dictionaries, 2000, pp. 1496–98.
30 Numbers of showers are rounded to the nearest tenth. City-proposed ratios for over five hundred clients were calculated on the basis of the city proposal that would add one fixture for every sixty extra clients. Queuing theory results assume the average shower is six minutes and the average use of a toilet is five minutes and that all clients take a shower and use the toilet within a three-hour breakfast or dinner period. The six-minute estimate of average time of a shower is taken from the affidavit of Robert H. White, Director of Service Operations in HRA's Family and Adult Services Office, October 12, 1982, paragraph 12. Five-minute estimate of average use of a toilet comes from P. J. Davidson and R. G. Courtney, "Revised Scales for Sanitary Accommodation in Offices," *Building and Environment* 11 (1976): pp. 51–56 and Goldstein et al., "Toilet Reading Habits in Israeli Adults," *Neurogastroenterology and Motility* (2009): pp. 21, 291–95.
31 McCain v. Koch, 502 N.Y.S.2d 720 (N.Y. App. Div. 1986), May 13, 1986.
32 Ibid.
33 Ibid.
34 Ibid.
35 Barbara Basler, "Ruling Widens Shelter Rights for Homeless," *New York Times*, May 14, 1986, p. B1.
36 Ibid.
37 *McCain v. Koch*, Index number 41023/83, Order, July 3, 1986.
38 *McCain v. Koch*, 511 N.E.2d 62, 62–63 (N.Y. 1987).
39 Ibid.
40 For an account of how "veto points" can be transformed into "opportunity points" and thus generate nonincremental change, see R. Shep Melnick, "Separation of

Powers and the Strategy of Rights: The Expansion of Special Education," in Marc K. Landy and Martin A. Levin, eds., *The New Politics of Public Policy* (Baltimore, MD: Johns Hopkins University Press, 1995), pp. 23–46.

41 Ibid., pp. 26–27.

42 Jonathan Soffer, *Ed Koch and the Rebuilding of New York City* (New York: Columbia University Press, 2010), chapter 19.

43 Alex Schwartz, "New York City and Subsidized Housing: Impacts and Lessons of the City's $5 Billion Capital Budget Housing Plan," *Housing Policy Debate* 10, no. 4 (1999): table 1.

44 Ibid., table 3.

45 Alan Finder, "Housing Plan Would Fix Up 5,200 Units," *New York Times*, December 24, 1986, p. B1.

46 Schwartz, "New York City and Subsidized Housing," figure 1.

47 Personal interview with Felice Michetti, December 13, 2011.

48 Personal interview with Ed Koch, February 19, 2010.

49 Ted Houghton, *A Description and History of the New York/New York Agreement to House Homeless Mentally Ill Individuals* (New York: Corporation for Supportive Housing, 2001), p. 29.

50 Schwartz, "New York City and Subsidized Housing," pp. 845–46. Low-income families got about 53 percent of the housing developed under the ten-year plan.

51 Judith Lynn Failer, *Who Qualifies for Rights? Homelessness, Mental Illness, and Civil Commitment* (Ithaca, NY: Cornell University Press, 2002), p. 13.

52 Jane F. Putnam, Neal L. Cohen, and Ann M. Sullivan, "Innovative Outreach Services for the Homeless Mentally Ill," *International Journal of Mental Health* 14, no. 4 (Winter 1985–1986): pp. 112–24.

53 Ibid., p. 24.

54 David Margolick, "Weighing the Risks and Rights of Homelessness," *New York Times*, December 8, 1985, sec. 4, p. 6.

55 Failer, *Who Qualifies for Rights?* p. 152, note 15.

56 Columbia University Community Services would later change its name to the Center for Urban Community Services.

57 Personal interview with Ellen Baxter, August 11, 2011.

58 Houghton, *A Description and History of the New York/New York Agreement to House Homeless Mentally Ill Individuals*, pp. 30–31.

59 Personal interview with Cynthia Stuart, chief operating officer, Supportive Housing Network of New York, September 8, 2014.

60 Personal interview with Edward Koch, February 29, 2010.

61 Memorandum from John E. Linville, vice president, Legal Affairs, and Luis R. Marcos, vice president, Mental Hygiene Services, New York City Health and Hospitals Corporation, to Directors of Psychiatry, September 9, 1987, 1, 2, 3. Italics in the original. Cited in Failer, *Who Qualifies for Rights*, p. 152, note 18.

62 Personal interview with Edward Koch, February 29, 2010.

63 New York City Health and Hospitals Corporation, Project HELP: Homeless mentally ill patients transported to Bellevue Hospital Pursuant to M.H.L. Sec. 9.37, October 28, 1987.

64 Luis R. Marcos, "Taking the Mentally Ill off the Streets: The Case of Joyce Brown," *International Journal of Mental Health* 20, no. 2 (Summer 1991): pp. 7–16.

65 Cited in Failer, *Who Qualifies for Rights?* p. 25.

66 Cited in Gregory E. Pence, *Classic Cases in Medical Ethics*, 5th ed. (Boston: McGraw Hill, 2008), chapter 15, p. 296.

67 Personal interview with Sam Tsembris, June 18, 2010.

68 Todd S. Purdum (based on reporting by Howard W. French, Michael Wines, and Todd S. Purdum), "Melee in Tompkins Sq. Park: Violence and Its Provocation," *New York Times*, August 14, 1988, sec. 1, p. 1; Janet Abu-Lughod, "The Battle for Tompkins Square Park," in Janet L. Abu-Lughod, ed., *From Urban Village to East Village: The Battle for New York's Lower East Side* (Cambridge, MA: Blackwell, 1994), p. 237.

69 C. Carr, "Night Clubbing: Reports from the Tompkins Square Police Riot," *Village Voice*, August 16, 1988, pp. 10, 17.

70 Robert D. McFadden, "Park Curfew Protest Erupts into a Battle and 38 Are Injured," *New York Times*, August 8, 1988, p. A1. The *Times* reported that "Mayor Koch reversed a police order that had kept the park closed from 1 a.m. to sunrise for the last month and directed that it remain open 'during the current heat wave' to cool passions. 'During this heat wave, we don't want to enforce a curfew and provoke another confrontation,' said Larry Simonberg, a spokesman for the Mayor."

71 Janet Abu-Lughod, "The Battle for Tompkins Square Park," in Janet L. Abu-Lughod, ed., *From Urban Village to East Village: The Battle for New York's Lower East Side*, p. 255.

72 James Barron, "Removal of Tompkins Sq. Homeless Is Set," *New York Times*, November 16, 1989, p. B1.

73 Frances Fox Piven and Richard A. Cloward, *Poor People's Movements: Why They Succeed, How They Fail* (New York: Vintage Books, 1979).

74 Tim Golden, "Cuomo and Dinkins Agree to House 5,225 Mentally Ill," *New York Times*, August 23, 1990, p. A1.

75 The New York/New York Agreement to House Homeless Mentally Ill Individuals, August 22, 1990, Section D: Placement Targets; Amendment, October 1993, Section 5. http://shnny.org/images/uploads/NYNYAgreement.pdf

76 Houghton, *A Description and History of the New York/New York Agreement to House Mentally Ill Individuals*, p. 3.

77 Personal interview with Cindy Freidmutter, February 9, 2012.

78 Houghton, *A Description and History of The New York/New York Agreement to House Homeless Mentally Ill Individuals*, p. 34.

79 Ibid., pp. 29–30.

80 *New York Times*, editorial, August 24, 1990, p. A28.
81 Houghton, *A Description and History of the New York/New York Agreement to House Homeless Mentally Ill Individuals*, p. 34.
82 Personal interview with Diane Baillargeon, February 24, 2012.
83 Personal interview with Cindy Freidmutter, February 9, 2012.
84 Ibid.
85 Ibid.
86 Personal interview with Diane Baillargeon, February 24, 2012.
87 Houghton, *A Description and History of the New York/New York Agreement to House Homeless Mentally Ill Individuals*, pp. 45, 3.

CHAPTER 3. HOMELESSNESS POLICY UNDER DINKINS

1 Manhattan Borough President's Taskforce on Housing for Homeless Families, *A Shelter Is Not a Home* (New York, March 1987).
2 Randall K. Filer, "What Really Causes Family Homelessness?" *NY: The City Journal* 1, no. 1 (Autumn 1990).
3 Barbara Basler, "Koch Limits Using Welfare Hotels," *New York Times*, December 17, 1985.
4 Susan V. Demers, "The Failures of Litigation as a Tool for the Development of Social Welfare Policy," *Fordham Urban Law Journal* 22, no. 4 (1994): article 7, p. 1027.
5 Peter Hellman, "Justice Freedman v. New York," *City Journal*, Spring 1997.
6 Michael A. Cardozo, "The New York City Corporation Counsel: The Best Legal Job in America," *New York Law School Law Review* 53 (2008–2009): 459.
7 Leslie Kaufman and David W. Chen, "City Agrees to Deal on Homeless Families' Right to Shelter," *New York Times*, September 18, 2008, p. B1.
8 Order, Freedman, J., Mar. 25, 1991, *McCain* (Index No. 41023/83).
9 18 NYCRR 352.3 (e) (2).
10 Order, Freedman, J., Mar. 25, 1991, *McCain* (Index No. 41023/83).
11 Preliminary order, Freedman, January 8, 1991, *McCain* (Index No. 41023/83).
12 Thomas Morgan, "Contempt Charge Faced in Placement of Homeless," *New York Times*, September 12, 1991, p. B6.
13 Memorandum decision, Freedman, September 10, 1991, *McCain* (Index No. 41023/83); Thomas Morgan, "Contempt Charge Faced in Placement of Homeless," p. B6.
14 Thomas Morgan, "New York Admits Failure of Homeless-Family Effort" *New York Times*, September 18, 1991, p. B3.
15 Todd S. Purdum, "Shelter Deadline Causes Angry Clash between Dinkins and Vallone," *New York Times*, October 3, 1991, p. B7.
16 Memorandum decision, Freedman, November 20, 1992, *McCain* (Index No. 41023/83).
17 Celia W. Dugger, "4 Dinkins Officials Found in Contempt on Housing Delay," *New York Times*, November 21, 1992, sec. 1, p. 1.
18 Celia W. Dugger, "Still at Odds over the Homeless," *New York Times*, November 23, 1992, p. B3.

19 Celia W. Dugger, "Dinkins to Appeal Contempt on Homeless," *New York Times*, December 15, 1992, p. B3.
20 *McCain v. Dinkins*, Supreme Court of New York, Appellate Division, First Department, 192 A.D. 2d 217; July 29, 1993.
21 Personal interview with Norman Steisel, June 24, 2010.
22 Personal interview with Cesar A. Perales, May 10, 2010.
23 Daniel Wise, "Alternate Dispute Resolution Was Key to Settlement of Homeless Litigation," *New York Law Journal*, January 23, 2003.
24 Note: "Implementation Problems in Institutional Reform Litigation," *Harvard Law Review* 91 (1977): p. 449.
25 Ibid.
26 Citizens Committee for Children of New York, *On Their Own: At What Cost; A look at Families Who Leave Shelters* (New York, 1992), illustration 1, p. 4.
27 Sam Roberts, "Metro Matters: City as Landlord; Homeless Force Policy Turnabout," *New York Times*, September 20, 1990, p. B1.
28 Edward F. Dejowski and Julie Ibanez, *Trends in Family Shelter Usage: Report to the New York City Human Resources Administration* (New York: Bureau of Management Information Systems, Human Resources Administration, 1992), p. 2.
29 Personal interview with Nancy Wackstein, November 12, 1992.
30 Ibid.
31 S. Roberts, "What Led to a Crackdown on the Homeless," *New York Times*, October 28, 1991, p. B1.
32 Thomas Morgan, "Advocates for Homeless Fault Housing Plan," *New York Times*, November 1, 1990.
33 David N. Dinkins with Peter Knobler, *A Mayor's Life: Governing New York's Gorgeous Mosaic* (New York: Public Affairs, 2013), pp. 183–84.
34 Personal interview with Nancy Wackstein, November 12, 1992.
35 J. Phillip Thompson, "The Failure of Liberal Homeless Policy in the Koch and Dinkins Administrations," *Political Science Quarterly* 111, no. 4 (Winter 1996): pp. 639–60; Gordon Berlin and William McAllister, "Homelessness: Why Nothing Has Worked, and What Will," *Brookings Review* 10, no. 4 (Fall 1992): pp. 12–17; Gordon Berlin and William McAllister, "Homeless Family Shelters and Family Homelessness," *American Behavioral Scientist* 37, no. 3 (January 1994): pp. 422–34; Gordon Berlin and William McAllister, "Homelessness," in Henry J. Aaron and Charles L Schultz, eds., *Setting Domestic Priorities: What Can Government Do?* (Washington, DC: Brookings Institution Press), pp. 63–99; Christopher Jencks, *The Homeless* (Cambridge MA: Harvard University Press, 1994), pp.104–5.
36 Personal interview with Norman Steisel, June 24, 2010.
37 Personal interview with Cesar A. Perales, May 10, 2010.
38 Cragg and O'Flaherty, "Do Homeless Shelter Conditions Determine Shelter Population? The Case of the Dinkins Deluge," *Journal of Urban Economics* 46 (1999): p. 377.
39 Ibid., p. 413.

40 Ibid., p. 380.
41 Ibid., p. 409.
42 Patrick Markee, "Bloomberg Administration Officials to *NY Times*: Up Is Down, Night Is Day, 2 + 2 = 5, Etc. Etc." *Coalition for the Homeless Blog*, posted June 1, 2011 at http://www.coalitionforthehomeless.org/bloomberg-administration-officials-to-ny-times-up-is-down-night-is-day-2-2-5-etc-etc.
43 Brian A. Jacob, and Jens Ludwig. "The Effects of Housing Assistance on Labor Supply: Evidence from a Voucher Lottery," *American Economic Review* 102, no. 1 (2012): pp. 272–304.
44 Dejowski and Ibanez, *Trends in Family Shelter Usage*, figure 1.
45 Celia Dugger, "Memo to Democrats: Housing Won't Solve Homelessness," *New York Times*, July 12, 1992.
46 Personal interview with Nancy Wackstein, May 24, 2010.
47 City of New York, *Mayor's Management Report*, September 17, 1990, p. 245.
48 New York City Housing Authority, Sally Hernandez-Pinero, "The Homeless and Public Housing in New York City," Testimony to New York City Council, undated, p. 2.
49 Ibid., p. 3.
50 Personal interview with Norman Steisel, June 24, 2010.
51 Personal interview with Sally Hernandez-Pinero, March 25, 1993.
52 *A Shelter Is Not a Home*, p. 8.
53 Ibid., p. 108.
54 James R. Knickman and Beth C. Weitzman, *A Study of Homeless Families in New York City: Risk Assessment Models and Strategies for Prevention*, final report, vol. 1 (New York: Health Research Program of New York University, September 1989).
55 Ibid., p. 30.
56 Ibid., p. 39.
57 Marybeth Shinn, Beth C. Weitzman, Daniela Stojanovic, and James R. Knickman et al., "Predictors of Homelessness among Families in New York City: From Shelter Request to Housing Stability," *American Journal of Public Health* 88, no. 11 (November 1998): pp. 1651–57, ABI/INFORM Global. This study found that "[i] ndividual characteristics associated with shelter entry did not prevent most families from becoming rehoused," p. 1654.
58 Marybeth Shinn, Judith S. Schteingart, and Nathanial Chioke Williams et al., "Long-Term Associations of Homelessness with Children's Well-Being," *American Behavioral Scientist* 51 (2008): 789. This study found that "[o]verall, the results suggest that a median of 55 months after first entering shelter and 39 months after last leaving it, formerly homeless children who remained with their mothers did not look enormously different from their continuously housed peers whose mothers used welfare. Nevertheless, almost all differences favored housed children," p. 802. An important qualification is that children who did not stay with their mothers at the time of the second interview were not included.

59 Siobhan M. Toohey, Marybeth Shinn, and Beth C. Weitzman, "Social Networks and Homelessness among Women Heads of Household," *American Journal of Community Psychology* 33, nos. 1/2 (March 2004). According to the authors,

> It does appear that there were some subtle long-term differences between formerly homeless and housed women but that formerly homeless women were not socially isolated. This finding, along with our finding that women on the verge of homelessness were better connected with social networks than were housed women, suggests that the more severe social deprivation other researchers have found among currently homeless women may be a temporary consequence of living in a shelter, rather than a central cause of homelessness.

60 New York City Commission on the Homeless, *The Way Home: A New Direction in Social Policy* (New York: February 1992), p. 21.

61 Personal interview with Nancy Wackstein, March 16, 2015.

62 Anthony Marcus, *Where Have All the Homeless Gone? The Making and Unmaking of a Crisis* (New York: Berghahn Books, 2006), pp. 68–69.

63 Celia W. Dugger, "Big Shelters Hold Terrors for the Mentally Ill," *New York Times*, January 12, 1992, sec. 1, p. 1.

64 Personal interview with Anne Teicher, March 17, 2015.

65 *New York City Five-Year Plan for Housing and Assisting Homeless Adults*, October 1991, p. 1.

66 Personal interview with Nancy Wackstein, March 16, 2015.

67 *New York City Five-Year Plan for Housing and Assisting Homeless Adults*, p. 62.

68 Ibid., pp. 67–68.

69 Sam Roberts, "Deciding on Sites for Shelters: A Faceless Numbers-Cruncher," *New York Times*, December 2, 1991, p. B3.

70 *A Shelter Is Not a Home*, p. 8.

71 Personal interview with Anne Teicher, March 17, 2015.

72 Personal interview with Nancy Wackstein, March 16, 2015.

73 Todd S. Purdum, "Dinkins Lists Possible Shelter Sites to Irate Protests on Many Fronts," *New York Times*, October 11, 1991, p. A1.

74 New York City Commission on the Homeless, *The Way Home: A New Direction in Social Policy* (New York: February 1992).

75 Ibid., p. 73.

76 Ibid., p. 7.

77 Ibid., p. 28.

78 Ibid., p. 9.

79 Ibid., p. 81.

80 Ibid., p. 15.

81 Sam Roberts, "Dinkins to Study Homeless Proposals," *New York Times*, February 22, 1992, sec. 1, p. 27.

82 Celia W. Dugger, "Panel's Report on Homeless Is Criticized by Dinkins Staff," *New York Times*, February 1, 1992, sec. 1, p. 1.

83 Ibid.

84 James C. McKinley Jr., "Dinkins Names a Manager for Agency for Homeless," *New York Times*, December 3, 1992, p. B3.
85 Personal interview with Muzzy Rosenblatt, April 9, 2010.
86 Celia W. Dugger, "Dinkins Plan for Homeless under Attack," *New York Times*, May 13, 1993, p. B1.
87 Celia W. Dugger, "Finding Ways to House All Vexes Leaders at Every Level," *New York Times*, July 6, 1993, p. A1.
88 Ibid.
89 Personal interview with Charles V. Raymond, April 9, 2010.
90 Personal interview with Norman Steisel, June 24, 2010.
91 Raymond is identified as Steisel's "protégé" in Celia W. Dugger, "A New Effort Aims to Raise Housing Aid," *New York Times*, May 30, 1993, sec. 1, p. 29, and as Steisel's "hand-picked candidate," in Celia W. Dugger, "Feud between Top Dinkins Aids Is Seen as Hurting Social Programs," *New York Times*, January 1, 1993, p. A1.
92 Dennis P. Culhane, "The Quandaries of Shelter Reform: An Appraisal of Efforts to 'Manage' Homelessness," *Social Service Review*, September 1992, pp. 428–40.
93 Personal interview with Charles V. Raymond, April 9, 2010.
94 *McCain v. Dinkins*, motion seq. no. 029, December 8, 1993.
95 James C. McKinley Jr., "Dinkins Names a Manager for Agency for Homeless," *New York Times*, December 3, 1992, p. B3.
96 Personal interview with Sam Tsemberis, November 24, 2014.
97 David L. Shern et al., "Serving Street-Dwelling Individuals with Psychiatric Disabilities: Outcomes of a Psychiatric Rehabilitation Clinical Trial," *American Journal of Public Health* 90, no. 12 (December 2000): p. 1873.
98 Personal interview with William Anthony, January 12, 2015.
99 Personal interview with Sam Tsemberis, November 24, 2014.
100 David L. Shern et al., "Serving Street-Dwelling Individuals with Psychiatric Disabilities: Outcomes of a Psychiatric Rehabilitation Clinical Trial," p. 1873.
101 Personal interview with Sam Tsemberis, November 24, 2014.
102 Personal interview with Sam Tsemberis, June 18, 2010.
103 Celia W. Dugger, "Giuliani Calls Dinkins Indecisive on Housing and Homeless," *New York Times*, August 5, 1993, p. B1.

CHAPTER 4. HOMELESSNESS POLICY UNDER GIULIANI

1 Personal interview with Joan Malin, March 29, 2010.
2 Ibid.
3 Ibid.
4 Shawn G. Kennedy, "Council Votes to Extend Life of Department for the Homeless," *New York Times*, September 7, 1995, p. B3.
5 Celia W. Dugger, "Giuliani Eases Stance on Plans for Homeless," *New York Times*, March 20, 1994, sec. 1, p. 1.
6 Personal interview with Joan Malin, March 29, 2010.
7 Dugger, "Giuliani Eases Stance on Plans for Homeless."

8 Personal interview with Joan Malin, March 29, 2010.

9 On how competitive political environments encourage policy entrepreneurship and facilitate the adoption of new policy ideas see Marc K. Landy and Martin A. Levin, eds., *The New Politics of Public Policy* (Baltimore, MD: Johns Hopkins University Press, 1995), p. 211 and pp. 278–79.

10 New York City Department of Homeless Services, "Reforming New York City's System of Homeless Services," May 1994, pp. 1, 6.

11 New York State Department of Social Services Administrative Directive 83 ADM-47. Section IV. A. I. 6: at 2.

12 New York State Department of Social Services Administrative Directive 94-ADM-20, Section IV, D.

13 Personal interview with Joan Malin, March 29, 2010.

14 New York City Department of Homeless Services, "Reforming New York City's System of Homeless Services," p. 4.

15 Kevin Sack, "Pataki Proposes to Deny Shelter to Homeless Who Break Rules: Shifting the Balance to Personal Responsibility," *New York Times*, April 15, 1995, p. A1. Also see New York State Department of Social Services, notice for proposed rule making for the enactment of 18 NYCRR 352.35, November 7, 1995.

16 Shawn G. Kennedy, "Judge Blocks a Bid to Deny Emergency Shelter," *New York Times*, November 17, 1995, p. B2.

17 *Callahan v. Carey*, Index No. 42582/79, "Memorandum in Support of Plaintiffs' Motion to Declare State 'Emergency' Regulations Null and Void," p. 8. (Sup. Ct. N.Y. County, filed Dec. 8, 1995).

18 President of the Borough of Manhattan, *A Shelter Is Not a Home: Report of the Manhattan Borough President's Task Force on Housing for Homeless Families* (New York: March 1987), pp. 121–22; and City Council of the City of New York, "Report of the Select Committee on the Homeless," November 24, 1986, p. 78.

19 Mayor's Advisory Task Force on the Homeless, "Toward a Comprehensive Policy on Homelessness," New York, 1987, p. 59.

20 New York City Commission on the Homeless, *The Way Home: A New Direction in Social Policy* (New York: February 1992), p. 32.

21 Department of Homeless Services, "Reforming New York City's System of Homeless Services," p. 6.

22 Personal interview with Joan Malin, March 29, 2010.

23 Thomas J. Main, "Shelters for Homeless Men in New York City: Towards Paternalism through Privatization," in Lawrence M. Mead, ed., *The New Paternalism: Supervisory Approaches to Poverty* (Washington, DC: Brookings Institution Press, 1997), table 5-1, p. 172.

24 Citizens' Budget Commission, "Department of Homeless Services," in *The State of Municipal Services in the 1990s: Social Services in New York City*, 1997.

25 Lynette Holloway, "City Plans Greatly Diminished Role in Homeless Shelters," *New York Times*, June 21, 1998, sec. 1, p. 32.

26 Janice M. Hirota, "Life and Work in City Shelters: Homeless Residents and Organizational Dynamics at the Borden Avenue Veterans Residence," City of New York Human Resources Administration, May 1991.
27 Salvation Army, Borden Avenue Veterans Residence, "What is BAVR?" New York, undated, p. 2.
28 Hirota, "Life and Work in City Shelters," p. 16.
29 Ibid., p. 21.
30 Alfred Peck, Isaac Pimentel, and Gerald Saunders, "Yesterday's Heroes, Today's Homeless: Strategies to Address African-American Veterans' Homelessness," Veterans Braintrust, Congressional Black Caucus, undated, pp. 2–3.
31 Hirota, "Life and Work in City Shelters," p. 41.
32 Ibid., p. iv.
33 Ibid., p. 60.
34 Sara Rimer, "Despite Pledge, Homeless Still in Hotel," *New York Times*, November 11, 1989, sec. 1, p. 29.
35 Carol Goar, "A Triumph of Urban Ingenuity," *Toronto Star*, November 26, 2003, p. A28.
36 Anthony Ramirez, "Neighborhood Report: Midtown; The Four Rules of Politics, by Nick Fish," *New York Times*, November 3, 1996, sec. 13, p. 6.
37 Personal interview with Rosanne Haggerty, April 29, 2015.
38 *McCain v. Giuliani*, Supreme Court, New York County, Part 30, Index No. 41023/83, November 22, 1994.
39 Personal interview with Kenneth Feinberg, August 18, 2011.
40 Ibid.
41 Leslie Kaufman, "One Constant in Homeless Litigation: New York v. the Judge," *New York Times*, November 12, 2002, p. B1.
42 Joyce Purnick, "For Homeless, a New Era Could Be Near," *New York Times*, March 3, 2005, p. B1.
43 Personal interview with Thomas Crane, December 14, 2010.
44 Personal interview with Steven Banks, November 25, 2013.
45 Lawrence Van Gelder, "Judge Asked to Halt Use of an Office for Homeless," *New York Times*, June 17, 1995, sec. 1, p. 23.
46 *McCain v. Giuliani*, index number 41023/83, Memorandum Decision, May 14, 1996, p. 12.
47 *McCain v. Giuliani*, index number 41023/83, Recommendations of the Special Masters, March 15, 1996, p. 1.
48 *McCain v. Giuliani*, index number 41023/83, Memorandum Decision, May 14, 1996, p. 34.
49 Personal interview with Thomas Crane, December 14, 2011.
50 Personal interview with Steven Banks, November 25, 2013.
51 94 ADM-20, New York State Office of Temporary and Disability Assistance, December 29, 1994, IV, D, p. 5

52 Celia W. Dugger, "Giuliani Relieved of an Obligation on the Homeless," *New York Times*, December 31, 1994, sec. 1, p. 1.

53 Ibid.

54 *McCain v. Giuliani*, index number 41023/83, Memorandum Decision, May 14, 1996, pp. 29–30.

55 94 ADM-20, III, p. 4.

56 *McCain v. Giuliani*, memorandum decision, March 3, 1998, p. 11.

57 Ibid., p. 14.

58 94 ADM-20, IV, D, p. 5.

59 *McCain v. Giuliani*, index number 41023/83, Memorandum Decision, May 14, 1996, pp. 29–30.

60 Matthew Purdy, "City to Revise Its Housing of Homeless," *New York Times*, February 2, 1995, p. B3.

61 Personal interview with Steven Banks, November 25, 2013.

62 *McCain v. Koch*, 502 N.Y.S.2d 720 (N.Y. App. Div. 1986), May 13, 1986.

63 Ibid.

64 *McCain v. Koch*, Order, July 3, 1986.

65 Ibid.

66 18 NYCRR 352.35 (e) 1.

67 18 NYCRR 352.35 (d).

68 *McCain v. Giuliani*, December 30, 1996, p. 7.

69 Ibid., pp. 16–19.

70 *McCain v. Giuliani*, May 27, 1997.

71 *McCain v. Giuliani*, Supreme Court of New York, Appellate Division, First Division 252 A.D. 2d 461; 676 N.Y.S. 2d 151; 1998 N.Y.App. Div. July 30, 1998.

72 Personal interview with Thomas Crane, December 14, 2011.

73 Virginia Breen and Joel Siegel, "Families Booted at Homeless Ctr.," *New York Daily News*, August 27, 1996, p. 10.

74 86 ADM-7, IV. A. 4, March 3, 1986. http://www.wnylc.net/Pdf/administrative-directives/old-admin-directives/86adm7.pdf.

75 Nina Bernstein, "Judge Orders City to Stop Housing Homeless in Office," *New York Times*, January 14, 1999, p. B3.

76 Nina Bernstein, "Giuliani to Order Homeless to Work for Their Shelter," *New York Times*, October 26, 1999, p. A1.

77 Ibid.

78 Ibid.

79 David M. Herszenhorn, "City Vows to Fight Order on Homeless Policy," *New York Times*, December 10, 1999, p. B12.

80 Personal interview with Joan Malin, March 29, 2010.

81 Personal interview with Gordon Campbell, October 24, 2011.

82 K. C. Baker and Joel Siegel, "Welfare Hotel Rule a Goner," *New York Daily News*, September 10, 1996.

83 Claire Serant, "Shelter Residents Protest Ouster," *New York Daily News*, October 9, 1996, Suburban section, p. 1.

84 Claire Serant, "Ex-Shelter to Become Luxury Inn," *New York Daily News*, March 20, 1997, Suburban section, p. 2.

85 Lynette Holloway, "City Plans Greatly Diminished Role in Homeless Staff," *New York Times*, June 21, 1998, sec.1, p. 32.

86 Messages and Papers from the Mayor, M-320, Communication from the Mayor—Mayor's veto and disapproval message of Introductory Number 317-A, July 24, 1998.

87 Mike Allen, "Defiance Reigns as Council Keeps Swinging at Mayor," *New York Times*, June 25, 1998, p. B3; Metro News Briefs: New York, "Giuliani Defies Council with Homeless-Bill Veto," *New York Times*, p. B5.

88 New York City Legislative Annual, 1998, Veto Report for Intro. 407-A (Local Law 57 in 1998) December 7, 1998.

89 New York City Council, Law Number 1998/057, enactment date: 12/17/1998. http://nyc.legistar.com/LegislationDetail.aspx?ID=432045&GUID=5E3ED12C-7ED3-45B8-97D3-C30B63021811&Options=&Search=

90 Nina Bernstein, "Clash over Shelter Exposes Deep Rift on Homeless Policy," *New York Times*, December 31, 1998, p. B1.

91 Personal interview with Martin Oesterreich, April 5, 2010.

92 Kemba Johnson, "My Favorite Martin," *City Limits*, July 1, 1999.

93 Personal interview with Martin Oesterreich, April 5, 2010.

94 Personal Interview with Steven Banks, December 9, 2013.

95 Nina Bernstein, "Homeless Shelters in New York Fill to Highest Level since 80's," *New York Times*, February 8, 2001, p. A1; personal interview with Martin Oesterreich, April 5, 2010.

96 Personal Interview with Mark Hurwitz, October 17, 2014.

97 Sam Tsemberis and Ronda F. Eisenberg, "Pathways to Housing: Supported Housing for Street-Dwelling Homeless Individuals with Psychiatric Disabilities," *Psychiatric Services* 51, no. 4 (April 2000): pp. 487–93, figure 1.

98 Personal Interview with Mark Hurwitz, October 17, 2014.

99 "NY/NY II," Supportive Housing Network of NY, undated, accessed at http://shnny.ore/budget-policy/nyc/ny-ny/ny-ny ii/; Connie Temple, Corporation for Supportive Housing, "Creating Supportive Housing through the NY/NY Agreements," Power Point presentation, September 30, 2009, slides 8–11.

100 Personal interview with Shelly Nortz, April 20, 2015.

101 David Gonzalez, "About New York; Street Name for Impasse: Homeless," *New York Times*, January 9, 1999, p. B1.

102 Personal interview with Shelly Nortz, April 20, 2015.

103 Raymond Hernandez, "Pataki and Giuliani Agree on Housing for the Mentally Ill," *New York Times*, April 22, 1999, p. B1.

104 Personal interview with Shelly Nortz, April 20, 2015.

CHAPTER 5. HOMELESSNESS POLICY UNDER BLOOMBERG

1 Leslie Kaufman, "City Shifts View on Homelessness," *New York Times*, June 16, 2004, p. 1.

2 Carine Barometre, deputy commissioner, Prevention Services, New York City Department of Homeless Services, "Preventing Homelessness in New York City," presentation at Fairfax County Virginia Summit, April 7, 2006. Accessed at http://www.fairfaxcounty.gov/homeless/summit/newyorkcity.pdf, June 18, 2012.

3 Accessed at http://www.nyc.gov/html/dhs/html/about/agencyintro.shtml, June 18, 2012. Emphasis in the original.

4 James Q. Wilson, *Bureaucracy: What Government Agencies Do and Why They Do It* (New York: Basic Books, 1989), pp. 38, 49.

5 M. Anne Hill and Thomas J. Main, *Is Welfare Working: The Massachusetts Reforms Three Years Later* (Boston: Pioneer Institute, 1998), pp. 51–71.

6 Thus the much-criticized HUD report of 1984 claimed that "for most people who become homeless, their condition is recent and likely to be temporary." U.S. Department of Housing and Urban Development, *A Report for the Secretary on the Homeless and Emergency Shelters* (Washington, DC: Office of Policy Development and Research, 1984).

7 Richard B. Freeman and Brian Hall, "Permanent Homelessness in America?" *Population Research and Policy Review* 6 (1987): p. 4.

8 Kim Hopper and Jill Hamberg, *The Making of America's Homeless: From Skid Row to New Poor, 1945–1984* (New York: Community Service Society, December 1984), pp. 62–63.

9 Thomas J. Main, "Homeless Families in New York City," *New York Times*, November 28, 1986.

10 Marybeth Shinn et al., "Predictors of Homelessness among Families in New York City: From Shelter Request to Housing Stability," *American Journal of Public Health*, November 1998, pp. 1651–57.

11 Daniela Stojanovic et al., "Tracing the Path out of Homelessness: The Housing Patterns of Families after Exiting Shelter," *Journal of Community Psychology* 27, no. 2 (1999): pp. 199–208.

12 Ibid.

13 Randall Kuhn and Dennis P. Culhane, "Applying Cluster Analysis to Test a Typology of Homelessness by Pattern of Shelter Utilization: Results from the Analysis of Administrative Data," *American Journal of Community Psychology* 26, no. 2 (1998): pp. 207–32.

14 Ibid., p. 226.

15 Ibid., p. 229.

16 For accounts of the role that professional consensus plays in precipitating nonincremental change, see Timothy J. Conlan, David R. Beam, and Margaret T. Wrightson, "Policy Models and Political Change: Insights from the Passage of Tax Reform," in Marc K. Landy and Martin A. Levin, eds., *The New Politics of Public*

Policy (Baltimore, MD: Johns Hopkins University Press, 1995), pp. 121–42; also see M. A. Hill and Thomas J. Main, *Is Welfare Working? The Massachusetts Reforms Three Years Later* (Boston: Pioneer Institute, 1998), chapter 3. For an account of the nature of public ideas see Mark H. Moore, "What Sort of Ideas Become Public Ideas?" in Robert B. Reich, ed., *The Power of Public Ideas* (Cambridge, MA: Harvard University Press, 1988).

17 Douglas McGary, "The Abolitionist," *Atlantic Monthly*, June 2004, pp. 36–39.

18 Personal interview with Nan Roman, April 3, 2006.

19 Personal interview with Philip F. Mangano, April 25, 2006.

20 Dennis P. Culhane, Stephen Metreaux, and Trevor Hadley, "Public Service Reductions with Placement of Homeless Persons in Supportive Housing," *Housing Policy Debate* 13, no. 1 (2002): pp. 107–63.

21 Personal interview with Connie Temple, April 23, 2015.

22 Sam Tsemberis, Leyla Gulcur, and Maria Nakae, "Housing First, Consumer Choice, and Harm Reduction for Homeless Individuals with a Dual Diagnosis," *American Journal of Public Health* 94, no. 4 (April 2004): p. 654.

23 In "The Curious Case of Housing First: The Limits of Evidence-Based Policy," *International Journal of Law and Psychiatry* 34 (2011): p. 278, Victoria Stanhope and Kerry Dunn report that

> [s]even of the eleven cities funded by CIHC (the federal Collaborative Initiative to Help End Chronic Homelessness) used some variation of the Housing First model and achieved 85% housing retention rates after 12 months. . . . The Department of Housing and Urban Development published the outcomes of their three-city, 12-month study of Housing First programs (one of which was Pathways to Housing) reporting an 84% housing retention rate for 12 months.

24 James Q. Wilson discusses the generally dismal track record of interagency councils and quotes approvingly Harold Seidman's judgment: "Interagency committees are the crabgrass in the garden of government. Nobody wants them, but everyone has them. Committees seem to thrive on scorn and ridicule." *Bureaucracy*, pp. 269–74.

25 Dina Temple-Raston, "Bloomberg Vows to Make Chronic Homelessness 'Extinct,'" *New York Sun*, June 24, 2004.

26 Personal interview with Lilliam Barrios-Paoli, senior vice president of the United Way of New York and cochair of the New York Coordinating Committee on Homelessness, November 12, 2004.

27 David Saltonstall, "Record 38,000 without Homes," *New York Daily News*, December 31, 2002, p. 10.

28 Ibid.

29 David Saltonstall, "A Plan to Help Homeless," *New York Daily News*, June 24, 2004, p. 2. For a more detailed account of the decision to switch from a ten-year to a five-year plan see John Cassidy, "Bloomberg's Game," *New Yorker*, April 4, 2005, p. 56. New York City mayors are term limited to a maximum of two

consecutive terms, or eight years. The city's official plan on homelessness, "Uniting for Solutions beyond Shelter," envisions a ten-year process. http://www.nyc.gov/html/endinghomelessness/downloads/pdf/actionbooklet/pdf, accessed December 15, 2015.

30 Leslie Kaufman, "City Shifts View on Homelessness," *New York Times*, June 16, 2004, p. 1.

31 Leslie Kaufman, "Mayor Urges Major Overhaul for Homeless," *New York Times*, June 24, 2004, p. 1. The quotation is from Joe Weisbord, staff director of Housing First, a housing advocacy group very critical of New York City in the past.

32 The City of New York, *Uniting for Solutions beyond Shelter: The Action Plan for New York City*, undated, p. 10. http://www.nyc.gov/html/endinghomelessness/downloads/pdf/actionbooklet.pdf, accessed December 14, 2015.

33 Ibid., p. 42.

34 Ibid., p. 5.

35 Ibid., pp. 4, 34.

36 Coalition for the Homeless, Advocacy Department, "New York City Homeless Municipal Shelter Population, 1983–Present," undated, http://coalhome.3cdn.net/9bf5aad273af9beaad_ldm6i6j2r.pdf, accessed January 21, 2014.

37 Leslie Kaurmann, "Mayor Urges Major Overhaul for Homeless," *New York Times*, June 24, 2004, p. B1.

38 Stipulation dated January 17, 2003.

39 Daniel Wise, "Alternate Dispute Resolution Was Key to Settlement of Homeless Litigation," *New York Law Journal*, January 23, 2003.

40 Personal interview with Thomas Crane, December 14, 2011.

41 Personal interview with Steven Banks, December 9, 2013.

42 Special Master Panel Agreement, January 17, 2003.

43 "Top Cases of 2003; Corporate Crime; Judicial Conduct; Government," *New York Law Journal*, February 23, 2004, col. 1, p. 15. Also see Daniel Wise, "Alternate Dispute Resolution Was Key to Settlement of Homeless Litigation," which reported on "the creation of a three-member panel with powers that, at least on paper, look more akin to those of an arbitrator than those of a mediator."

44 Personal interview with Thomas Crane, December 14, 2011.

45 Personal interview with Steven Banks, November 25, 2013.

46 Personal interview with Thomas Crane, December 14, 2011.

47 New York City Family Homelessness Special Master Panel, *Report on the Emergency Assistance Unit and Shelter Eligibility Determination*, June 23, 2004, p. 5.

48 *Report on the Emergency Assistance Unit and Eligibility Determination*, p. 7.

49 New York City Family Homelessness Special Master Panel, *Report on the Emergency Assistance Unit and Shelter Eligibility Determination*, p. 1.

50 Leslie Kaufman, "For Homeless Families in City, Stricter Rules and Quicker Aid," *New York Times*, November 17, 2004, p. 1.

51 Cassi Feldman, "Cruel to Be Kind," *City Limits*, September/October 2005.

52 Michael Saul, "Plan New Facility for Homeless," *New York Daily News*, November 17, 2004, p. 20.
53 David Saltonstall with Mark Fass, "Despised Homeless Intake Office to Be Gutted," *Daily News*, June 27, 2004, p. 24.
54 Interview with Rebecca Chew, January 24, 2012.
55 Jennifer Egan, "To Be Young and Homeless," *New York Times*, March 24, 2002, sec. 6, col. 1, Magazine Desk, p. 32.
56 Feldman, "Cruel to Be Kind"
57 Michelle O'Donnell, "Judge Rules in City's Favor on Housing Homeless Families," *New York Times*, August 17, 2005, p. B2.
58 Personal interview with Vida Chavez-Downs, February 27, 2006.
59 Ginia Bellafante, "Rare Sympathy for the Landlord," *New York Times*, February 26, 2012, sec. MB, p. 1.
60 Howard Husock, "Reining in Housing Vouchers," *New York Sun*, November 3, 2004, p. 11.
61 Leslie Kaufman, "Homeless Families Blocked from Seeking U.S. Housing Aid," *New York Times*, October 20, 2004, p. B1.
62 Michael Cragg and Brendan O'Flaherty, "Do Homeless Shelter Conditions Determine Shelter Population? The Case of the Dinkins Deluge," *Journal of Urban Economics* 46 (1999): pp. 377–415.
63 Leslie Kaufman, "Homeless Families Blocked from Seeking U.S. Housing Aid."
64 Howard Husock, "Reining in Housing Vouchers."
65 Leslie Kaufman, "Homeless Families Blocked from Seeking U.S. Housing Aid."
66 Personal interview with Linda Gibbs, July 25, 2005.
67 New York City Family Homelessness Special Master Panel, Letter to the Court, January 16, 2005. For a news report on the issuance of the SMP's findings see Leslie Kaufman, "Deal on Legal Aid Lawsuits for Homeless Breaks Down," *New York Times*, February 16, 2005, p. B3.
68 Personal interview with Steven Banks, December 9, 2013.
69 Affirmation of Thomas Crane, February 2006, p. 26.
70 Ibid., pp. 14–15.
71 Personal interview with George Nashak, October 19, 2014.
72 Ibid.
73 Personal interview with Shelly Nortz, April 20, 2015.
74 Personal interview with Connie Temple, April 23, 2015.
75 Personal interview with George Nashak, October 19, 2014; Tanveer Ali, "Hess vs. Homelessness: Chat with DHS Commish," *City Limits*, August 7, 2006.
76 Personal interview with Sam Tsemberis, November 24, 2014.
77 Personal interview with George Nashak, October 19, 2014.
78 Personal interview with Robert Hess, March 26, 2010.
79 Personal interview with Scott Auwarter, assistant executive director, BronxWorks, October 19, 2011.

80 Mosi Secret, "Smaller Shelters and Persuasion Coax Homeless off Bronx Streets," *New York Times*, October 18, 2011, p. A1; HOPE 2011, The NYC Street Survey, slide 8. http://www.nyc.gov/html/dhs/downloads/pdf/hope11_results.pdf, accessed December 15, 2015.

81 HOPE 2014, The NYC Street Survey, slide 7.

82 "Decision of Interest; New York County Supreme Court; Justice Helen E. Freedman; DOI; Court Appoints 'Special Masters' to Investigate Erroneous Denials of Emergency Shelter to Homeless," *New York Law Journal*, November 27, 2007, p. 26.

83 Ibid.

84 *McCain v. Bloomberg*, Supreme Court of New York County of New York, Index no. 41023/83, Affidavit of John Mollenkopf, August 2007.

85 Ibid. The three members of the new special master panel were former appellate division justices Hon. Betty Weinberg Ellerin and Hon. E. Leo Milonas, and former Legal Services Corporation president, Alexander Forger, Esq.

86 Daniel Wise, "City Seeks to End Court Oversight of Homeless Shelters," *New York Law Journal*, November 21, 2007, col. 1, p. 1.

87 *Bloomberg Businessweek*, Company Overview of Lawyers Committee for Civil Rights under Law, Executive Profile, Alexander D. Forger Esq. Accessed January 8, 2014.

88 Personal interview with Steven Banks, December 19, 2013.

89 Ibid.

90 Michael A. Cardozo, "The New York City Corporation Counsel: The Best Legal Job in America," *New York Law School Law Review* 53 (2008–2009): p. 459.

91 Daniel Wise, "City, Legal Aid Agree to Settle 25-Year-Old Homeless Suits," *New York Law Journal*, September 18, 2008, p. 1.

92 Editorial, "Good Riddance," *New York Daily News*, September 19, 2008, p. 28.

93 Personal interview with Steven Banks, December 9, 2013.

94 Ibid.

95 *Boston v. City of New York*, Index No. 402295/08, Final Judgment, September 17, 2008, pp. 1–2.

96 New York City Independent Budget Office, Inside the Budget, Number 157, "Has the Rise in Homeless Prevention Spending Decreased the Shelter Population?" August 7, 2008, p. 4. http://www.ibo.nyc.ny.us/newsfax/insidethebudget157.pdf, accessed December 15, 2015.

97 Ibid.; Tina Moore with Adam Lisberg, "Bloomy Defends Homeless Program," *New York Daily News*, October 2, 2010, p. 6.

98 Abt Associates, *Final Report: Evaluation of the Homebase Community Prevention Program*, June 6, 2013, p. 3. http://www.abtassociates.com/AbtAssociates/files/cf/cf819ade-6613-4664-9ac1-2344225c24d7.pdf, accessed December 15, 2015; Cara Buckley, "To Test Housing Program, Some Are Denied Aid," *New York Times*, December 9, 2010, p. A1.

99 Tina Moore, "City's Cruel Test for Poor Families: 200 Denied Aid Are Being Treated Like 'Rats in a Lab Experiment,'" *New York Daily News*, September 30, 2010, p. 6.

100 States News Service, Statement from the Manhattan Borough President on Department of Homeless Services' Home Base Program, October 5, 2010. https://www.highbeam.com/doc/1G1-238778110.html, accessed December 15, 2015.

101 Tina Moore, "Uproar by Pols over 'Cruel Test' of City Homeless," *New York Daily News*, October 1, 2010, p. 4.

102 Ibid.

103 Tina Moore, "'Serious Ethical Questions': Council Members Grill Officials over Denying Homeless Services for a Study," *New York Daily News*, December 10, 2010, p. 30.

104 Tina Moore with Adam Lisberg, "Bloomy Defends Homeless Program."

105 Abt Associates, *Final Report: Evaluation of the Homebase Community Prevention Program*, p. 13.

106 Ibid., p. 14.

107 Peter Hellman, "Justice Freedman v. New York," *City Journal*, Spring 1997.

108 Alan Feuer, "The Hidden Homeless," *New York Times*, February 5, 2012, sec. MB, Metropolitan Desk, p. 1.

109 New York City Department of Homeless Services press release, PR-149-11, May 11, 2011.

110 Interview with Rebecca Chew, January 24, 2012.

111 Ibid.

112 Coalition for the Homeless, "State of the Homeless 2009: A Proven Way to Reduce Family Homelessness during the Economic Recession," April 23, 2009, p. 4. http://www.coalitionforthehomeless.org/wp-content/uploads/2014/06/StateoftheHomeless2009.pdf, accessed December 15, 2015.

113 Howard Husock, "Reining in Housing Vouchers," *New York Sun*, November 3, 2004, p. 1.

114 Ibid.

115 Coalition for the Homeless, "Homeless Families at Risk: Hazardous Conditions in the Housing Stability Plus Program," February 2007, p. 2, written by Lindsey Davis, edited by Patrick Markee. http://www.coalitionforthehomeless.org/wp-content/uploads/2014/06/HomelessFamiliesAtRiskReport2007/wAppendx.pdf, accessed December 15, 2015.

116 Sewell Chan, "Critics See Flaws in a Program to Help the Homeless Pay Rent," *New York Times*, May 8, 2006, p. B2.

117 Leslie Kaufman, "With a Record Number of Homeless Families, the City Vows to Improve Aid," *New York Times*, March 19, 2007, p. B1.

118 Ibid.

119 Coalition for the Homeless, Advocacy Department, "New York City Homeless Municipal Shelter Population, 1983–Present," undated, http://coalhome.3cdn.net/9bf5aad273af9beaad_ldm6i6j2r.pdf, accessed January 21, 2014.

120 Leslie Kaufman, "With a Record Number of Homeless Families, the City Vows to Improve Aid," p. B1.

121 New York City Department of Homeless Services, "New Rental Strategy Rewards Work and Prepares Clients for Independent Living through Matched Savings," April 25, 2007. http://www.nyc.gov/html/dhs/html/communications/pr042507.shtml, accessed July 21, 2014. This document explains the matched savings feature of Advantage as follows:

> A key tool in the Work Advantage program is a savings program that will provide clients with a financial cushion when rental assistance ends. While clients are receiving the rental subsidy, which will account for almost 100% of their rent, they can contribute up to 20% of the rent amount to a savings account that will be matched at the end of the program. In addition, clients will pay $50 in rent directly to the landlord, which will also be matched and added to the client's savings. For instance, after one year, a family with a monthly rent of $1,070 who was saving at a rate of 20% per month could end up with nearly $6,000 in a savings account, including the client savings and City matching funds.

122 Personal interview with Robert V. Hess, March 26, 2010.

123 Coalition for the Homeless, Advocacy Department, "New York City Homeless Municipal Shelter Population, 1983–Present."

124 New York City Department of Homeless Services, *A Progress Report on Uniting for Solutions beyond Shelter*, Fall 2008, p. 2. http://www.nyc.gov/html/dhs/downloads/pdf/progress_Report.pdf, accessed December 15, 2015.

125 Commissioner Robert V. Hess explained the revised requirements for the Advantage program as follows:

> Clients entering year one of the Advantage NY program will be required to be employed for at least 20 hours per week, and participate in an additional 15 hours per week of housing searches or HRA-approved work activities. Clients will also be required to contribute 30 percent of their gross monthly income toward rent during their first year of participation in the program.
>
> For year two, the subsidy will be available to those who are employed for 35 hours per week and remain compliant with program rules. The revised program has raised the income threshold as well, to where clients must continue to have an income that is less than 200 percent of the federal poverty level—an improvement to our previous program which set the cap at 150 percent of the federal poverty level. During the second year, participants will be required to contribute the greater half of their monthly rent, or 30 percent of their income, toward their housing costs.

Testimony of Commissioner Robert V. Hess for City Council Hearing, General Welfare Committee, "Oversight: Update on DHS' Advantage NY and Homebase Programs" Thursday, April 15, 2010.

126 Julie Bosman, "Plan Would Require Homeless to Work to Qualify for Rent Subsidies," *New York Times*, April 14, 2010, p. A20.

127 New York City Office of Comptroller, "Audit Report on the Monitoring of the Work Advantage Program by the Department of Homeless Services," Audit Number: MG10-060A, Release Date: July 15, 2010. http://comptroller.nyc.gov/reports/audit/?r=07-15-10_MG10-060A, accessed December 15, 2015.
128 New York City Department of Homeless Services, "The 411 on Advantage: Myths and Facts," undated. http://www.nyc.gov/html/dhs/html/communications/pb072810.shtml, accessed December 15, 2015.
129 Diana Scholl, "Critics of Homeless Program Fight to Save It," *City Limits*, March 11, 2011.
130 Patrick Markee and Giselle Routhier, Coalition for the Homeless, "The Revolving Door Spins Faster: New Evidence That the Flawed 'Advantage' Program Forces Many Formerly-Homeless Families Back into Homelessness," February 16, 2011. http://www.coalitionforthehomeless.org/wp-content/uploads/2014/06/BriefingPaper-TheRevolvingDoorSpinsFaster2-16-2011.pdf, accessed December 15, 2015.
131 Associated Press, "NYC: 15,000 Ex-homeless Families Losing Rent Help," March 17, 2011; Mosi Secret, "City Says State Is Forcing Cuts to Program for the Homeless," *New York Times*, March 11, 2011.
132 Markee and Routhier, Coalition for the Homeless, "The Revolving Door Spins Faster."
133 Remarks by Seth Diamond at No Way to Pay: What's Next for Homeless Families in NYC, a forum held by the Milano School's Center for New York City Affairs May 3, 2012. http://www.nyc.gov/html/dhs/downloads/pdf/commissioner_remarks_05032012.pdf.
134 DHS complied a collection of thirty-four press and radio stories from March and April 2011 on the coming end of Advantage. There were also several television news stories.
135 Mosi Secret, "City Sees End to Rental Aid for Homeless," *New York Times*, June 1, 2011, p. A1.
136 Coalition for the Homeless, Advocacy Department, "New York City Homeless Municipal Shelter Population, 1983–Present."
137 Personal interview with Richard Motta, November 22, 2011.

CHAPTER 6. HOMELESSNESS POLICY UNDER DE BLASIO

1 Heather Mac Donald, "No Managers Need Apply," *City Journal*, Eye on the News, March 11, 2014.
2 Personal interview with Steven Banks, May 29, 2015.
3 City of New York, Department of Homeless Services, Press Release, "DHS Launches Largest Homelessness Prevention Campaign Ever: 'Imagine' Campaign Encourages Families to "Read Out, Before a Shelter Is Your Only Option," March 16, 2015. http://www1.nyc.gov/assets/dhs/downloads/pdf/press-releases/1-15-Homebase-Campaign-Press-Release-Draft.pdf, accessed December 15, 2015; Department of Homeless Services Testimony, New York City Council General Welfare Committee, Preliminary Budget Hearing for Fiscal Year 2016, March 17,

2015, http://www1.nyc.gov/assets/dhs/downloads/pdf/testimony/preliminary_budget_testimony_3.17.14.pdf, accessed December 15, 2015.

4 Personal interview with Steven Banks, May 29, 2015.

5 Personal interview with Lilliam Barrios-Paoli, May 1, 2015.

6 Leslie Kaufman, "With a Record Number of Homeless Families, the City Vows to Improve Aid," *New York Times*, March 19, 2007, p. B1.

7 Personal interview with Patrick Markee, June 5, 2015.

8 Greg B. Smith, "Pathways to Misery: Troubled Nonprofits' Clients Face Evict," *New York Daily News*, September 7, 2014, p. 6; Greg B. Smith, "It's My Life on Fear Street: Ailing Firm puts Mentally Ill at Risk," *New York Daily News*, September 14, 2014, p. 10.

9 Personal interview with Lilliam Barrios-Paoli, May 1, 2015.

10 Ibid.

11 Ibid.

12 New York City Department of Homeless Services, *2015–2017 Operational Plan*, March 2015, p. 3. http://www1.nyc.gov/assets/dhs/downloads/pdf/operational-plan-2015-2017.pdf, accessed December 15, 2015.

13 Personal interview with Gilbert Taylor, May 7, 2015.

14 Personal interview with Steven Banks, May 29, 2015.

15 For accounts of the role that professional consensus plays in precipitating nonincremental change, see Timothy J. Conlan, David R. Beam, and Margaret T. Wrightson, "Policy Models and Political Change: Insights from the Passage of Tax Reform," in Marc K. Landy and Martin A. Levin, eds., *The New Politics of Public Policy* (Baltimore, MD: Johns Hopkins University Press, 1995), pp. 121–42; also see M. A. Hill and Thomas J. Main, *Is Welfare Working? The Massachusetts Reforms Three Years Later* (Boston: Pioneer Institute, 1998), chapter 3. For an account of the nature of public ideas, see Mark H. Moore, "What Sort of Ideas Become Public Ideas?" in Robert B. Reich, ed., *The Power of Public Ideas* (Cambridge, MA: Harvard University Press, 1988).

CONCLUSION

1 Wallace S. Sayer and Herbert Kaufman, *Governing New York City* (New York: Russell Sage Foundation, 1960), p. 720.

2 Jewel Bellush, "Clusters of Power: Interest Groups," in Jewel Bellush and Dick Netzer, eds., *Urban Politics New York Style* (Armonk, NY: Sharpe, 1990), p. 334.

3 David A. Snow, Sarah A. Soule, and Daniel M. Cress, "Identifying the Precipitants of Homeless Protest across 17 US Cities, 1980 to 1990," *Social Forces* 83, no. 3 (March 2005): p. 1184.

4 Donna Wilson Kircheimer, "Sheltering the Homeless in New York City: Expansion in an Era of Government Contraction," *Political Science Quarterly* 104, no. 4, (Winter 1989–1990): pp. 607–23.

5 The City of New York, Executive Budget, Fiscal Year 2014, Office of Management and Budget, Message of the Mayor, p. 3. http://www.nyc.gov/html/omb/downloads/pdf/mm5_13.pdf, accessed December 15, 2015.

6 Sarah Kellermann, "Is Deinstitutionalization Working for the Mentally Ill?" (New York: Department of Mental Health, Mental Retardation, and Alcoholism Services, 1982), p. 9.

7 Adjustment for inflation calculated using CPI Inflation Calculator, Bureau of Labor Statistics.

8 Los Angeles Homeless Services Authority, "2014–15 Proposed Budget by Programs and Funding," June 30, 2015.

9 Daniel M. Cress and David A. Snow, "The Outcomes of Homeless Mobilization: The Influence of Organization, Disruption, Political Mediation, and Framing," *American Journal of Sociology* 105, no. 4 (January 2000): 1086. The article does not indicate in what year the Oakland Union of the Homeless achieved the housing project.

10 Donna Wilson Kirchheimer, "Sheltering the Homeless in New York City," *Political Science Quarterly* 104, no. 4 (Winter 1989–1990): p. 623.

11 For an account that recognizes both the accomplishments and the limitations of La Guardia's housing policy, see Thomas Kessner, *Fiorello H. La Guardia and the Making of Modern New York* (New York: Penguin, 1989), chapters 4 and 5, pp. 320–36.

12 See Roger Burrows and Brian Loader, *Towards a Post-Fordist Welfare State?* (London: Routledge, 1994).

13 Kirchheimer, "Sheltering the Homeless in New York City," p. 615.

14 Ibid., p. 616.

15 Barrett A. Lee, Chad R. Farrell, and Bruce G. Link, "Revisiting the Contact Hypothesis: The Case of Public Exposure to Homelessness," *American Sociological Review* 69, no. 1 (February 2004): pp. 40–63.

16 Joel Blau, *The Visible Poor: Homelessness in the United States* (Oxford: Oxford University Press, 1992), p. 4.

17 Ana Maria Arumi and Andrew L. Yarro, with Amber Ott and Jonathan Rochkind, *Compassion, Concern, and Conflicted Feelings: New Yorkers on Homelessness and Housing* (New York: Public Agenda Foundation, 2007).

18 Personal interview with Edward Koch, February 19, 2010.

19 Frances Fox Piven and Richard A. Cloward, *Poor People's Movements: Why They Succeed, How They Fail* (New York: Vintage Books, 1979), p. 36.

20 "Residents of Welfare Hotel Seize City Office to Demand Permanent Housing," *New York Times*, January 10, 1989, p. B2; Sara Rimer, "Homeless Organize to Fight for Themselves," *New York Times*, January 26, 1989, p. B1; Jesus Rangel, "Self-Help at a Shelter," *New York Times*, sec., part 3, p. 67; Gloria Gasper, *"Parents on the Move": A Qualitative Study of a Self-Help Organization of Homeless Parents*, unpublished Ed. D. dissertation, University of Massachusetts, 1991.

21 Jimmy Breslin, "Homeless Raise Voices to Bring Down Roof," *Sun Sentinel*, December 15, 1986 (syndicated column); Theresa Funiciello, *Tyranny of Kindness: Dismantling the Welfare System to End Poverty in America* (New York: Atlantic Monthly Press, 1993), pp. 176–77.

22 Joyce Purnick, "Location Isn't Everything," *New York Times*, September 28, 1997, sec. 7, p. 18. This article is a review of John Jiler, *Sleeping with the Mayor* (St. Paul: Hungry Mind Press, 1997).

23 Michel Marriott, "Homeless in Park Sticking to a Cause," *New York Times*, November 28, 1988, p. B3.

24 Funiciello, *Tyranny of Kindness*, pp.162, xvii.

25 Daniel P. Moynihan, *The Politics of a Guaranteed Income: The Nixon Administration and the Family Assistance Plan* (New York: Vintage, 1973); Lawrence M. Mead, *Beyond Entitlement: The Social Obligations of Citizenship* (New York: Free Press, 1986); Leslie Lenkowsky, *Politics, Economics, and Welfare Reform: The Failure of the Negative Income Tax in Britain and the United States* (Lanham, MD: University Press of America, 1986).

26 Thomas J. Main, "Nonincremental Change in an Urban Environment: The Case of New York City's Human Resources Administration," *Administration & Society* 37, no. 4 (September 2005): pp. 483–503.

27 Lawrence M. Mead, "The Rise of Paternalism," in *The New Paternalism: Supervisory Approaches to Poverty* (Washington, DC: Brookings Institution, 1997), p. 2.

28 Sam Tsemberis, Leyla Gulcur, Maria Nakae, "Housing First, Consumer Choice, and Harm Reduction for Homeless Individuals with a Dual Diagnosis," *American Journal of Public Health* 94, no. 4 (April 2004): pp. 651–56, figure 4.

29 Deborah K. Padget, Leyla Gulcur, and Sam Tsemberis, "Housing First Services for People Who Are Homeless with Co-Occurring Serious Mental Illness and Substance Abuse," *Research on Social Work Practice* 16, no. 1 (January 2006): pp. 74–83, figure 4.

30 Ibid., p. 654.

31 Ronni Michelle Greenwood et al., "Decreasing Psychiatric Symptoms by Increasing Choice in Services for Adults," *American Journal of Community Psychology* 36, nos. 3/4 (December 2005): pp. 223–38.

32 Ronni Michelle Greenwood, Ana Stefanici, and Sam Tsemberis, "Pathways Housing First for Homeless Persons with Psychiatric Disabilities: Program Innovation, Research, and Advocacy," *Journal of Social Issues* 69, no. 4 (2013): p. 649.

33 Personal interview with Sam Tsemberis, November 24, 2014.

34 Dina Temple-Raston, "Bloomberg Vows to Make Chronic Homelessness 'Extinct,'" *New York Sun*, June 24, 2004.

35 Personal interview with Linda Gibbs, July 25, 2005.

36 John Hull Mollenkopf, *A Phoenix in the Ashes: The Rise and Fall of the Koch Coalition in New York City Politics* (Princeton, NJ: Princeton University Press, 1992), p. 70.

37 Ibid., p. 193.

38 Ibid., pp. 157–58, 185, 198.

39 Personal interview with Edward Koch, February 29, 2010.

40 Personal interview with Len Koerner, December 14, 2011.

41 Steven Kelman, *Making Public Policy: A Hopeful View of American Government* (New York: Basic Books, 1988), p. 10.

42 Jonathan Soffer, *Ed Koch and the Rebuilding of New York City* (New York: Columbia University Press, 2010), p. 294.
43 Mollenkopf, *A Phoenix in the Ashes*, pp. 21, 148, 150.
44 The rebuilding of marginal housing, the crime drop, and the improved public transportation are discussed in Michael Gecan, "Getting Better All the Time: Inside New York's Quiet Success Stories," *Village Voice*, December 30, 2003.
45 Clarence N. Stone, *Regime Politics: Governing Atlanta, 1946–1988* (Lawrence: University Press of Kansas, 1989), p. 227.
46 Floyd Hunter, *Community Power Structure: A Study of Decision Makers* (Garden City, NY: Anchor Books, 1963).
47 Stone, *Regime Politics*, p. 176.
48 The words quoted in this sentence come from a passage from *The Prince* by Machiavelli, quoted by Stone in *Regime Politics*, p. 183. The full passage reads, "Nothing makes a prince so much esteemed as to carry on great enterprises."
49 Robert Coldwell Wood, *1400 Governments: The Political Economy of the New York Metropolitan Region* (Cambridge, MA: Harvard University Press, 1961), pp. 1–2.
50 Theodore J. Lowi, *At the Pleasure of the Mayor: Patronage and Power in New York City, 1989–1958* (New York: Free Press of Glencoe, 1964), p. 218.
51 Ibid.
52 John J. Harrigan and Ronald K. Vogel, *Political Change in the Metropolis*, 7th ed. (New York: Longman, 2003), pp. 16–17.
53 For a convincing account of the power of the rights strategy in U.S. policymaking, see Marc K. Landy, "The New Politics of Environmental Policy," in Marc K. Landy and Martin A. Levin, eds., *The New Politics of Public Policy* (Baltimore, MD: Johns Hopkins University Press), pp. 207–27.
54 The phrase "opportunity points" comes from R. Shep Melnick, "Separation of Powers and the Strategy of Rights: The Expansion of Special Education," in Marc K. Landy and Martin A. Levin, eds., *The New Politics of Public Policy* (Baltimore, MD: Johns Hopkins University Press, 1995), pp. 23–46.
55 For a discussion of policy feedbacks see M. Weir, A. S. Orloff, and T. Skocpol, "Introduction: Understanding American Social Politics," in M. Weir, A. S. Orloff, and T. Skocpol, eds., *The Politics of Social Policy in the United States* (Princeton, NJ: Princeton University Press, 1988), p. 25.
56 Greenwood, Stefanici, and Tsemberis, "Pathways Housing First for Homeless Persons," p. 649.
57 Personal interview with Deborah Padgett, January 23, 2015.

INDEX

ABOUT THE AUTHOR

Thomas J. Main is Associate Professor at the School of Public Affairs, Baruch College, City University of New York. He holds a Ph.D. in Politics from Princeton University and an M.P.A. from the Harvard Kennedy School of Government. He has been writing on the subject of homelessness in New York City for more than thirty years.